Art as an Agent for Social Change

# Personal/Public Scholarship

*Series Editor*

Patricia Leavy (*USA*)



VOLUME 8

The titles published in this series are listed at *brill.com/pepu*

# Art as an Agent for Social Change

*Edited by*

Hala Mreiwed, Mindy R. Carter and Claudia Mitchell

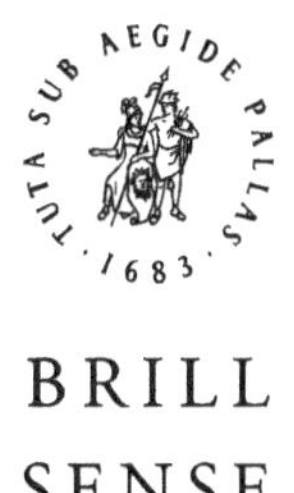


BRILL
SENSE

LEIDEN | BOSTON

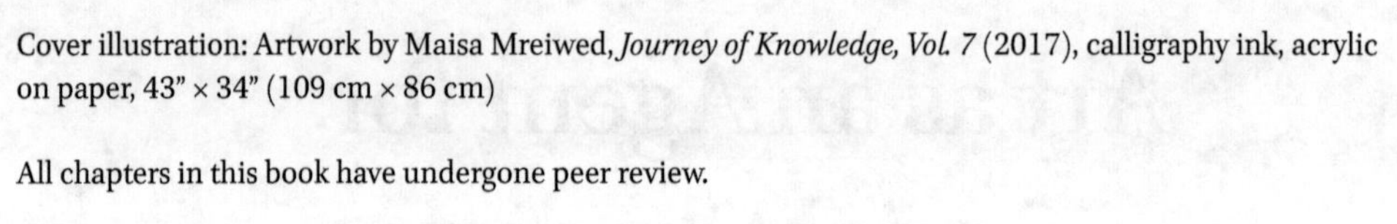

Cover illustration: Artwork by Maisa Mreiwed, *Journey of Knowledge, Vol. 7* (2017), calligraphy ink, acrylic on paper, 43" × 34" (109 cm × 86 cm)

All chapters in this book have undergone peer review.

The Library of Congress Cataloging-in-Publication Data is available online at http://catalog.loc.gov

Typeface for the Latin, Greek, and Cyrillic scripts: “Brill”. See and download: brill.com/brill-typeface.

ISSN 2542-9671
ISBN 978-90-04-44285-6 (paperback)
ISBN 978-90-04-44286-3 (hardback)
ISBN 978-90-04-44287-0 (e-book)



This book is printed on acid-free paper and produced in a sustainable manner.

# Advance Praise for
# *Art as an Agent for Social Change*

"*Art as an Agent for Social Change* deftly explores the connections between art and social change through a rich telling of the journeys of knowledge work of artists, researchers, educators and activists. The cover artwork lingers as a 'framework' for future journeys of knowledge production highlighting the necessity of introspection, but also interaction, interdependence, interconnectedness, and intersection required for wholesome scholarship for social change in complex and uncertain times. The editors have brought together a powerful text that opens up possibilities for innovation in connecting art, research, teaching and community activism, enabling the authentic and respectful interbeing of individuals and communities, vitalising the work they do. The interdisciplinary text makes a timeous and important contribution to the field of arts-based research."
– **Naydene de Lange, Professor Emeritus, Nelson Mandela University, Port Elizabeth, South Africa**

"A superb collection of provocative, educative, and imaginative artful narratives that celebrates arts and their significance in bringing about personal, social, and ecological transformations. Given the inclusive, holistic, contemplative, and collaborative nature of the contributions, this volume emphasizes interconnection, hope, well-being, and empowerment and contributes to a burgeoning global movement for social justice and change. An important read for all educators!"
– **Ashwani Kumar, President, Arts Researchers and Teachers Society, Canada**

"In a time of dire need for social change, this book offers a captivating collection of 'snapshots' that showcase the transformational power of arts in education. It allows us to witness inclusive research practices, recognize multiple global perspectives, challenge pre-conceived perceptions, and appreciate arts-based methodological approaches with the goal of re-imagining education."
– **Sara Hashem, PhD, Arts Educator, McGill University, Canada**

*In loving memory of*
*Doreen Starke-Meyerring*

*We will forever be inspired by your vision, generosity and passion for education, research, the arts, wellbeing and their interconnections.*

∵

# Contents

# Foreword

As an artist, educator, and researcher who has worked in the field of art for social change in Canada and abroad for over 40 years, I am delighted to see this very approachable and useful book.

Anyone needing to be convinced of the transformational power of arts-infused education needs to read this collection of detailed and sometimes provocative essays. If you are already integrating art for social change into your work, you will be offered a panoply of methods and guiding philosophies, and you will be able to hear the voices of project participants as they describe the changes they experienced. Readers who are simply curious about education and art for social change (ASC) may well become converts to these effective and enlivening approaches to teaching and learning.

Comprehensive methodological detail, excellent references to seminal scholarly publications, and, especially, the voices of participant learners (or co-creators) come together to produce a persuasive validation of education through participatory arts. This book challenges us to think critically about what really matters.

The collection includes work from Canada and the US, Norway, India, Hong Kong, and South Africa. The authors describe how they integrated visual, performance, and literary arts into their work, recount what happened during these processes and provide analyses of impacts.

Despite the diversity of contexts and approaches, these essays reveal remarkably common themes and findings. In many of these case studies—referred to as "snapshots" by the editors—we read about how participants experienced self-empowerment and new agency; how they further developed curiosity and awareness; and how a sense of possibility and active engagement was nurtured. Silence was transformed into expression. Bodies, minds and emotions were connected—head, hands and hearts—reminding us all that they are inseparable.

Many of the writers explore how ASC builds community, penetrates cultural barriers, and destroys stereotypes. Through exposure to the arts, to collective and individual artmaking, as well as to dialogue and reflection, a more inclusive and expansive view of the world inside and outside of the classroom is nurtured. Critical perspective is developed in the framework of a broader and more detailed understanding of both local and global issues.

In a time of profound polarisation (and some would say deep cynicism), the experience of inclusion and equity, of listening and imagining, and of dialogue through metaphor becomes a powerful tool for emancipation. These educators, scholars, and community activists address issues of social and environmental justice (including the human rights of children), of trauma and oppression, and suggest actions that can be taken to encourage new ways of being and acting in the world. Over and over, we read about how energising and effective these unpredictable and surprising processes can be.

Risk-taking and risk-evaluation come along with these approaches and some of these projects lead to an entry into areas beyond the usual and conventional. Writers suggest that these processes demand a critical re-imagination of the power and role of the educator (as we begin to think about the teacher as *facilitator* rather than as traditional *instructor*) and of the researcher (as we learn to view participants as active co-researchers rather than as passive subjects). They also question and challenge the long-lived hierarchical systems within which many teachers and students operate, and pose questions about how educators, themselves, are educated.

The examples in this book describe a growing global movement. The battle to legitimise ASC work is being waged around the world, aided by the now extensive and compelling evidence of its positive impact on individuals and communities, and its power to accomplish even systemic change.

This collection of provocative pieces offers us stories rather than just masses of data. Since ASC approaches put more emphasis on *process* rather than on the ultimate art objects or events, the authors suggest that the impacts of both process and product must be evaluated in different qualitative, quantitative, and art-based ways.

It is notable that the few longitudinal studies that exist refer to how former students are able, many years later, to remember the pictures they painted and the songs and dances they performed then. A story told by a father to a former teacher comes to mind: the sudden memory of a poem about violence that he and classmates had created ten years earlier had stayed his hand when he was just about to strike his partner. Once the door is opened ....

Since technocratic and data-driven forces sometimes overpower our ability to connect with each other in more than superficial ways, I hope that readers will enjoy the messages of generosity, inclusion, expansiveness, and hope that permeate this book. *Art as an Agent for Social Change* offers inspiring approaches to education and research, and to changing the world.

We are born with great powers of imagination. When we are encouraged to use and share this capacity, change becomes more than a desire: we create new understandings and possibilities.

Perhaps readers of this book will be inspired to write a poem, to dance or to sing, to draw an image or to share a story!

*Judith Marcuse*
Founder and Artistic Director, Judith Marcuse Projects
Founder and Co-director, International Centre of Art for Social Change
Senior Fellow, Ashoka Canada

# Acknowledgments

We have many people (and institutions) to thank in helping us bring this collection together. Beginning at the beginning, we would like to acknowledge the members of the Artful Inquiry Research Group (AIRG) 2018 Committee for their generosity in planning and convening the *Art as an Agent for Social Change* symposium which took place in the Faculty of Education, McGill University, October 12–13, 2018: Lori Beavis, Lynn Butler-Kisber, Emmy Côté, Alisan Funk, Lidoloy Chavez Guerra, Maria Ezcurra Lucotti, and Sheryl Smith-Gilman. We also acknowledge the artists from No Bad Sound Studios (NBS) and the support of all the volunteers, presenters and attendees at the conference.

We are particularly grateful to Patricia Leavy, first for her provocative key-note presentation at the *Art as an Agent for Social Change* symposium, and later for her enthusiastic support for our book proposal as part of her Brill | Sense series Personal/Public Scholarship. We also thank John Bennett and Jolanda Karada at Brill | Sense for their support, and prompt and encouraging responses to all our questions.

Supported by Patricia and John, we issued the call for chapter proposals for this book. We were delighted with the many submissions from across Canada, the US, South Africa, Norway and China. We thank all the contributors for their commitment to the project of art for social change and wish to acknowledge their engagement both as authors and reviewers.

We are also grateful to the artist and art educator Maisa Mreiwed for use of her artwork *Journey of Knowledge, Vol. 7* (2017) for our book cover.

We offer a special acknowledgement to Dr. Judith Marcuse for so generously agreeing to write the foreword for this book. Her own work in art for social change leads the way and is an inspiration.

We thank Avril Rios Torres for her assistance with the preparation of the final manuscript.

We are forever indebted to Dr. Ann Smith who, with her exceptional editing skills, so ably kept the process going and ensured a total fairness in relation to maintaining both brevity and 'to the point' sharpness of all the chapters.

Finally, we would like to thank our funders, the Artful Inquiry Research Group (AIRG) and the Distinguished James McGill Professor Fund.

# Figures and Tables

## Figures

## Tables

# Notes on Contributors

## Editors

*Mindy R. Carter*
is an Associate Professor in the Department of Integrated Studies in Education at McGill University, Canada. Her research focuses on teacher identity, and on using the arts to foster culturally responsible pedagogies. Carter has received Fonds de recherche du Quebec (2015–2018) and Social Sciences and Humanities Research Council funding (2017–2020) to explore how pre- and in-service teachers can use drama education and theatre to learn and teach about reconciliation in Quebec classrooms. She is currently the Vice-President of the Canadian Society for the Study of Education's Curriculum Studies special interest group and the Chair of the Artful Inquiry Research Group (AIRG) at McGill.

*Claudia Mitchell*
is a Distinguished James McGill Professor in the Department of Integrated Studies, Faculty of Education, McGill University, Canada, and an Honorary Professor in the School of Education, University of KwaZulu-Natal, South Africa. Her research interests focus on participatory arts-based methodologies, girlhood studies, teacher identity, and the prevention of gender-based violence with Indigenous girls and young women in South Africa and Canada, and across various countries in Eastern and Southern Africa, West Africa, and East Asia Pacific.

*Hala Mreiwed*
is a PhD candidate and a course lecturer in the Faculty of Education at McGill University, Canada. Her research focuses on Child Rights Education (she is a consultant in this area and is a board member of the Canadian Coalition for the Rights of Children); her interests—personal, academic, and professional—lie in the areas of child rights, equity in education, the impact of war-trauma on education, teacher education and training, community-building in classrooms, children's media and creative drama.

## Authors

*Esther Armaignac*
is a PhD student in the Department of Integrated Studies in Education at McGill University, Canada. Her research focuses on the use of popular culture along with participatory action research practices based on critical media lit-

eracy and feminist pedagogy, in sex education courses to encourage teenagers to develop critical thinking about issues related to gender and sexuality.

*Makram R. Ayache*
is a Lebanese-Canadian, theatre artist, educator, and academic based in Toronto. His research focuses on queer and Arab representation in Canadian theatre as part of a conversation about media representations of Arabs/Muslims. Most recently, his poem "These Old Jackets and Crowns" was published in *Nimrod International Journal.*

*Dan Berkley*
trained as both a physicist and a circus clown, doing the latter professionally and touring with Ringling Brothers Circus among others. Coaching circus led him to teaching. He earned his Master's degree through the New York City Teaching Fellows program and currently teaches physics in Chicago Public Schools.

*Rébecca Bourgault*
is an assistant professor at Boston University, USA, and a community artist, holds an EdD in Art & Art Education from Teachers College, Columbia University in NYC, an MFA from the University of Calgary, and a BFA from Concordia University, Canada. Her research interests include socially engaged art practices and arts-based research methods and pedagogies.

*Trinh Ngoc Phuong Bui*
has a Master's of Education and is an International Student Advisor at Thompson Rivers University, Canada. She has expertise in international education, student services, mindfulness, and educational psychology. Her interest lies in mindfulness, higher education, feminist pedagogy, Buddhism pedagogy, critical theory, and social and ecological justice.

*Casey Burkholder*
is an Assistant Professor in the Faculty of Education at the University of New Brunswick, Canada. Her work focuses on mobilising DIY media making practices with young people to address issues of concern in local contexts. Her research focuses on New Brunswick-based DIY activism with queer, trans, and non-binary youth and teachers.

*Avivit M. Cherrington*
is a research associate at the Faculty of Education at Nelson Mandela University. She locates her work in community psychology with an interest in positive psychology, agency, and participatory citizenship. Using her expertise in the

application of various participatory visual methods specifically framed by a critical, research-as-change design, she explores these concepts as catalysts for cultivating transformative praxis towards social justice.

*Amber C. Coleman*
is originally from Columbus, Georgia, and a PhD student in Art and Visual Culture Education at the University of Arizona, USA. She is currently a Graduate Assistant at the Tucson Museum of Art. Her research interests include Black feminist theory, art and museum education, and critical pedagogy.

*Deanna Del Vecchio*
is a PhD candidate in Social Justice Education at the University of Toronto, OISE, Canada. She studies the use of visual methodologies by social science researchers, focusing on the U.S.-Mexico borderlands. Her career in education has included classroom teaching, community-based learning, outdoor education, and teacher training.

*Victoria L. Dickman-Burnett*
recently graduated with a PhD in Education and Community-Based Action Research and Quantitative and Mixed Research Methodologies from the University of Cincinnati. Victoria's research focuses on participatory sexual violence prevention programs for high school youth at the intersection of art, literature, and prevention science.

*Alisan Funk*
is the head of the Bachelor program in circus at the Stockholm's University of the Arts. She is a circus coach, performer, and creator, pursuing a PhD in Education at McGill University. She researches circus education, including the technical and creative aspects of contemporary and classical circus performance.

*Kristen P. Goessling*
is an Assistant Professor of Human Development and Family Studies at Pennsylvania State University, Brandywine, USA. A committed engaged scholar, she leads interdisciplinary projects that align in the designing of spaces of belonging in which people learn and build meaningful relationships in the pursuit of social change.

*Ka Lee Carrie Ho*
(University of Saint Joseph) earned her Master's degree from Middlesex University, UK and her PhD in Creativity and Early Childhood Education from the Education University of Hong Kong. Her transdisciplinary arts-based research

focuses on aesthetics, spirituality, SEN support, and applied theater from the perspective of postmodernism.

*Madeline Hoak*
is a NYC-based circus performer, professor, and producer. She teaches aerial acrobatics at Pace University and founded the aerial arts program at Muhlenberg College, Pennsylvania, USA. She designed and is pursuing a master's degree at NYU in Circus Studies focusing on spectatorship and the cultural relevance of contemporary circus.

*Kerri Kennedy*
is an interdisciplinary artist, specialising in visual, media, and performance art. Her work explores untraditional approaches to old and new media and combines different modes of production in hybrid forms. Kerri's work has been screened at the Trent Film Society's Snowdance Short Film Festival, where her video *Digital Landscape* was awarded Best Experimental Film in 2016.

*Sage Kincaid*
is associate curator of education at the Georgia Museum of Art. She earned an MA in Cultural Studies with a focus on Art Museums from Brandeis University, and is a PhD candidate in Art Education at the University of Georgia, USA.

*Frans Kruger*
is a lecturer in the Faculty of Education at the University of the Free State, South Africa. His research interests include posthumanist pedagogies, African philosophy of education, ecojustice, and post-qualitative inquiry.

*Jodi Latremouille*
earned her PhD in Educational Research at the Werklund School of Education, University of Calgary, and is a sessional instructor in the Master of Education program at Thompson Rivers University, Canada. Her research interests include hermeneutics, ecological and feminist pedagogy, social and environmental justice, life writing, and poetic inquiry.

*Amélie Lemieux*
is Assistant Professor of Literacies in the Faculty of Education at Mount Saint Vincent University, Canada. Her research interests include young people's digital practices and aesthetic-laden processes in education, and posthuman methodological frameworks. She published *Mapping Holistic Learning* (with Boyd White; Peter Lang, 2017) and received a Lieutenant-Governor's Medal for academic excellence and community engagement.

*Leah Lewis*
is an Assistant Professor in Counselling Psychology. As a registered arts therapist and Canadian Certified Counsellor, her arts-informed research is in community arts therapy practice and health areas. Her current projects include The Hearthstone Community Art Hive (SSHRC) and The Dialysis Project (Canada Council for the Arts, ArtsNL).

*Xuemei Li*
is Associate Professor in Memorial University's Faculty of Education, Canada, and has led and participated in many funded projects on newcomer (immigrant, refugee, and international student) language, social, settlement, and career issues in Canada. Her research also covers cross-cultural identity reconstruction, English academic writing, and TESL/TEFL methodology.

*Warren Linds*
is Associate Professor, Applied Human Sciences, Concordia University, Canada. His research uses applied theatre to address social justice issues. He was Co-Principal Investigator in the research intervention project Acting Out! But in a Good Way, which linked well-being and the arts with Indigenous youth in Saskatchewan, Canada.

*Wai Luk Lo*
earned his PhD in Theatre Studies from City University, New York, USA. He has been teaching and conducting research for more than 20 years. He is currently an Honorary University Fellow of Hong Kong Baptist University. His research interests include dramaturgy, Hong Kong drama, history and the aesthetics of Chinese cinema.

*Judith Marcuse*
(LL.D., Hons.) has worked for five decades in the arts as dancer, choreographer, director, producer, educator, consultant, writer and lecturer. Her experiences have supported her internationally-recognized work in community-engaged art for social change (ASC) spanning over 20 years. Founder of the International Centre of Art for Social Change, she is a recipient of major awards, including an honorary doctorate, and a Lifetime Achievement Award from the Canadian Network for Arts and Learning.

*Heather McLeod*
is a Full Professor at Memorial University, Canada, and has won national, university, and faculty awards for teaching in which she uses qualitative and arts-based research approaches. Her current funded research initiatives include the

Art Hive community project, a poetry project, and an exploration of becoming a researcher/developing an academic identity.

*Amy Migliore*
is a PhD candidate in Art Education at The Pennsylvania State University, USA, and is interested in how agentic voices can be cultivated through studio-based practices. She has been an art educator at the secondary level for twenty years and was an adjunct professor at Kutztown University of Pennsylvania.

*Lisa A. Mitchell*
is Assistant Professor in the School of Education at St. Thomas University, Canada, and specialises in Music and Arts-based education and research and is an active musician and photographer. Her teaching and research focus on curriculum and pedagogy, integrated, interdisciplinary, and intercontextual approaches to teaching and teacher education, collaborative and inclusive practices in diverse classrooms, and narrative methodologies.

*Karen Morris*
is an MEd candidate, Educational Leadership, at High Point University Leadership Academy, USA. She is an Administrative Intern in Winston-Salem/Forsyth County Schools. Former Arts Magnet Director at RJ Reynolds High School, she was the 2019 NC Arts Administrator of the Year. She is a North Carolina A+ Schools Fellow.

*Marguerite Müller*
is a lecturer in the Faculty of Education at the University of the Free State, South Africa. At present, she teaches in the discipline of Curriculum Studies. In her research, she employs arts-based, narrative, and post-qualitative inquiry to explore issues of social justice and educator subjectivity in the higher education space.

*Giang Hoang Le Nguyen*
is a PhD student in Educational Studies at Brock University, Canada, and has research interests in social justice education, photovoice as a visual art form in educational research, photo-story as an arts-based research method, and English language teaching in an era of globalisation and neoliberalism.

*Tone Pernille Østern*
has a Doctor of Arts in Dance from the Theatre Academy at Uniarts Helsinki, Finland. She is a dance artist and Professor in Arts Education with a focus on Dance at NTNU Norwegian University of Science and Technology.

*Kathleen Pithouse-Morgan*
is Professor of Education at the University of KwaZulu-Natal, South Africa. Her work has given rise to a distinctive formulation of *poetic professional learning* as a literary arts-based mode for researching and enriching professional learning. In 2019, she received the South African National Excellence in Higher Education Teaching and Learning Award.

*Deborah Randolph*
(International Scholars Group) is an independent researcher and museum educator. She has served as Curator of Education at the Southeastern Center for Contemporary Art. She holds a PhD in Education from UNC-Chapel Hill, USA. Her research interests include arts integration, museum environmental resilience, and arts and social justice.

*Jacqueline Reid-Walsh*
is an Associate Professor at The Pennsylvania State University, USA, cross-appointed between the Departments of Curriculum and Instruction and Women's, Gender and Sexuality Studies. She has authored numerous works including a recent book called *Interactive Books: Playful Media Before Pop-ups* (2017)

*Rosemary C. Reilly*
is a Full Professor in Applied Human Sciences at Concordia University, Canada. She is a Member Scholar Academic of the International Institute for Qualitative Methodology. Her research interests include the impact of trauma on communities, collective healing strategies, and posttraumatic growth, and the use of qualitative and arts-based methodologies.

*Matt Rogers*
is an Associate Professor in the Faculty of Education at the University of New Brunswick, Canada, and an Atlantic Canadian Filmmaker. His research focuses on youth-centered participatory filmmaking and documentary inquiry as a knowledge mobilisation tool.

*Sheryl Smith-Gilman*
is the Assistant Director of Undergraduate Teacher Education Programs in the Department of Integrated Studies in the Faculty of Education at McGill University, Canada. Her areas of interest focus on teacher education and on early childhood pedagogy including attention to children's development, cultural identity, and meaning making through arts-based approaches.

*Callan Steinmann*
is curator of education at the Georgia Museum of Art. She holds a Master's in Museum Education from UT Austin and a PhD in Art Education from the University of Georgia, USA, where she teaches museum education and courses on museum studies.

*Mariam Ugarte*
is a teacher in the Health department of PACC vocational school, Quebec, Canada. She holds a Bachelor's degree in Education and a Masters in Human Systems Intervention from Concordia University, Canada. Previously, she worked as a labor and delivery room nurse. She always uses some form of creativity to facilitate learning.

*Sue Uhlig*
is a PhD candidate in Art Education at The Pennsylvania State University, USA. Her research explores the entanglement of collecting as pedagogy, research, and artistic process and product. She also teaches online classes as a lecturer in the School of Design, Art and Performance at Purdue University, USA.

*Amanda Claudia Wager*
is a Tier II Canada Research Chair in Community Research in Arts, Culture & Education at Vancouver Island University, Canada. As an interdisciplinary scholar, her community engaged research and teaching encompasses literacies, languages, and the arts with local youth, families, and communities.

*Boyd White*
is Associate Professor in the Department of Integrated Studies in Education, Faculty of Education, McGill University. Early in his career Dr. White was a printmaker, painter, and art educator. Currently his key teaching and research interests are in the areas of philosophy and art education, particularly on the topic of aesthetics and art criticism.

CHAPTER 1

# In Focus

## *Snapshots of Social Change through the Arts*

*Mindy R. Carter, Claudia Mitchell and Hala Mreiwed*

## 1 A Brief History

In 2014, Mindy R. Carter and Sara Hashem founded the Artful Inquiry Research Group (AIRG) at McGill University with the aim of creating an exchange platform for faculty and graduate students who engage in arts-based research practices. AIRG helps connect communities of arts-based researchers and educators by focusing on how making art and engaging in relational art practices affect one's research. By formalising the many arts interests across the Faculty of Education, Carter and Hashem anticipated creating more collaborations and cross-fertilisation of knowledge of benefit to the Faculty and its community by establishing a dynamic interdisciplinary group of scholars. To this end, the Artful Inquiry bi-annual symposium, led by scholars, researchers, students, and practitioners, was established in 2016 as an interdisciplinary forum for sharing scholarship, practices, and research on artful inquiry and methods in K-University schooling, community-based practices and beyond. Workshops, panel discussions, and individual paper presentations at the Symposium explored two questions in particular: How do we continue to develop the tools for creating, researching, and teaching in/through/with art? How are creative forms of inquiry and representation supported and sustained in communities within and beyond academia?

After the second AIRG symposium in 2018 (with co-conference chairs Mindy R. Carter and Hala Mreiwed), we noted increased interest in finding ways in which art-making and artistic engagement could be agents of/for social change in research and teaching, and in community collaborations. This interest was based on a topic, "Art as an agent for social change" addressed during the two-day symposium held in the Faculty of Education at McGill University (Montreal, Quebec). To engage more deeply with the concerns raised by this topic, Claudia Mitchell suggested the production of a co-edited book. With this synergy and a commitment to disseminate some of the work emerging from the symposium and beyond, the book took shape in relation to three main themes: (1) Community building; (2) Collaborations; and, (3) Teaching & Pedagogy. These themes bring into focus a number of key issues: the ways in which


DOI: 10.1163/9789004442870_001

educators address art as an agent for social change in their curricula and in their classrooms; collaborations and the impact they have on those involved including the community in which they took place; artful practice as an internal process looking at how art can be incorporated for social/public/personal change and possible interconnections; and, the role of art in enabling critical discussions of power asymmetry.

The artwork on the cover of this book, Maisa Mreiwed's calligraphy ink, acrylic on paper, *Journey of Knowledge, Vol. 7* (2017), is emblematic of these key issues and themes on art as an agent for social change. As this Montreal-based artist states, the work takes as its inspiration the rich history of the Atwater Library in Montreal and its contributions to the community.

> Seven Medallions, two parrots as well as specific architectural elements and symbols from the building tell the story of the Library's innovative and creative journey of producing and promoting knowledge in the arts and sciences. The Library has been a place of gathering and learning for the community since it first opened its doors as the Mechanics Institute in the 19th century. The artwork is inspired by the library's journey of knowledge with the parrots signifying the strength, intelligence, and beauty of coming together as individuals and as members of the community. (Artist's statement, 2020)

## 2 Snapshots

As a special feature of the book, each of the 24 chapters that follow is a snapshot of sorts, brief in length and seeking to be provocative either explicitly or implicitly about art and social change. The snapshot, of course, may sound like something old-fashioned, produced with a hand-held Brownie instamatic camera from an earlier era, or in a contemporary era of mobile phones and other devices, an image produced from what has become an ambition to photograph everything indiscriminately, including the ubiquitous selfie. Snapshots, in photography, are often defined as spontaneous pictures of a subject that provide the viewer with a quick illustration and starting point for deeper engagement. To this point, each chapter, more in its brevity (all are 3750 words or fewer) than content, offers the reader an up-close example of how art can provoke, educate, and/or (re)imagine in one small way how subjectivities can shift and change. Our choice to use the concept of snapshot as a metaphor for these short pieces comes from several sources. Many of the chapters work with the visual, so drawing on photography seems particularly appropriate. Numerous researchers and theorists have also used similar metaphors to make sense of how in-depth interviews or research data across sectors can be honoured in form and function through textual snapshots, portraits, vignettes, assemblages, or postcard conventions for individual participants (see Carter, 2016; Derrida, 1987).

We were also inspired by several other book projects that have placed the arts at their centre and have incorporated terminology that reflects an arts focus. The chapters in Pillay, Pithouse-Morgan, and Naicker's (2017) edited book, *Object Medleys: Interpretive Possibilities for Educational Research*, uses the notion of a medley to refer to assemblages of writing, with each chapter in the book made up of three or four short object stories. In another book, co-edited by Pithouse-Morgan, Pillay, and Mitchell (2019), *Memory Mosaics: Researching Teacher Professional Learning Through Artful Memory-work*, the metaphor of the mosaic is used. As the authors note in a follow-up article in which they discuss the idea of the metaphor of the mosaic, "The metaphor opened up a collaborative, creative, yet contained, thinking space that assisted us in bringing into dialogue unique instances of memory-work as visual, poetic, and prose texts, moving across authors, and continents, cultures, and contexts, and personal beliefs and values" (Mitchell, Pithouse-Morgan, & Pillay, 2020). Put together, the snapshots, as summarised below, are like an ocean that garners strength and power when rivers flow into it. In this book, subjectivities become forces that are unstoppable. This, we propose, is the essence of art working as an agent for change.

## 3 About the Snapshots

### 3.1 *Community Building*

Recognising the significance of the social in art for social change, the first set of snapshots focuses on community building. At the core of this section is the question: What role does community building play in bringing forth social change through the arts? To explore this, we must begin with our understanding of the meaning of community. For us, community represents the coming together of differences that foster respect for individual identities, inclusion, collaboration, empowerment, and feelings of safety. By the idea of coming together, we do not imply the loss of anyone's own identity or the promotion of sameness (for a more in-depth discussion on the definition of community, see Furman, 1998; Greene, 1995; Mreiwed, Carter, & Shabtay, 2017), but, rather, the sharing of narratives and "ways of being together, of attaining mutuality, of reaching toward some common world" (Greene, 1995, p. 39). It is essential to recognise that while we are all independent beings, we live together in a world that is interconnected and interdependent; through the communities that we build together, we can celebrate and share our differences and also bring to light what we have in common and empower each other as we grow as individuals, members of our communities, and part of the global community.

The first chapter in this section "'Imagining Things being Otherwise': Rethinking Community and the Art Museum Experience" by Callan Steinmann and Sage Kincaid sets the stage for the exploration of the social in art for social change. The authors explore opportunities for meaningful participatory encounters with objects and people in the museum space. They address the role of visitor-centered, socially responsive approaches in two public programs in a campus art museum in challenging traditional conceptions of museum going and offer visitors new ways of being and performing community in an art museum space. By exploring the "Otherwise" of the art museum experience and space, this chapter brings to the fore the power of participatory programming in creating and enhancing a sense of community mindfulness.

The role of art in building community, enhancing creativity, and bringing forth social change is also evident in education. Sheryl Smith-Gilman's "Voices from the Heart: Using Community and Art to Foster Social Change in Pre-service Teachers" explores how the arts can be integrated to cultivate classroom community, foster empathy, and promote individual and collective growth and development that can lead to social change. For this to happen, it is essential to create a safe space in the classroom in which risk and experimentation can take place so that creativity and imagination are fostered. This chapter addresses the practice-theory gap in arts-based educational research and demonstrates the powerful impact of art on teaching and learning as well as its potential to extend beyond the classroom.

In the "Art Hive: A Relational Framework for Social Change," Leah Lewis, Heather McLeod, and Xuemei Li explore the role and impact of community Art Hives in bringing diverse groups together in Newfoundland and Labrador. In their consideration of Art Hives, they focus on increasing awareness and respect for cultural identities and histories, fostering understanding and knowledge, and building social connections in the process.

Rosemary C Reilly's "The Murder Next Door: Developing Healing Responses and Building Community Following Trauma Using Research-informed Theatre," focuses on a project that allowed individuals to engage in formulating healing community responses. Using data from three case studies of community trauma, Reilly created a reader's theatre presentation. The theatrical presentation involved post-performance discussions that formed the foundation for audience members' creativity and problem-solving, using their own real-life communities for reference. This functioned as a starting point for policy discussions on how to address trauma effectively and promote community healing outside of an existing real-life traumatic event and its emotional and psychological wake.

The role of theatre as an agent for social change and in empowering the individuals involved is also explored in "Lost in Transition: Brecht's Theatre as a Social Change Agent for Youth Empowerment in the Time of the 20th Anniversary of Hong Kong Handover" by Wai Luk Lo and Ka Lee Carrie Ho. In this chapter, the authors discuss how Brecht's *The Caucasian Chalk Circle* was adapted and performed by a youth theatre in 2016, when Hong Kong was approaching the 20th anniversary of its handover back to China, with a re-interpretation of what empowerment means to the young people of the 21st century. Thirty novice youth performers trained together and collaborated on both the script and six Cantonese songs during six workshops and 200 hours of rehearsals. The youth experienced changes in their self-perception, some noting that they acquired a stronger self-image, and a certain level of comfort stemming from the release of personal and social anxiety.

In "Making Stone Soup: Arts-Based Organisational Interventions and Participants' Sense of Wellbeing, Communication and Teamwork," Mariam Ugarte and Warren Linds address the different arts-based organisational interventions used in a project in a hospital in Kalyandurg, Andhra Pradesh, India, to improve communication and participation among all staff members and, in turn, foster a feeling of wellbeing and empowerment in the nurses. The authors explore the various methods used (dialogic circles, improvisation, storytelling, painting, and puppet making) and show how these methods helped the researcher and the participants to arrive at a place of collaborative work and trust. This also led to a stronger sense of wellbeing, and to improved communication and teamwork.

Then Avivit M. Cherrington's "Visions of Hope in Education: Fostering Student Teachers' Identities of Becoming Agents of Change through a Photo Competition and Exhibition" addresses one of the challenges for teacher education programmes in South Africa, which is to foster hope in student teachers who are able to be responsive to the realities experienced by the country's vastly divergent school contexts. The author explores how engaging with participatory hope-enhancing arts-based activities such as photography might motivate critical self-reflection among the students, shifting their identities towards becoming teachers who are agents of change.

Finally, In "Empty Jars: Using Memoration to Confront the Settler Colonial Project through Arts-Based Research," Deanna Del Vecchio uses creative practice as visual methodology with a focus on the personal change required for social change as she reflects on her identity as a white woman art educator reading Indigenous feminist scholarship. She presents "Typology of Preserves," a series of photographs in a grid format and applies the aesthetic conventions of German photographers Bernd and Hilla Becher (1972–2009) to the photos of the glass jars that her grandmother used for preserving tomatoes and other produce from her Toronto backyard after emigrating from rural Italy in the 1960s.

### 3.2 *Collaborations*

There is arguably not a more important moment in history where relationality and fostering an ethic of care for/with the other, is more important. The rise of extremism in all sectors is undeniable. Globally, we are dealing with the rise of fascism, economic interdependence, and the effects of pandemics such as the Coronavirus (COVID 19), and climate change. Collaboration is one way through which we can begin to create and sustain interconnections among and between systems to unite and heal. What it means to work with others on a joint project underpins the snapshots of collaboration in their focus on how the arts can help to understand more deeply what it means to work relationally for positive social change.

In their consideration of this theme, Amélie Lemieux and Boyd White in "Walking with Wonder: Attunement to the Senses and Relationality in Photographic Inquiry" offer reflections on walking as an artful practice that is an internal, private process that may nonetheless foster public educational change and growth. Taking inspiration from land artist Richard Long, whose artistic practice involves solitary walks across isolated territories and environmental interactions with nature, Lemieux and White reflect on place, space, and time and human↔natural world intra-actions. These engagements are interrogated using phenomenological hermeneutics as a way to engage in conversations on post-qualitative frameworks such as a/r/tography, posthumanist studies, and participatory visual inquiry. These interrogations result in the writing of ekphrastic poetry and photographic records, as the co-authors explore their walking rituals in their respective cities, Halifax and Montreal. The rituals guide the authors towards shared intersections of pathways to reflections on walking and education. While this chapter portrays collaboration between two academics, their hope is to promote wider participation within the education community and beyond.

Next, in "Expression and Action for Change: A Contemporary Arts Center and School Collaboration," Deborah Randolph and Karen Morris present a collaboration between a public arts magnet high school and a contemporary arts center during the exhibition *Dispatches*, featuring artists whose work reflected political, social, and ecological issues. The collaboration resulted in student and faculty reflection, expression, and action while they examined identities and their place in the world with others. The result was a more inclusive school climate. The process unfolded over four months and included field trips, artists' visits. and student expression and action. Student learning went beyond increasing the ability to think critically across disciplines; students responded according to an expanded social conscience. Experiences at the arts center were enhanced by school visits with ten contemporary artists, who brought an on-the-ground perspective to current issues. Students from the entire school created art based on *Dispatches*, made real by the artists' visits, and activated through student conversations, expressions, and actions.

"Moving beyond Celebration Toward Action: Affordances and Tensions in Screening and Audiencing Cellphilms and Participatory Verbatim Films" by Casey Burkholder and Matt Rogers explores participatory verbatim films (dramatic recreations of research texts) and cellphilms (cellphone + film production) as they are screened for different audiences in complicated, and sometimes contradictory ways. Reflecting on their experiences in screening films emerging from two projects with youth in New Brunswick, Canada, they ask: What is the role of a facilitator when audiencing participatory verbatim films and cellphilms? What are the facilitator's responsibilities in screening in different spaces (e.g. at a film festival, to teachers, to youth peers, at schools)? By exploring how these two projects were screened in community settings and at film festivals, this chapter considers the overlapping and distinct opportunities and challenges to screening a girl-led participatory verbatim film (*Social Proof*) and a queer youth-produced cellphilm (*Nackawic Needs a GSA Now!!*).

Extending the possibilities and potential of using film for collaborative educational purposes, is the chapter entitled "Cameraless Film-Making in the Education Classroom: A Professor-Student Artistic Collaboration" by Lisa A. Mitchell and Kerri Kennedy. This research explores Mitchell & Kennedy's experiences as an Arts Education professor and a student film-maker respectively, as they collaborated on designing and delivering a cameraless film-making workshop in the Bachelor of Education program at Trent University in Peterborough, Ontario. The workshop was delivered in six Education classes over a period of 18 months to approximately 150 teacher candidates. A framework of Appreciative Inquiry (AI) was used to explore both (a) the collaborative working relationship between the professor and student, and (b) the film-making experience itself and how participants responded to engaging in the collaborative cameraless film-making process. Data includes participant interviews, workshop photos, and four resulting short digital films. Findings from this research highlight four themes: (1) flattened hierarchy, (2) hybrid teaching, (3) personalised learning, and (4) and affective expression.

Next, Tone Pernille Østern, in her chapter, "Choreographic Processes as Poetic, Political, and Pedagogical Action in Contemporary Times," diffracts through this ongoing choreographic research project by exploring the question of how choreography can become socially engaged when the working structures focus on collaboration. The author, a choreographer/teacher educator/researcher, understands choreography as a choreographic-pedagogical entanglement. In this entanglement poetical, pedagogical, and political dimensions crystallise. As a result of her diffractions through the artistic research material, the author proposes *contemporary times* as concept and as necessary disturbance and friction in order to push choreography-as-action into the world. Choreography is poetical-pedagogical-political entanglement, and in this, choreography can contribute not only to artistic, but also to pedagogical and social change.

In their chapter, Madeline Hoak, Alisan Funk, and Dan Berkley bring their professional careers in the circus arts to explore "Teaching the Mind-body: Integrating Knowledges through Circus Arts." Building on a deep interest and involvement with other academic domains, including physics, history, and education they find that combining circus arts with these traditionally academic subjects motivates circus students to engage with their own learning processes. Through an exploration of their own collaborative pedagogical discussions based on their experiences of teaching students of circus arts, the authors identify three common ways in which students experience agency through the integration of circus practice and academic knowledges. First, students are able to build new knowledge from their domains of comfort into domains of discomfort. Second, combining physical and academic knowledge expands student access to creative solutions, thereby expanding their knowledge horizons. Finally, collaboration enables community building, which elicits the development of trust in new situations.

The three authors, Giang Hoang Le Nguyen, Trinh Ngoc Phuong Bui, and Jodi Latremouille, of the next chapter, "Contemplative Arts-Based Practices in Education: Weaving Our Way towards Social and Ecological Justice through Transcultural Storymaking," find inspiration through the act of *storymaking* as an active and ethical creative response to the ecological and social times in which we live today. In this three-part life writing narrative, they braid their reflections regarding the contemplative art genres of Photo-Story, life writing, holistic teaching practices, and creative mindfulness art. This work takes place across diverse international backgrounds and life experiences. Through a combination of methodological approaches, including Indigenous and Eastern philosophies, and ecological ways of knowing, the authors wonder, individually and collaboratively, how one/they might make and re-make individual and collective stories through the contemplative arts. Their hope is that a holistic education oriented towards a more hopeful, humane, and just world can take shape.

Finally, Sue Uhlig, Amy Migliore, and Jacqueline Reid-Walsh in "The Generative Act of Critical Pedagogy: Animating Children's Books and Games as Research Practice," highlight how critical pedagogy can be an animated and generative act of research. The authors use a course housed in the Department of Curriculum and Instruction in an American university as a case study in which they recount their own pedagogical experiences in the critical examination of children's books, toys, and games. The approach to the course encouraged arts-based responses through animations with the aim to provoke thinking and impel deeper connections to content and to each other. The framework of a participatory animation afforded learners and researchers the opportunity to question how art activates the space outside the classroom and moves into the public sphere through engagement with toys and children's books. What emerged from these creative animations was an interactive, engaging, and responsive pedagogy that listens, looks deeper, and invites mutual recognition. In this manner, historical books, toys, and games for children are linked to the present and shown to aid in teaching about an interconnectedness that makes way for critical examination and creative acts of research.

### 3.3 *Teaching and Pedagogy*

How can those teaching in universities, colleges, and schools navigate pedagogical spaces through art, and how might art contribute to bringing about social change? A unifying feature of the "Art for Social Change" symposium that inspired this book in the first place was the idea of the arts and artistic expression as a medium for supporting professional learning, and for advancing the use of classroom practices that seek to make a difference.

Thus, we begin this final set of snapshots with Kathleen Pithouse-Morgan's "Our Words Flowing into Wide Futures: Making a Difference through Poetic Professional Learning." Pithouse-Morgan has collaborated with many others to engage the power of poetic inquiry for researching and performing professional learning. Here she shows how she looked back over this scholarship in South Africa to ask the question, "What difference can poetry make to professional learning?" The chapter demonstrates how the experience of poetry making, especially when it is collective, can permeate professional learning research and practice with imagination, feeling, and sensory impressions in ways that intensify and interconnect self-insight, care for others, and social awareness.

Also writing of South African Higher Education, the next chapter by Margaret Müller and Frans Kruger, "Eight Weeks, Eight Verses: Using Arts-Based Inquiry to Explore Educator Subjectivity and Reflexivity during a Time of Social Change" explores the complexity, messiness, and intertwined nature of personal and professional experiences during a time of social change in the country. In recent years student protests at South African institutions of higher education have highlighted and intensified calls for decolonisation and the transformation of curricula and pedagogy. The authors use art to foreground the entanglement of educator subjectivity, memory, and experience in relation to this specific context.

Then Victoria L. Dickman-Burnett, in "Dear Artemisia: Art as Transformation in Sexual Violence Prevention," discusses the transformative power of art in the context of a high school sexual violence prevention program. To highlight the transformative power of art, this chapter is written in the form of a letter to Artemisia Gentileschi, a baroque painter and rape survivor. Gentileschi is famous for the trial resulting from her rape at the hands of her mentor as well as for her paintings, which depict feminine rage realistically. The combination of art and survivorship makes Gentileschi the ideal intended audience for such a letter.

Keeping with the idea of students' creative productions to address sexual violence, Esther Armaignac, in her chapter "Fiction for Social Change: Addressing Gender in and through Popular Films," asks the question: "How can popular culture and creative practices be used to engage students in discussing gender roles, norms related to gender, consent and sexual harassment? As she notes, fiction can be a powerful way of engaging readers, and, as such, fiction can function as a strong critical tool. This chapter explores how popular culture and creative practices can be used to engage secondary students in discussing issues related to gender and sexuality.

Makram Ayache's chapter, "Unconscious Acts: An Auto-ethnographic Investigation into Euro-centric White Normative Consciousness in Theatre Training Programs in Canada," interrogates how white normative consciousness can have an impact on the racialised students in classical conservatory actor training programs. The author examines a micro-incident in which a seemingly innocuous comment made by a professor, "I saw a child of war," can be explained as an orientalist analysis of his brown body in performance.

Next, Rebecca Bourgault, in "A Pedagogy of Presence: Attending to Context, Process, Being, and Belonging," elaborates on an experimental use of a pedagogy of presence introduced in an open studio at a shelter for homeless women. Part social art practice tinged with quiet activism and part meditation, in borrowing from theories of adult learning, she describes how the qualities of presence at the open studio offered a calming and centering counterpoise to the precarious living situation experienced by participants. She considers how this lived awareness of the value of presence enhances human connections through shared art-making, listening, and a sense of social belonging.

Amber C. Coleman's chapter, "Conceptualising a Black Feminist Arts Pedagogy: Looking Back to Look Forward" explores how Black women's experiences can be better included in art educational practices. Recognising how much Black women's perspectives matter and have value in discussions of art pedagogy, she notes that their art educational experiences are often under-represented. She looks at how Black feminist arts pedagogy centres the experiences and knowledges of marginalised groups and calls for the collaborative construction of meaning and for practices of social justice So that art-making can become a tool of empowerment.

Appropriately, the final chapter in this section and in the book as a whole, is Amanda Claudia Wager's and Kristen P. Goessling's "Working toward Sustainable Creative Social Justice Practices: Advancing Equity and Justice in the Academy." As they say, sustainability is key. Drawing on their various identities as scholars-activists-educators-artists, the authors share a critical pedagogical commitment to supporting the development of the critical consciousness of students and colleagues. In their chapter they demonstrate the potential of incorporating arts into different types of curriculum for generating social and personal change through a reciprocal process made possible through art-based pedagogical practices.

•••

The importance of bringing together in one place so many examples of artists, educators, arts educators, and community groups using the arts for social change, reminds us of, and connects us to a larger community of practice in which becoming through being can be lived. This collective and collaborative interconnected work breaks down hierarchies of what knowledges are worth knowing (and who gets to decide what they are) by beginning with making, doing, and feeling on a human embodied level that provokes connections and interconnections betwixt and between many variables.

We invite you, as readers, to consider the spaces between the snapshots, and the blurred borders that quick pictures might elicit so that memory, imagination, and your own readings of the possibilities and potential for hope that these snapshots conjure up might become a part of your own imaginaries.

## References

Carter, M. (2016). Postcards from prison: An autophenomenological inquiry. *Journal of Curriculum Theorizing, 31*(1), 72–87.

Derrida, J. (1987). *The post card: From Socrates to Freud and beyond.* University of Chicago Press.

Furman, G. C. (1998). Postmodernism and community in schools: Unravelling the paradox. *Educational Administration Quarterly, 34*(3), 298–328.

Greene, M. (1995). *Releasing the imagination: Essays on education, the arts and social change.* Jossey-Bass.

Mitchell, C. Pithouse-Morgan, K, & Pillay, D. (2020). Mosaic-ing memory in teacher education and professional learning. *Other Education: Journal of Educational Alternatives, 9*(1), 7–20.

Mreiwed, H., Carter, M., & Shabtay, A. (2017). Building classroom community through drama education. *Australia Journal of Drama, 44*(1), 44–57. https://doi/10.1080/14452294.2017.1329680

Pillay, D., Pithouse-Morgan, K., & Naicker, I. (Eds.). (2017). *Object medleys: Interpretive possibilities for educational research.* Sense.

Pithouse-Morgan, K., Pillay, D., & Mitchell, C. (Eds.). (2019). *Memory mosaics: Researching teacher professional learning through artful memory-work.* Springer.

# PART 1

## *Community Building*

∴

CHAPTER 2

# "Imagining Things Being Otherwise"

## *Rethinking Community and the Art Museum Experience*

*Sage Kincaid and Callan Steinmann*

Guided by Maxine Greene's assertion "that imagining things being otherwise may be a first step toward acting on the belief that they can be changed" (1995, p. 22), in this chapter we examine how community was experienced by participants in two public programs—Studio Workshop and Morning Mindfulness—at the Georgia Museum of Art. Through the practices of artmaking and mindfulness, these programs challenge traditional conceptions of museum-going and offer visitors new ways of being and performing community in an art museum space. Studio Workshop is an artmaking program for adults featuring studio practice in response to works of art in the museum. Morning Mindfulness invites deep engagement with works of art using guided contemplative practice and encouraging an attentive way of being. Both programs prioritise visitor response and agency, inviting new ways of connecting with other participants, the museum space, and works of art.

## 1 Evolving Theory and Practice in Art Museum Education

The museum field has undergone an ideological evolution over the last several decades, described twenty years ago by Stephen Weil as a shift from museums "being about something to being for somebody" (1999, p. 1). Beginning in the 1800s, museum practice prioritised the object over all else, and the role of the curator was to transmit art historical knowledge and expertise to the visitor. Postmodern art theory of the mid-20th century had a widespread impact on aesthetic education as art educators embraced what Olivia Gude (2004) called "a suspicion of totalizing discourses and grand narratives," rejecting "the belief that there is one right way to organize and understand things" (p. 13). The museum transitioned from being an essentially modernist institution, seeking to transmit objective and universal truths, to what we call the post-museum, an institution that recognises that reality is shaped both individually and collectively (Hooper-Greenhill, 2000). In the post-museum, museum practice is socially responsive, understanding that interpretation and meaning making are "dialogical, cyclical, *and* built/mediated/revised based on personal

 | DOI: 10.1163/9789004442870_002

understandings of the world" (Kletchka, 2018, p. 301, original emphasis). This constructivist, visitor-centered paradigm of museum practice (Sami & Michaelson, 2016) acknowledges that works of art are not static objects with a singular meaning, but, rather, objects of experience (Wood & Latham, 2014) that can be interpreted differently depending on the context within which individuals find themselves.

Visitor-centered museum education programs reflect these shifting goals as museum educators have reoriented their practices toward programming and pedagogy that is responsive to the diverse communities they serve (Anderson, 2012). Today's museum educators understand that meaning-making is at the core of the art museum experience and, as Simon (2010) has noted, they strive to create opportunities for visitors to engage actively with museum collections, spaces, and each other through participatory encounters with works of art. By "cultivating a culture of experimentation" (p. 316), art museums can collaborate with visitors and break down hierarchical divisions between institutions and the people they serve. As Rika Burnham and Elliott Kai-Kee (2007) have written, museum educators of today "ask that museums be not only places where people can participate in their own acts of constructing meaning but also places where we redefine the visitors themselves from information seekers to seekers of experience, of reflection, of imagination" (p. 12).

### 1.1 *Researching Visitor Experience in Museums*

Scholarship in the museum field over the last twenty to thirty years reflects these theoretical shifts in museum philosophy and growing interest in visitor experience. Using a range of research methodologies, visitor studies seek to uncover the attitudes, values, experiences, and opinions of museumgoers. Eilean Hooper-Greenhill (2006) has written that in order to understand the visitor experience, museum professionals cannot merely observe people in the galleries, but must, instead, explore the subjective perspective of individual visitors. "In terms of how visitors are conceived," she wrote, "there is a shift from thinking about visitors as an undifferentiated mass public to beginning to accept visitors as active interpreters and performers of meaning-making practices within complex cultural sites" (p. 362).

Research into visitor experience over the past several decades by Falk and Dierking (2013), has shown that the museum experience is a complex, personal process influenced by many nuanced factors including interactions among the visitor's personal context (life experience, background, and expectations), sociocultural context (cultural background and social dimensions of the visit), the physical context (architecture of the building and exhibition design) and time. As each visitor brings their own set of life experiences, preferences, and knowledge to the museum, museum staff can no longer dictate a "one-size-fits-all" interpretation to visitors but must, instead, become "a collaborator in the meaning-making process" (Lankford, 2002, p. 146).

Programs like mindfulness, slow looking, and artmaking in museum spaces invite audiences to respond, ponder, connect, and question—decidedly active ways of being that challenge traditional hierarchical models of museum authority and empower visitors with the tools to direct their own museum experiences.

### 1.2 *A Phenomenological Approach*

Considering the urgent need for museum educators to reflect critically on current practice, and that reviews of literature in the field revealed no empirical research that specifically addresses the visitor experience in either artmaking or mindfulness museum programs, we conducted two separate studies. By exploring how participants experience these public programs, both studies aimed to address a gap in the literature and better understand how to connect meaningfully and creatively with museum audiences.

Both studies used qualitative research methods. This approach focuses on a holistic view of the research situation, moving away from a modernist epistemology to one that acknowledges the situatedness and complex nature of human experience. Within the framework of qualitative research, a phenomenological approach is appropriate for an investigation of visitor experience because it seeks to understand the participants' lifeworlds, or lived experiences of the world (Dahlberg, Dahlberg, & Nyström, 2008; Vagle, 2014; van Manen, 1990). Phenomenology is, in essence, the study of the structures of lived experience in people's everyday lives. It emphasises the inseparability of experience from the world and asserts that the body is the primary site through which we know the world (Merleau-Ponty, 1945/1995). In understanding museum visitor experience—as well as the role of researcher—as embodied and situated, we can acknowledge the myriad contexts that visitors bring with them and move closer to an understanding not only of the experience for participants, but also an interpretation of the meaning of the experience (Dahlberg & Dahlberg, 2020).

## 2 Setting and Program Descriptions

Both research projects described here took place at the Georgia Museum of Art (GMOA), the campus museum of the University of Georgia and Georgia's official state museum of art. Founded in the 1940s, today the museum is home to over 12,000 works of art, including 19th- and 20th-century American art, contemporary works, and a European art collection. As both a university museum and the official state art museum, GMOA serves a broad range of audiences at the university, in the Athens community, and statewide. Admission is free, and the museum's unofficial mottos are "Free Inspiration" and "Art for Everyone." The museum offers a variety of on- and off-site programming for all ages, including family programs, K–12 tours, film screenings, student nights for UGA students, and more.

### 2.1 *Studio Workshop*

The Studio Workshop program at the Georgia Museum of Art began in 2015. Geared toward adult visitors, the program combines studio practice with gallery exploration, offering participants the opportunity to explore artistic media and techniques and connect to the museum and its collection. Each Studio Workshop session consists of four consecutive meetings on Thursday evenings from 6:30 to 8:30. Sessions are limited to fifteen participants. No prior studio art experience is required. Sessions are led by Athens-area teaching artists, and each class pairs studio practice with object-based experiences. During the course of a single class, the group might sketch and draw inspiration from objects in the galleries, view selections of works of art pulled from storage in the Collection Study room, and experiment with various artistic media in the Studio Classroom. Studio Workshop sessions have encompassed a range of topics including watercolor and gouache, drawing basics, printmaking, fibre arts, calligraphy, biomorphic acrylics, bookbinding, and more. Steinmann's doctoral research focused on Studio Workshop, and she gathered data from January 2016 through March 2017, including observations, field notes, interviews, photography, participant artwork, and written reflections from fourteen adult participants.

### 2.2 *Morning Mindfulness*

Morning Mindfulness was also started in 2015, and occurs every other Friday from 9:30 to 10:30 a.m. during the school year for a total of sixteen sessions. The program is free and open to the public, no experience is necessary, and yoga mats and meditation pillows are provided. Each session attracts twenty to forty people, with participants ranging from college students to retirees. The program begins with a brief introduction by museum staff and then is led by a mindfulness instructor who guides the group in breathing exercises and contemplative looking at works of art. Morning Mindfulness concludes with reflection about what participants noticed and experienced. In the context of this program, mindfulness is understood as "the awareness that emerges through paying attention on purpose, in the present moment, and non-judgmentally to the unfolding of experience" (Kabat-Zinn, 200, p. 145). For Kincaid's doctoral research, she collected data from January to November 2018 from twelve interviews, fifteen observations, and fifty written narratives.

## 3 Finding Community

The two doctoral studies were conducted independently. Steinmann and Kincaid each used similar phenomenological approaches to data collection, including participant observation, photography, written reflections, and semi-structured interviews. While the phenomenon of each individual program is distinct and unique, later comparison of findings revealed many intriguing parallels in the ways in which community manifested during the two programs. In the following sections, we present a description of findings related to how participants of both Studio Workshop (SW) and Morning Mindfulness (MM) experienced community. We conclude with recommendations for developing museum programming that creates a sense of community.

Community in the context of these two art museum programs is understood as comprising three categories that are always on the move, together, in a fluid, responsive interaction. Participants experience community not just with other people in the group, but also within a space (with the space) and within the exchange that occurs between the viewer and a work of art (with the art). Community in these programs is a praxis and can be understood as an ever-evolving communion between participants and their environment. Below, we describe the structure of this experience in three parts.

### 3.1 *Community Builds through Shared Experience*

In both programs, participants experienced community with others in the program through the act of being and doing together in a shared experience. The programs created openings for people to connect with one another as they participated in program activities, noticed how others engaged with the space and works of art, and shared perspectives and knowledge along the way. Participants in both programs described a special "group energy," often comparing how their experience differed from meditating or making art alone, which for many people had felt "isolating" or "lonely" in the past. One participant noted that "[i]n a community with art, I think it helped me learn more, and I can grasp more than if I did it by myself" (MM). Participants were also guided by the embodied experience of other participants; one interviewee said, "Creativity breeds creativity … So [inspiration comes] not just from the work of art that we see, or that we talk about, it's also the works of art that are being created by others in the space" (SW). Another interviewee observed that "when we're not talking to each other, to me, it is still community in that we came together and then you learn from the experience of others" (MM).

Participants in both programs also experienced community by sharing perspectives, information, and interpretations of works of art. Conversation or reflections on works of art often resulted in richer understandings than if individuals viewed art alone. One interviewee commented on this sharing of different perspectives,

> It reminded me of lying in the grass and looking at the sky and seeing shapes in the clouds, and how you'll see something completely different from the next person ... I wasn't expecting to hear somebody say something so different from what I was thinking. (SW)

Building meaning together resulted in richer connections. One participant noted,

> It was so neat because one person would chime in and then another person would piggyback off what the last person said. It felt like there's a sense of little bits of connection coming together. I could feel more and more connection growing in the group. (MM)

A creative learning community was built from seeing the embodied experience of others and considering the unique perspectives of different participants.

### 3.2 *Community Builds in a Place Apart*

Participants in both programs experienced community when they felt a sense of fellowship with the museum. The museum offered a special place where participants could feel connected to the space and receptive to an unfolding of the experience at hand, either in Studio Workshop or in Morning Mindfulness. Within each program, participants were aware of being in a place apart from their usual habits. They noticed the overall atmosphere of the space itself, using descriptive language like "special," "calm," and "meditative" to evoke the feeling of being in the museum. Many likened entering the museum to crossing over a boundary into a different atmosphere, for example,

> It's like church or something. I'm not sure how to put it exactly, it's just a special place to be. Some of it has to do with the art, obviously, but it's not just that ... It feels like you're in a very special, fancy place. (SW)

Another participant noted that

> the museum setting, that's the unifying, comforting thing. I mean from the time you walk in the door, because the museum in and of itself has a calming effect, at least it does for me and a kind of quiet cathedral-type feeling. I think there's something about the light in the early morning and then the excitement of going up the stairs to the galleries. (MM)

Interviewees also noticed that being in the museum had an impact on their state of mind. Upon entering the museum, one participant said, "It really re-centered my approach. It was a great transition from leaving the workday … to entering into this new place where you're going to refocus your attention on art" (SW) and another

> felt transformed when I walk in the door. I know I'm in a different setting and it kind of frees my emotions and brain up a little bit. And then the different activities that we do kind of reinforce it and also expand into kind of another place. (MM)

### 3.3 *Community Builds with Art*

In both programs, participants experienced a sense of community with the works of art in the museum. Program activities invited participants to explore objects in the galleries through close looking, guided beholding exercises, drawing, photography, writing—all approaches that encourage active engagement, personal connection, and contemplation. Participants noticed the significance of being physically with art objects.

> You can look at slides all day long. You can look at books, and the photographs [of works of art] are beautiful. But seeing something in the flesh is different. It's like the difference between looking at a travel magazine and actually going to France. It's different when you see it with your own eyes … whatever you bring to it that day is going to change your attitude about it. Being there is different. Seeing it with your own eyes, seeing the real thing. (SW)

Participants in both programs also described a distinct sense of communion with the artists who created the objects. One interviewee observed that "[i]t's nice to just stand there and to really absorb the art. I feel like you're looking into a window of somebody's consciousness, into a window of somebody's thoughts or even another time space reality" (MM). The embodied acts of mindfulness meditation and artmaking practice created a bridge of experience, allowing group members to reach across time and space to connect with the humans behind the works of art. One participant mused, "I've stopped to smell the roses before, but this was different ... This was different because I had to interact with art, the work of another human" (MM). Another noted,

> Being around the centuries' worth of artwork inspires me ... I feel closer to the artists themselves. Getting to see the works up close, trying to figure out how the artists worked and what influenced them, gives me new ideas for my own work and a sublime feeling of my place in art making's long history. (SW)

Another interviewee described her experience as a "collaboration with the museum pieces in a way" (SW).

## 4 Conclusion

Through mindfulness and artmaking, participants experience a sense of community not only with each other but with the museum, works of art, and the artists who created the art in the museum. In this space of communion, program participants experience the museum in a new way and value the connections forged through participatory engagement. Through the practices embodied in these two programs, museum educators can aid in a "conscious participation" (Eisner, 2002, p. 24), creating space for community building, and exploring new ways of being in the museum, as illustrated by this participant's experience.

> It's learning a different way. It does help, I don't want to say train, but it does help maybe retrain or breakdown these perceived rules that some of us might have picked up that this is how you're supposed to do or be. (MM)

The important work of moving museums toward breaking down "perceived rules" and being more socially responsive is ongoing, but we offer the following as essential components for building community through public programs.

- *Welcoming visitors into the museum for a special experience.* By participating in a designated museum program, individuals can feel a sense of belonging in the museum space. While museumgoers can often feel that museums are intimidating or uninviting, guidance from museum staff and program instructors offer support and scaffolding for the experience. The specialness of the museum space can help participants "uncouple from the ordinary" (Greene, 1984, p. 124), as the environment helps them engage in the work at hand. Repeat visits with the same group members and instructors, in the same spaces, can also create a sense of comfort and familiarity with the museum as an institution over time.

– *Creating openings for visitor agency and participation.* While offering guidance and support, these programs also provide ample opportunity for participants to become active agents in their own museum experience. Maxine Greene (1986) has written that art educators must create "atmospheres that foster active exploring rather than passivity, that allow for the unpredictable and the unforeseen" (p. 57). In the museum, open-ended participatory activities that allow visitors to move freely through the galleries, choose which works of art to focus on, and engage in shared conversation and reflection with one another can create openings for surprising, unprescribed moments of meaning-making to occur.
– *Inviting deep, personal engagement with works of art.* Through both guided activities and open-ended exploration, these programs invite visitors to experience works of art through active engagement. Extended looking, sketching, writing, and beholding exercises encourage slowing down, allowing participants to "notice what there is to be noticed," and in turn "achieve them as variously meaningful" (Greene, 1995, p. 6).

Programs like Studio Workshop and Morning Mindfulness activate the museum in ways that can lead to transformative experiences that help people make connections between themselves and works of art, one another, and the world around them. Building community in a museum provides participants with a space in which they feel comfortable and embrace new ways of being with each other and art, which can, in turn, further help to erode the rigid hierarchical structure of modernist museum practice. These are small steps in imagining things being otherwise. It is our hope that by reimagining ways of being in the museum and forging connections with art and each other, we are moving closer to what Greene (1984) calls "transforming the petrified world" (p. 134).

## References

Anderson, G. (2012). A framework: Reinventing the museum. In G. Anderson (Ed.), *Reinventing the museum: The evolving conversation on the paradigm shift* (2nd ed., pp. 1–10). AltaMira Press.

Burnham, R. & Kai-Kee, E. (2007). Museum education and the project of interpretation in the twenty-first century. *The Journal of Aesthetic Education, 41*(2), 11–13.

Dahlberg, H., & Dahlberg, K. (2020). Open and reflective lifeworld research: A third way. *Qualitative Inquiry, 26*(5), 458–464.

Dahlberg, K., Dahlberg, H., & Nyström, M. (2008). *Reflective lifeworld research.* Studentlitteratur AB.

Eisner, E. (2002). *The arts and the creation of the mind.* Yale University Press.

Falk, J., & Dierking, L. (2013). *The museum experience revisited.* Left Coast Press, Inc.

Greene, M. (1984). The art of being present: Educating for aesthetic encounters. *The Journal of Education, 166*(2), 123–135.

Greene, M. (1995). *Releasing the imagination: Essays on education, the arts, and social change.* Jossey-Bass.

Gude, O. (2004). Postmodern principles: In search of a 21st century art education. *Art Education, 57*(1), 6–14.

Hooper-Greenhill, E. (2000). *Museums and the interpretation of visual culture.* Routledge.

Hooper-Greenhill, E. (2006). Studying visitors. In S. Macdonald (Ed.), *A companion to museum studies* (pp. 362–376). Blackwell.

Kabat-Zinn, J. (1994). *Wherever you go, there you are: Mindfulness meditation in everyday life.* Hyperion Books.

Kletchka, D. C. (2018). Toward post-critical museologies in U.S. art museums. *Studies in Art Education, 59*(4), 297–310.

Lankford, E. L. (2002). Aesthetic experience in constructivist museums. *The Journal of Aesthetic Experience, 36*(2), 140–153.

Merleau-Ponty, M. (1995). *Phenomenology of perception* (C. Smith, Trans.). Routledge. (Original work published 1945)

Samis, P., & Michaelson, M. (2016). *Creating the visitor-centered museum.* Routledge.

Simon, N. (2010). *The participatory museum.* Museum 2.0.

Vagle, M. (2014). *Crafting phenomenological research.* Routledge.

van Manen, M. (1990). *Researching lived experience: Human science for an action sensitive pedagogy.* The State University of New York Press.

Weil, S. (1999). From being about something to being for somebody: The ongoing transformation of the American museum. *Daedalus, 128*(3), 229–258.

Wood, E., & Latham, K. (2014). *The objects of experience: Transforming visitor-object encounters in museums.* Left Coast Press.

CHAPTER 3

# Voices from the Heart

## *Using Community and Art to Foster Social Change in Pre-Service Teachers*

*Sheryl Smith-Gilman*

One of the most important areas of attention to cultivating any classroom community lies in the interactions between educators and their students. Those connections are at the very heart of teaching. The quality of such exchanges may even influence students as to the kind of relationships they will develop over their lifetimes. There is no scientific formula to assure a successful and positive classroom environment. However, a classroom that exhibits an atmosphere of respect, empathy, and supportive interactions characterises a climate conducive to healthy experiences for teaching and for learning (Phipps, 2016). The classroom community can reflect caring that includes skillful teaching, along with empowering learners to be responsible in their work together. Maxine Greene (1995) encourages us to contemplate "a community that is always in the making, marked by an emerging solidarity, a sharing of certain beliefs" (p. 39). Consequently, a classroom community is also intentional and dependent on the ongoing active contributions of its students and teachers (Mreiwed, Carter, & Shabtay, 2017; Carter, 2014). How they co-construct learning as a cohesive, respectful, safe, open, and interactive place is what may lead to the fostering of a warm, yet challenging experience for all involved as Carter (2014) has reminded us.

I have always believed that educators who welcome diversity in their classrooms will work arduously to create a cohesive community. These are the teachers who well understand the importance of a child's positive self-identity and will take measures to create space for every child's social and emotional comfort. Classroom practice that pursues positive learning experiences, inclusiveness, and security for each learner is the goal of teachers who respect diversity and seek to contribute to the human and social growth of their students. Such teachers are modeling and creating a community of learners in their classrooms. Indeed, there have been advancements in how diversity is celebrated, and support for social justice has been substantial (Cole, 2014; Fiorello, 2010), yet how teachers deal personally and professionally with issues related to diversity and inclusion are sometimes problematic. Regrettably, many elementary school systems continue to foster prescriptive objectives, standardised measurements, and demonstrate limited interest in creating classroom

 | DOI: 10.1163/9789004442870_003

community (Pinar, 2004; Carter, 2015). And so, I wonder how soon-to-be teachers address the needs of diversity issues in order to generate effective, safe, and collegial learning environments.

As a professor in a university teacher education program, I think about how I can support future educators to think broadly and intentionally about issues of diversity such as race, culture, language, inclusion, and social and economic influences so that they do not unknowingly perpetuate their own biases or cultural and economic values in their classrooms. How can my pre-service teachers come to recognise the value of their own points of view and the boundaries of their self-identity while at the same time holding space to care for and nurture the varied abilities of young children? How can I sensitise my students to understand children deeply and to solidify community? In Quebec, for example, teachers often feel challenged by the task of creating true communities since they are presented with diverse inclusive classrooms along with Ministry demands to foster homogeneity, particularly of the language of instruction. New immigrants to Quebec have no choice but to attend French schools; they are placed in mixed-age so-called special classes or classes d'accueil.[1] The focus is on language and language alone; this is the introduction of these children to Quebec culture.

With the goal of fostering empathy and having conversations, I challenge my pre-service teachers, through an arts-based methodology, to unlock their own potential to represent what will be meaningful to their own practice for they, too, are part of the diverse population in our university. Specifically, can my pre-service teachers welcome all young children, those leaders of intuition and imagination? I believe an empathetic approach needs to come first in the practice of teaching. Gallagher and Thordarson (2018) have pointed out that empathy leads to authentic listening and feeling toward people's experiences, laying foundations for establishing community within a classroom.

Accordingly, as a pertinent and habitual exercise in a mandatory course I teach, Kindergarten Classroom Pedagogy, I launch initial discussions with attention to caring and listening to children—an empathetic approach. My students are in the second year of their teacher education program and are beginning their methods courses of study. I encourage them to examine how they envision their possible role as a teacher, and to contemplate the image they hold of the young child. My belief in commencing this trajectory of study defends the idea that their teaching and learning reflects their thoughts and the mental images they have of children. Such grounding is at the heart of the kind of community that must be created in a classroom of young learners just starting school. Establishing a classroom community implies creating an environment in which learners come together for common objectives or goals. A strong classroom community extends that definition to underscore feelings of empowerment for students, and the responsibility and motivation to interact socially.

Notably, profound attention to the image of the child first emerged from the Reggio Emilia approach to early childhood education (Rinaldi, 2001). It focuses on the central contemplation of the question, "What is your image of the child?" since there are many conceivable images. Malaguzzi (1994) suggests that teaching begins with how the child is viewed. He explained,

> There are hundreds of different images of the child. Each one of you has inside yourself an image of the child that directs you as you begin to relate to a child. This theory within you pushes you to behave in certain ways; it orients you as you talk to the child, listen to the child, observe the child. (p. 52)

Given Malaguzzi's suggestion that there may be hundreds of different images, attending to young learners with empathy and mindfulness to diversity calls for discussion about how children might be taught. According to the Reggio Emilia approach, a positive image of the child has to be retained as central to all teaching and learning. Gandini (1993) insisted that all children bring curiosity, preparedness, potential, inquisitiveness, and interest to constructing their learning. Such principles are founded on ethics related to quality care, including bringing adults and children together and creating community.

Therefore, our beginning class discussions respond to the question, "What is your image of the child?" Some of my students' immediate responses have included the words: naïve; silly; wild; cute; sponges. I then ask my students to consider issues they think young children may encounter today. My students' responses deepen our conversation and significant discussion topics emerge such as early introduction of technology, child health and obesity, immigration and language challenges, and standardised goals remaining constant while developmental appropriateness and culture are ignored. Unfortunately, such concerns have led to a decrease in children's overall success and have hindered their ability to be creative (Cutcher & Cook, 2016).

Consequently, as a first assignment, I take my pre-service teachers through an empathetic journey that considers their image of the child. I have them select a medium in which to create an arts-based representation that depicts their image of the child, based on values for teaching they deem essential. This assignment has many objectives. First, I aim to model a process of framing learning to help reconnect my pre-service teachers with their own creativity which often gets lost along the way during their years of schooling. Additionally, I hope the exercise will support my students to uncover the needs of their future students and help them approach diverse Kindergarteners, who are developing at varying rates. Purposefully, I aim to generate a community of Education student learners who will grow into their teacher identities and consider values that go beyond materials and strategies (that are still important) and build learning in an environment that embraces community. Vecchi (2010) has reminded us that teachers today are often seduced by techniques and that they tend to implement them with young children with a simplified knowledge of the child's expressive and creative potential. With their careful consideration of their image of the child, I aim to support my pre-service teachers to contemplate who children are, socially and emotionally, first, and then to teach without restricting these children's learning to predetermined schemes.

When we shared these completed assignments of a particular class, I was completely taken aback by my pre-service teachers' meticulous considerations. Presentations included performances of poetry relating that the child is a curious being, dioramas portraying children at different kinds of play to illustrate the image of the child as having potential, and a mobile created out of clay formations consisting of children's emotionally expressive faces, as well as books and other representations that depicted the child as a learner. However, one image of the child, created by a group of four future educators, brought many of us to tears during their presentation—the child as having rights (Figure 3.1).[2]

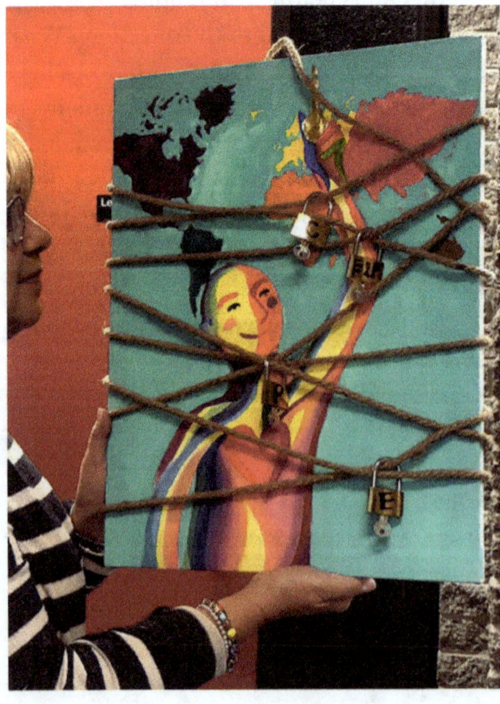

FIGURE 3.1
The child as having rights

This group explained they had painted a child intentionally, using a variety of colours to represent every child, culture, gender, religion, race, and ability. The heart at the center of the child's chest depicts the loving soul they believe all children possess. The maps in the background of the painting represent the homelands of the artists, these future teachers who collaborated on this image of the child. They were four young women whose rights were challenged during their own early years in education. These pre-service teachers, immigrants from Syria, Hong Kong, the US, and Colombia, shared their stories about how their rights to an education were taken away from them at a young age. They disclosed how they were denied freedom of expression, protection, the right to play, and the right to be educated. Their loss of rights, represented by the ropes surrounding the painting and actual locks that were fastened, constrained them from ever getting what was duly theirs. This group researched the UN Convention on the Rights of the Child (CRC) and the Canadian Charter of Human Rights and Freedoms and, to represent these, painted a golden key in the child's hand, making clear their view of the child as demanding and having rights. These student teachers demonstrated their own mindset regarding social change and promising their students a better future than the past they had each endured as children. Such a powerful statement illustrates how the arts can provide opportunity for voices to be heard, allowing others to listen and have conversations. And, as each quoted right to education, play, security, and freedom was read aloud, the young women unlocked the locks, removed the ropes, and set the painting, and, by implication, the child, free.

## 1 The Arts and Community

Our exercise of learning to understand the implications of the image of the young child affected us all and this was indeed a personal, powerful, and affecting experience as we created a community of learners in our university classroom. The use of the arts brought about a shift in thinking about the self and others in educational settings. New understandings emerged for our class community; a change occurred amid an exercise of trust and risk taking in which dialogue was valued and encouraged. The pre-service teachers' acts of disclosure, spoken through their artistic representation, produced trust. The artistic ways of knowing proved to be meaningful tools that allowed my pre-service teachers to be heard, to tell their stories, to test their theories, and share understandings interactively. When we consider what art means and does, we speak of extensions to our thinking and to our considerations. The function of art is to create impact or sensors of meaning making, sensors that may distinguish all that is unbearable, discomforting, and unacceptable in the world.

Undeniably, the arts here developed empathetic sensors that were unleashed. This group of students released their stories and their emotions through the arts, and authentic listening happened for us all. Indeed, such risk-taking and listening are crucial elements for creating strong empathetic bonds (see Gallagher & Thordarson, 2018), the foundation for developing a trustworthy community. Yet, sensors can also have the capacity to prompt extensions of meaning, to harmonise communities providing pathways out of darkness, releasing oppression, and softening injustices.

Importantly, the pre-service teachers' explorations of various art mediums supported their attempts to challenge ideas from their own perspectives, and, importantly, in a space that was comfortable for them (see Wright, 2003). When my students had opportunities to be actively involved in the arts, they had opportunities to be honest, transparent, and work with discomfort, strengthening their community of learners. Their backgrounds allowed them to recognise various possibilities about children, to acknowledge the gift of education, and it provided them with different conduits into teaching. Greene (2004) maintained that a process of transforming awareness through artistic experiences underscores how teachers can implement the arts to develop knowledge along with creating spaces for dialogue, relationships, and a deeper awareness of possibilities. What emerged as significant was a formation of teacher identity and self-esteem, central to fostering a mindset of possibilities for community building. My students' reflections acknowledged that they now felt more comfortable with taking risks and believed that they could reach out better to all students. Their diverse perspectives expressed through the arts led to new insights and created a community of learners whose knowledge was broadened creatively and empathetically.

## 2 The Self in Community

As I mentioned earlier, I feel compelled to echo my sentiments about the importance of sensitising my pre-service teachers to begin their practice with empathy so that their diverse students will be welcomed authentically. The empathetic approach directed us all to what was essential to consider during our course of study. With better understandings of various images of the child, my students demonstrated profound thoughtfulness about who they were planning for and thus developed a mindful approach to Kindergarten teaching and learning.

The opening activity I proposed to my pre-service teachers aligns with acknowledging that I, too, learn from my community and I engage with my students as I hope they will engage with their future students. Lilian Katz (2010) has called this "the principle of congruity" (p. 22), a way of ensuring consistency and harmony between the way one educates student teachers and the way one hopes they will teach in the future. The process of inquiry through an arts-based methodology supported me and my pre-service teachers in self–realisations and in the recognition of what is important to us all in early childhood teaching. The creative opportunities found in arts-based methods have allowed me to witness future teachers embracing values of learning in support of not only academics, but with profound attention to the social and emotional development of every child they will teach. Beginning with the self offered grounding in how pre-service teachers envision their students and led to a heart-felt responsibility for generating and producing positive images of a classroom community. I cannot help but repeat how authentic and powerful the experiences were.

Many studies in education have confirmed the efficacy of social and emotional learning programs for students (see Greenberg et al., 2003; Zins et al., 2004) but there is a paucity of research that explores how a teacher's social and emotional competence impacts the classroom community and how it can have a positive consequence on student outcomes (see Jennings & Greenberg, 2008). In the presence of 21st-century demands, teachers must maintain reflexivity in order to create a genuine classroom community. Indeed, personal values help us connect to what will be implemented every day in a classroom. Such self-reflection will place educators in the position of mirroring what they expect from their own students—social and emotional competence. In the end, how teachers choose to communicate, develop relationships, and situate themselves personally will be foundational. Mindful consideration of personal perspectives will support the responsibility of creating a classroom community that is fair and nurturing for all learners. As seen in my university classroom, the arts served as the communicative tool for theory and practice. The lessons learned were shared and driven by a freedom to explore in artistic ways, thus impacting views on teaching and learning.

We cannot ignore the fact that as teachers we need to have knowledge of subject areas, of children's learning styles and cognitive development, of children's social and emotional development, of culturally responsive education, and of how to address the needs of diverse classrooms of learners. Their professional obligations expect teachers to remain current in gaining knowledge about emerging research and improved practices. However, we know that knowledge of oneself is integral to social change; Parker Palmer (1997) has pointed out that we teach who we are, and without knowing ourselves how can we teach others? A focal part of working with children calls on knowing one's core dispositions.

- How does one observe oneself and others?
- How does one handle conflict?
- What does one consider integral to developing and sustaining
- relationships?
- What is one's comfort level interacting with diverse populations?
- What about heart, aesthetics, and culture?
- What about the unique child?

These questions reverberate into others.

- What is learning?
- What is social justice in and when teaching?

The responses to such personal questions might help pre-service teachers and, certainly, educators in general, to identify their own abilities, weaknesses, and necessary areas of growth in professional learning. This does not necessarily imply we need to find answers or definite outcomes. Rather, such inquires lead to developing a passionate identity in support of a community of learners, thus strengthening outlooks for a true educational community. The objective here is for teachers to consolidate personal stances into visions that will foster a set of effective teaching outlooks when they are generating that classroom community. Ultimately, such reflection is an ongoing process that remains at the heart of teaching and the heart of community. If teachers stand firm in believing that all children have the right to an education, are capable of inquiry and of being active constructors of knowledge, then we help develop a community of young learners who will explore throughout their years in school, and perhaps beyond. My plan to sensitise and support my pre-service teachers in looking and listening well to their future students, in acknowledging and working with the various images of children they might have, was effective. Social change came about in a community because initial learning was rooted in my students taking responsibility for their own vision, for personal learning first, and for growing with others.

## Notes

1 Classes d'accueil in Quebec are classrooms dedicated to teaching immigrant children and youth to read and write in French.

2 Students have given written permission to show and discuss their work.

## References

Carter, M. (2014). Drama and theatre education in Canada: A snapshot. *McGill Journal of Education/Revue des sciences de l'éducation de McGill, 49*(1), 237–245. https://doi.org/10.7202/1025780ar

Carter, M. (2015). A critical, a/r/tographical enquiry into the meaning and purpose of performing "Gallop Apace." *Journal of Educational Enquiry, 14*(1), 52–63. http://www.ojs.unisa.edu.au/index.php?EDEQ/article/view/1024/726

Cole, R. W. (2014). *Educating everybody's children: Diverse teaching strategies for diverse learners* (2nd ed.). Association for Supervision and Curriculum Development.

Cutcher, A., & Cook, P. (2016). One must also be an artist: Online delivery of teacher education. *International Journal of Education and the Arts, 17*(3). http://www.ijea.org/v17n13/index.html

Fiorello, P. (2010). *Diverse teaching methods for diverse classrooms: A guide for elementary education.* Association for Supervision and Curriculum Development.

Gallagher, A., & Thordarson, K. (2018). *Design thinking for school leaders.* Association for Supervision and Curriculum Development.

Gandini, L. (1993). Fundamentals of the Reggio Emilia approach to early childhood education. *Young Children, 49*, 4–8. https://www.jstor.org/stable/i40102590

Greene, M. (1995). *Releasing the imagination: Essays on education, the arts and social change.* Jossey-Bass.

Greene, M. (2004). Carpe diem: The arts and school structuring. In G. Diaz & M. B. McKenna (Eds.), *Teaching for aesthetic experience: The art of learning* (pp. 17–31). Peter Lang.

Greenberg, M. T., Weissberg, R. P., Obrien, M. U., Zins, J. E., Fredericks, L., & Resnik, H. (2003). Enhancing school-based prevention and youth development through coordinated social, emotional and academic learning. *American Psychologist, 58*, 466–474.

Jennings, P. A., & Greenberg, M. T. (2008). The pro-social classroom: Teacher social and emotional competence in relation to student classroom outcomes. *Journal of Educational Research.* https://journals.sagepub.com/doi/10.3102/0034654308325693

Katz, L. (2010). How young children learn: Part l. In S. Schmidt (Ed.), *Key issues in early years education: A reader* (pp. 9–14). Routledge.

Malaguzzi, L. (1994). Your image of the child: Where teaching begins. *Child Care Information Exchange, 3*, 52–94. https://www.childcareexchange.com/article/your-image-of-the-child-where-teaching-begins/5009652/

Mreiwed, H., Carter, M., & Shabtay, A. (2017). Building classroom community through drama education. *Australia Journal of Drama, 44*(1), 44–57. https://doi/10.1080/14452294.2017.1329680

Palmer, P. (1997). *The courage to teach.* John Wiley & Sons.

Phipps, H. (2016). *Children speaking with children. Visualizing engagement through contemporary Canadian picture books in French classrooms* (Unpublished doctoral dissertation). McGill University, Montreal.

Pinar, W. F. (2004). *What is curriculum theory?* Lawrence Erlbaum Associates.

Rinaldi, C. (2001). The image of the child and the child's environment as fundamental principle. In L. Gandini & C. P. Edwards (Eds.), *Bambini: The Italian approach to infant toddler care* (pp. 45–53). Teachers College Press.

Vecchi, V. (2010). *Art and creativity in Reggio Emilia: Exploring the role and potential of ateliers in early childhood education.* Routledge.

Wright, S. (2003). *The arts: Young children and learning.* Pearson Education.

Zins, J. E., Weissberg, R. P., Wang, M. C., & Walberg, H. J. (2004). *Building academic success on social and emotional learning.* Teachers College Press.

CHAPTER 4

# Art Hive

## *A Relational Framework for Social Change*

*Leah Lewis, Heather McLeod and Xuemei Li*

## 1 Introduction

In line with the work of Timm-Bottos (2006), we have been researching various applications of the Art Hive framework in community settings in Newfoundland and Labrador (NL) since 2015. Between 2015 and 2017 our projects included newcomer programming with immigrant and refugee youth in a local high school in the form of weekly pop-up art hive sessions. Our focus was on establishing a sense of belonging and inclusion in a new place and art making in a social context. Adler's Crucial Cs (children need courage, they need to connect with others, feel capable, and know that they count,) as Bettner and Lew (1990) have reminded us, informed our observations of how the hive process affected the experiences of newcomer students. The next round of sessions responded to the requests of newcomer young people to invite local students to participate with them in studio sessions; here social engagement increased. Outcomes demonstrated that the Art Hive sessions provided space for social connection and exchange, fostered creative competency, and supported social connection. Students experienced a home-like support and felt noticed by others. A student-curated exhibit and open house was hosted by the young people who took charge of mini-printmaking workshops and demonstrated an overall pride in ownership of the hive space and program.

Based on our high-school programming and responding to a call for more permanent Art Hive programming, we expanded our Art Hive to a studio located in a local Indigenous organisation, where we have been hosting community-embedded programming since November 2018. In addition to having shifted from a pop-up style to a permanent rented studio space of our own, our participant focus has also evolved and expanded from a newcomer-only process focusing on inclusion and belonging, to an expanded and integrated culturally diverse engagement that includes newcomer young people and families, as well as Indigenous young people, families, and elders whom we have met through our hosting agency, our region's Native friendship centre.

In the Art Hive model, a profound power of relationship, based in and created through artmaking, informs our experiences and our perceptions

 | DOI: 10.1163/9789004442870_004

and practice of community-based scholarship. We find ourselves engaging more intentionally with the colonial history of our region in response to our developing relationship with our Indigenous colleagues who, as mentioned above, are our current studio hosts. Inevitably, we ponder our roles as research collaborators and practitioners responding to current calls for reconciliation.

In this chapter we reflect on the cultural context of our research that includes both recent immigration and a long, complex, and traumatic colonial history that has affected our Indigenous communities. We consider our learning as scholars and educators, and also as socially invested citizens producing new knowledge collectively and collaboratively. Our experiences with newcomer young people at a local high school segued into an expanded cultural landscape with the addition of Mi'kmaq, Inuit, and Innu participants. This expanded relationship has informed the ways in which identity and context affect knowledge creation; our research process has inevitably been shaped by our current socio-political context in NL in relation to both the complex colonial history of our province and its current engagement with reconciliation, as well as to the current shifting cultural landscape being created currently by increasing immigration.

We reflect critically on what it means to engage in responsible and accountable knowledge creation when identities are informed by oppressive colonial histories, trauma, and/or profound othering that results from the refugee experience of being a newcomer. Through the relational framework of an Art Hive, we strive to increase our awareness of cultural identities and histories in order to avoid inflicting repeated harm through disrespect and practice based on cultural appropriation (Baskin, 2016; Vowel, 2016).

## 2 Art Hives as Practice

While considered therapeutic spaces, Art Hives are not clinically modeled; they do not engage with concepts of treatment in response to diagnosis (Allen, 2008; Timm-Bottos, 2016). Rather, Art Hives are publicly accessible studio spaces that are grounded in a community art therapy approach that sees art making as the primary site of engagement and exchange. This differs from medical model art therapy approaches that engage with clinical diagnosis and assessment and operate out of clinical settings, such as psychiatry units and hospitals. Art Hives, based on holistic wellness models, are community-situated. They provide free programming, including access to art making materials, and provide a loose form of facilitation by practitioners familiar with community art therapy practice and a person-centred and non-evaluative style of facilitation. Art Hives privilege human connection, independence, and autonomy as vital to holistic wellness and functioning. Through art making practice in a shared and collective setting that might be called a held space, hives focus on the person over the art, while also acknowledging the art as an extension of the artist. Allen (2008) has described hive practitioners as being the space holders possessing a compassionate disinterest in the art-making process. It is the creative doing that is encouraged as the site through which connection is achieved.

Art Hives intentionally consider cultural nuance and safety and do not rely on common spoken language (Kapitan, 2015). Instead, the primary shared activity is creative process via media and technique in art making. Creative process is accessed within the collaborative space and is supported through non-evaluative input that does not judge or evaluate technique, but is, instead, descriptive and reflective. Such nuanced moving away from critique encourages exchange and conversation that is art-focused while at the same time acts as a means for joining in relationship (Christensen, 2011). The act of making as well as creative exploration and discovery at the site of the individual is a focal point for developing communication and connection (Moon, 2002). We highlight technique as contributing to participant comfort and sense of ease in the act of making art. We provide materials that minimise anxiety and self-scrutiny about art making by introducing techniques that require little skill but produce satisfying outputs. Small pallet cardboard, off-loom weaving, paper weaving, Styrofoam printing, and papier mâché sculpting all provide creative engagement with satisfying outputs while demanding little knowledge of technique.

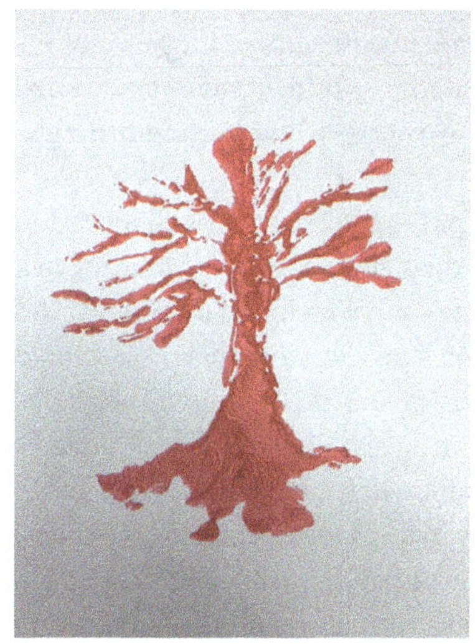

FIGURE 4.1
Styrofoam printing technique

## 3 The Open Studio Project and Its Background

Our first project, The Open Studio, took place in collaboration with Holy Heart High School in St. John's, which hosts the bulk of local newcomer programing (Lewis, McLeod, & Li, 2018). Newcomer students hailed from a wide variety of countries including Syria, Eritrea, and Ethiopia. The demographic landscape of NL is historically Euro-Christian, with visible minorities representing less than 2% of the total population (Statistics Canada, 2012). This contrasts with other Canadian cities, like Montreal or Toronto, where visible minorities represent approximately 40% (Association for New Canadians [ANC], 2017). Following an influx of Syrian newcomers in 2016 in response to Syria's humanitarian crisis, NL sponsored approximately 300 Government Assisted Refugees, 200 of whom were from Syria (ANC, 2017). Over 1,000 newcomers were sponsored between 2017 and 2018 in all and the provincial government has committed to increasing immigration to 1,700 per year by 2022, As is clear, NL is experiencing a historical shift in population diversity. Government response has involved welcome programming, identifying the needs of newcomers including language learning and employment, as well as supporting social interaction as a feature of fostering mental wellbeing (Gilroy Inc., 2005).

Positive changes have also been happening in high schools. Students from refugee families with financial constraints and low parental educational attainments are most vulnerable to increased barriers to completing their education (Bitew & Ferguson, 2010). Earlier local research in NL indicated that the support for newcomer children, particularly refugee children with educational gaps, is insufficient (Burnaby, 2010; Sarma-Debnath & Castano, 2008). Currently, new guideline documents by the Department of Education (DOE), 2010, and a new Literacy Enrichment and Academic Readiness for Newcomers (LEARN) program that assists newcomer students to bridge their educational gaps and prepare them for joining mainstream classes, better attend to newcomer students' educational needs.

Beginning in 2015 we facilitated weekly pop-up sessions in collaboration and consultation with newcomer students (Lewis et al., 2018), culminating in a student-led open house and art show. Our data source included interviews and focus groups with both students and teaching staff who took part. We gained an in-depth understanding of the applicability of an Art Hive and its activities to culturally diverse contexts. Themes included access to social space that feels like home and learning English in a non-evaluative space (Lewis et al., 2018). Our data addresses experiences of inclusivity in a space in which art making is the primary activity and in which academic evaluation is irrelevant. Additionally, our findings supported a further five weeks with newcomers the following year, during which students opted to invite local peers to join in the Art Hive sessions. Focus group outputs from this second set of sessions highlighted the role and importance of hope in being a newcomer to NL.

## 4 The Hearthstone Community Art Hive

Our second project, the Hearthstone Community Studio Art Hive, (hereafter Hearthstone) started in late 2018. It is informed by our work in the high school and participants' desire to expand programming to merge newcomer and local groups. Hearthstone is funded by Canada's Social Sciences and Humanities Research Council (SSHRC). Our studio, located in downtown St. John's, is in a shared space hosted by First Light Centre, our local native friendship center, where we hope to remain after our initial pilot phase of two years. We have established ourselves and now avoid the disruption of set up and break down that is inherent to pop-up programming. Permanence allows for continuity of programming, flexibility of art making activity, constant availability of materials for visiting participants, and overall continued community presence and visibility. We host closed programming with specific groups, as well as open-studio sessions for anyone wishing to attend. Our participants continue to include newcomer populations and other diverse groups. Our group work also includes working with adults transitioning from the prison system, a group of trans youth, and seniors. Additionally, we have collaborated with First Light to provide closed programming with Indigenous families. Since permanency allows for time to establish our space and our community relationships, we have been getting to know our immediate community. Participant art decorates the walls, there is a table for self-service tea and coffee to which members contribute snack food, and our cupboards are full of card stock, acrylic and tempera paint of many colours, collage supplies, glue, pencils, markers, art books and more. We have found that our materials change in response to the space and cultural needs of participants. In consultation with our Friendship Centre colleagues, we now include caribou leather, seal skin, and beading materials since these are culturally meaningful to our local Mi'kmaq and Inuit members, and offer enhanced opportunities for learning and cultural exchange.

As a multidisciplinary academic team consisting of an arts therapist, art educator, and newcomer scholar we reflect on the past four years from pedagogical and scholarly perspectives. Through our lived experiences of community, our reflective stance is informed by arts scholarship, identity, culture, and colonial history. We explore the nuances of culturally informed research that is community situated and collaborative as a core feature of culturally safe and inclusive scholarship. This is presented through the community art engagement of our Art Hive experiences, partnerships, and developing relationships. We find ourselves critically considering our roles and responsibilities in such work. This means engaging with our own privilege, which includes cultural assumptions that are informed by colonial histories. We remain aware of the precariousness that often surfaces when privilege meets challenge for change (see Lu, 2012; Maracle, 1996, 2017; Vowel, 2016).

## 5 Fostering a Socially Engaged Studio: Relationship, Space, and Social Justice

### 5.1 *Art Hive as Relational*

A core feature of Hearthstone's being a socially engaged space is our consideration of the significance of relationship in how programming is planned and facilitated. The island of Newfoundland is the original home territory of the Beothuk and Mi'Kmaq, while Labrador is the home of Innu and Inuit peoples. We understand that personal connection and consideration of this context is important to Art Hive practice. Part of that connecting is informed by the positioning of the hive facilitator or therapist. The identity of the practitioner is an important part of the creative work. Moon (2002) has pointed out the significance of holistic practitioner identity that cannot operate in isolation from personal, family, and other aspects of their life. The perspective of the practitioner informs how connecting with others and relationship-building occurs. This includes an assumption that for both practitioner and participant the artistic perspective, or, put differently, the engagement with metaphor and symbol, contributes to "attending to the stories of our own lives" (p. 33). It is in relating to creative process through relationship that we begin to access a heightened awareness of our life events, which inevitably includes the cultural contexts with which we engage. Creative process is further fostered through the consideration of language, the two Rs of relationship, which are responsibility and reciprocity (Baskin, 2016), and supportive non-evaluative support.

### 5.2 *The Two Rs of Relationship*

The core components of relationship are the two Rs of responsibility and reciprocity (Baskin, 2016). Responsibility in relation to cultural history and formed identity implies learning about this history and the importance of cultural imagery and ritual, as well as seeking out important information so as to understand how cultural appropriation can happen. Reciprocity is the way we respond within relationships. Decision making occurs in a relational context, informed by the two Rs. Inherent in reciprocity is shared responsibility that is non-evaluative but supportive within the creative process. This emphasises the learning that occurs at the site of relational engagement and exchange.

## 5.3 *The Language of Connecting*

In both Art Hive spaces, language played a role in relation to connection along with careful consideration of the relevance of identity as it relates to spoken language and other forms of communication. In our high school pop-up Art Hives, the space was animated by multiple languages, and exchanges took place in students' language of origin. This style of exchange continues at Hearthstone, with the addition of Indigenous languages including Innu-aimun and Inuktitut. Welcome signs are translated into these languages and cultural images, such as ulus (Inuit carving knives) are depicted in artwork.

## 5.4 *Art Hive and Context, Art Hive as Cultural Space*

We argue that justice must be part of practice, and we consider how Art Hives challenge oppressive structures through active engagement with publicly shared spaces that foster identity through relationship building and mutually creative processes. Because Art Hives are grounded in philosophies of social justice and feminism and based on community practice models, we consider how notions of justice contribute to the interplay of relationships within a creative space. Baskin (2016) has noted that in helping contexts Indigenous knowledge does not differentiate the importance of body and mind, so "there is no separation between physical health and mental health" (p. 196). Wellness is a holistic and inherently collective concept. Individual mental health and wellness exist in conjunction with community wellness; when a community thrives, so do the individuals in it. Justice-oriented intent, especially in cultural contexts that are negotiating colonial histories, can contribute to an enhancement of identity and cultural pride (Baskin, 2016).

In the Art Hive space, identity is considered through the techniques learned, shared and practised, and through cultural artifacts like talking sticks, as well and the materials available for use. Identity is also supported by the ways in which cultural images are displayed and shared since this informs how and whether cultural exchange takes place. The Art Hive protects and invites; on behalf of community members, we protect how the space is used, and we invite all to attend, participate, and contribute. Baskin (2016), Vowel (2016), and Moon (2002) have all highlighted the importance of critical awareness of the power of space and context for culturally safe and inviting practice.

We need to keep two questions in mind: "Does space foster connection and encourage emerging identity?" and "How might space be at odds with participant identity and culture?"

### 5.5 *Hive Programming Merges Relationship and Space*

Environmental space is important for wellness (Baskin, 2016; Timm-Bottos & Reilly, 2015; Vowel, 2016; Maracle, 2017). Land, animals, birds, and fish all live alongside humans and our wellness is linked to theirs. Through this understanding of connection, we must share space, responsibility, and consider reciprocity. Land and space should represent participants' contexts by engaging with and learning about imagery and cultural materials. When programming reflects community and responds to communal need, it is a form of enacting just ways of being together and this helps to acknowledge the value of cultural images and materials. It is significant that health and wellness are a result of a holistic relationship with others, self, and environment (Baskin 2016; Timm-Bottos & Reilly, 2015; Vowel, 2016).

## 6 Concluding Thoughts

In this chapter we have engaged with what it means to practice responsible scholarship with different communities. We recognise the need to make room for much subjectivity since identity is a diverse and broad concept.

In our exploration of the Art Hive framework and the ways in which it aligns with culturally sensitive work, we privilege relationship-building and shared ownership of art-making practice with the aim of fostering independence and autonomy for and with Art Hive participants. We acknowledge the significance of the studio as a space in which knowledge creation, informed by materials and technique, can take place. Practicing cultural humility informs our community scholarship and our engagement with Indigenous ways of knowing.

Positive relationships that avoid assumptions and are open to learning include a recognition of responsibility in the work process. For us, art making, and arts focused programming precedes scholarship. The research, while its goal is to foster new perspectives and knowledge, is always secondary to creative programming and participant engagement. We conclude that in practicing culturally safe relational scholarship, we critically engage the complex colonial histories and marginalisation in Newfoundland and Labrador.

## References


Allen, P. (2008). Commentary on community-based art studios: Underlying principles. *Art Therapy: Journal of the Americal Art Therapy Asssociation, 25*(1), 11–12.

Association for New Canadians, Newfoundland and Labrador. (2018). *ANC 2017–2018 annual report.* http://www.ancnl.ca/publications-resources

Baskin, C. (2016). *Stong helpers teachings: The value of Indigenous knowledges in the helping professions* (2nd ed.). Canadian Scholars' Press.

Berryman, M., Soohoo, S., Nevin, A., Arani Barrett, T., & Ford, T. (2013). *Culturally responsive methodologies at work in education settings.* Emerald Group Publishing Limited.

Bettner, B. L., & Lew, A. (1990). *Raising kids who can.* Connexions Press.

Bitew, G., & Ferguson, P. (2019). Parental support for African immigrant students' schooling in Australia. *Journal of Comparative Family Studies, 41*(1), 149–165.

Burnaby, B. (2010). *The devil is in the details: Access for newcomer learners to ESL and ABE programs in St. John's.* The Coalition on Richer Diversity and the Refugee and Immigraqnt Advisory Council.

Christensen, M. C. (2011). Using feminist leadership to build a performance based, peer education program. *Qualitative Social Work, 12*(3), 254–269.

Kapitan, L. (2015). Social action in practice: Shifting the ethnocentric lens in cross-cultural art therapy encounters. *Art Therapy: Journal of the American Art Therapy Association, 32*(3), 104–111.

Lewis, L., McLeod, H., & Li, X. (2018). The open studio: Exploring immigrant and refugee youth experiences of belonging through community-based arts practice. *Cultural and Pedagogical Inquiry, 10*(1), 5–21.

Lu, L. (2012). Journey women: Art therapy in a decolonizing framework of practice. *The Arts in Psychotherapy, 39*(3), 192–200.

CHAPTER 5

# The Murder Next Door

## *Developing Healing Responses and Building Community Following Trauma Using Research-Based Theatre*

*Rosemary C. Reilly*

Traumatic events involving murder profoundly affect community residents and their relationships with their families and neighbours. Appropriate responses to such trauma typically include providing individual therapy, but trauma is also a collective experience. Community-level trauma damages the basic tissue of social life, rupturing the bonds that attach people to each other and involves a shocking and gradual realisation that the community is no longer an effective source of support (Erikson, 1976). This results in a loss of interpersonal connection, a pervasive sense of sorrow and purposelessness, disorientation, low community morale, and a loss of community identity (Raphael, 1986).

Little attention is given to local initiatives that address nonclinical healing of the community as a whole. Trauma may decrease or increase a community's sense of communality, the cohesive threads that bind a community together and create an environment in which individuals can lead enriching lives. Research highlights that how a community responds post-trauma can make the difference between members experiencing posttraumatic stress which leads to relationships becoming antagonistic, fractured, and alienated (see Reilly, 2011) or posttraumatic growth which is the positive psychological change that results from the successful struggle with challenging life circumstances. Posttraumatic growth is not about returning to the same life one lived prior to the trauma but is, rather, about undergoing significant shifts in thinking and relating to the world that contribute to a process of deeply meaningful change (Calhoun & Tedeschi, 2006).

Collective trauma must be transformed in and by the community. Since mutual social support forms the foundation for psychologically rebuilding community, relationships with family, co-workers, and neighbours become a primary source of recovery and healing. This allows communities not only to bounce back, but to "bounce forward" as indicated by Manyena, O' Brien, O'Keefe, and Rose (2011) and move from a sense of powerlessness towards pride and deep-rooted attachment. Most communities have outlined plans to deal

 | DOI: 10.1163/9789004442870_005

with natural disasters and emergencies, but municipal officials and community leaders have little guidance on how to address psychological or emotional community trauma and its aftermath. When trauma strikes, it affects everyone. It is not uncommon for residents to feel less positive, less energetic, and unable to enjoy life in the aftershock of a trauma; they are less able to generate and implement healing strategies themselves. Therefore, it is imperative that strategies for local community healing be identified prior to the occurrence of trauma. The project I discuss in this chapter created an opportunity for community members to engage in just such formulations. Using principles of research-based theatre (Belliveau, 2015) I created a readers' theatre presentation about the murder of a family in a close-knit small town. I theatricalised research data gleaned from three case studies of community trauma in an urban community (two domestic homicides), a rural one (the murder of a young girl), and a school community (a mass shooting). This performance functioned as a starting point for discussions on how to promote community healing effectively outside of an existing real-life trauma and its emotional and psychological wake.

## 1 Research-Based Theatre

Theatre is increasingly employed as a method and methodology in scholarly settings. It has been validated as a tool to critically and effectively collect and analyse data, educate audiences about significant issues, enliven and enrich the dissemination of research findings, shape public policy, advance social change by engaging and addressing issues of social justice, oppression, and marginalisation, and intervene in human systems, promoting attitude and behaviour change.[1] Theatre has the ability to capture and communicate complicated knowledge about multifaceted social realities and relationships in ways that affect the heart and mind in connecting the audience personally to the genuine experiences portrayed in the performance. When they are theatricalising data, researchers show, not tell, the results of their research, thus creating three-dimensional portraits of their data. These portraits allow "one to retain, at least somewhat, the human dimensions of the life experience qualitative research attempts to study … to not lose research participants in the data or not transform them into dehumanized stereotypes" (Donmoyer & Donmoyer, 2008, p. 216). Research-based theatre has taken on many forms from verbatim theatre to performance ethnography and from documentary theatre to ethnodrama (Belliveau, 2015).

### 1.1 *Readers' Theatre*

Readers' theater is a sub-genre of theatre in which actors hold scripts, staging is simplified, scenery is limited to stools and ladders, and costumes, if used at all, are little more than articles of clothing intended to suggest, rather than represent, a character (Donmoyer & Donmoyer, 2008). I chose this format for my research-based drama since it is, by design, a stylised rather than a realistic form; readers' theatre is presentational rather than representational. Whereas representational forms attempt realism, presentational forms ask audience members to fill in what has been intentionally omitted onstage and, in the process, co-construct with the actors the meaning of the work. In my theatre project, this created the optimal amount of *aesthetic distance* (Bleuer, Chin, & Sakamoto, 2018)—a space between an overly emotional state regarding the murder of a woman and her young children, and the overly rational state of typical research objectivity. This aesthetic distance allowed audience members to use all their intellectual and emotional resources to develop empathic and perceptive responses regarding beneficial community healing strategies.

### 1.2 *Playwriting*

Saldaña (1998) has noted that ethnotheatre has inherent ethical issues regarding the presentation of participants' experiences – exposing intimate conflicts, distorting personal histories, and violating privacy – in essence, the so-called juicy stuff that fuels good storytelling may, in fact, challenge the researcher's ethical obligation to do no harm. This was my primary concern since I had witnessed the effects of the stigma attached to communities and their members during the aftermath of a murder. Therefore, rather than presenting the findings from one case, I drew on the themes that emerged from the three separate ones mentioned above, and created a fictitious amalgamation of events, characters, situations, and interactions. Since the purpose of the performance was to create a context in which to generate healing strategies, the events of the play unfold following the murder which is never depicted in the play but is only referenced. I focused on those themes that are generally unnoticed to emphasise the hidden impact of them on community members. For example (see the scene below), I highlight the internal conflicts felt by the owner of the house where the murder had occurred, and show how this impacted him personally and economically. In the play, I cycle back-and-forth between verbatim presentations of the data in the form of monologues (to lend veracity and authenticity) to imagined, private interactions that expose the more painful effects of this community trauma. The play lasts approximately 50 minutes and uses a structure similar to that of *The Laramie Project* (Kaufman, 2001).

## 2 An Excerpt from the Murder Next Door

ACT [1] SCENE [1]

*The scene is a cramped real estate office. There is a desk, a telephone, and some piles of paper—neat but busy. Chuck Branden is seated; he is writing and examining some files. After a few moments, he glances up, as if realizing that someone else has come into the office.*

CHUCK

I have lived in Lawton my whole life. It's the sense of community that keeps us here. So, do I think it's changed since the murders? Obviously, there was the horror and the shock … Oh, and the media, of course.

(*Sigh*)

But has it changed us?

There were the piles of teddy bears and ceramic angels, and candles. And tons of flowers on the porch of the house. The folks over at the Kiwanis put together a trust fund for Kevin. He survived only because he wasn't home at the time. So, when he's ready to leave his aunt's place, to live on his own or go to college or whatever, he'll have something. And the school where Jamie and Michelle went, they planted a tree. It's all about dealing with the hurt, if that makes sense.

Me?

(*Pause*)

As the owner, I just had to be practical, but I tried to be human about it. That started the moment I met the Martins, ah … Joanne's parents. There was no way that they could go into that house. That made all sorts of sense to me. Okay fine, I'll be the go-between. So I asked them, "What do you want? What sorts of things are important to you?" So they made a list. Sentimental stuff, mostly. We searched the house high and low for everything we could, and eventually, I think we found everything on the list. Well, actually … I don't know if we ever found Joanne's wedding ring.

(*Pause*)

The hardest part?

(*Pause*)

I suppose it was the time right after it happened. I first went into the house after the police had taken … whatever evidence they needed. It wasn't pleasant to deal with physically. My business partner, Jim, and I ripped everything apart, right down to the ground. All the carpets out and new carpets put in. All the walls, completely scrubbed down and disinfected. We repainted everything. It was the only way you could deal with it. Because, we had to re-rent it.

(*Pause*)

I guess, one of the twinges of guilt I felt throughout this whole thing was about Mr. Martin, and how he felt. He would have loved to see the house just demolished. As a dad, I could relate to that. That's what I found hard: Chuck the human being versus Chuck the landlord. We just didn't have a choice. Maybe if we did, we might have bulldozed the whole thing.

(*Pause*)

There's still a stigma attached to that house. One of the guys who moved in afterwards had a priest come in to bless the house, I guess, or whatever they wanted.

(*Pause*)

So, do I think Lawton's changed? I'm not sure.

(*Blackout*)

This scene sets out the question, "Has this trauma changed this close-knit community?" The readers' theatre performance attempts to demonstrate how.

## 3 Readers' Theatre Performance as Data Collection

### 3.1 *Method*

A focus group methodology was used during the post-performance discussions to create a reflective and collaborative problem-solving space. Since focus groups are a socially-oriented technique for capturing data (Krueger & Casey, 2009), this was the best method to elicit the audience's perceptions, feelings, attitudes, and ideas concerning the themes of the research, provide the ground for understanding the impact on the community, and afford an interactive, dynamic source of data regarding strategies for fostering community healing. The post-performance discussions lasted approximately 45 minutes. Attendees were divided into groups of four to five to maximise their airtime. One simple question was posed: "If you were a member of this community, what would be some of the strategies you would find beneficial and effective to help the community to heal itself?"

### 3.2 *Setting and Participants*

The readers' theatre script was piloted twice on two different university campuses to test its effectiveness. Participants were recruited by open invitation through an advertisement linked to a research seminar, and a full description of the theatre presentation was included. No preparation was required. Although both pilots were with academic researchers and university students older than

18, audience members were encouraged to approach this experience as a person who lived in a neighbourhood where this might occur. In total, 45 participants attended the pilot performances and the post-performance discussions.

### 3.3 *Data Collection and Analysis*

Data were collected on flipchart paper during the focus groups by a facilitator who recorded the contributions of the participants and by participants who were also encouraged to record their own thoughts and suggestions. In this way, all data were anonymised in an aggregate form. The data were analysed using the constant comparative method, a systematic inductive process used for categorising and comparing qualitative data.

### 3.4 *Ethical Considerations*

Research ethics approval was obtained from the University Human Research Ethics Committee. Strategies for minimising potential harm to research participants included a poster outside the performance space alerting audience members to the focus of the play and its allusion to murder (although the exposure to violent content was far less than is the case in the average TV show). This caveat was repeated from the stage area prior to the performance and reiterated before the post-performance discussion. I also emphasised that anyone could leave the performance space at any time, or choose to remain but not voice comments during the discussion. A short break followed the performance to allow audience members to leave inconspicuously. The verbal consent script stressed that if audience members remained, this implied their consent to participate. A sheet with psychological resources was also provided.

## 4 Findings from the Performances

At both performances, all audience members stayed for the post-performance discussion, which was lively and varied. Participants engaged conceptually with the piece by offering a range of informed, diverse opinions on policy issues and possible solutions for community healing. Additionally, participants engaged emotionally by disclosing and discussing what this might mean if it occurred in their own communities.

Beneficial strategies for healing generated in the focus group discussions tended to gather around five main themes outlined below.

### 4.1 *Acknowledgement of Community Trauma as a Civic Responsibility*

Building on the idea that every community has an emergency preparedness plan, participants suggested, as a proactive response, that a community trauma team be struck as a regular feature of municipal services. This team would be knowledgeable about community trauma, and trained in various aspects of community-building post-trauma. It then could be activated when needed. As well, participants noted that plans for responding to community trauma needed to be considered as a long-term (at least a year) investment that would be developed in phases and be responsive to the unique needs of the community.

A crucial first step many participants advanced was the public acknowledgement by local officials and leaders that this was a community issue and responsibility. Addressing the stigma and isolation that trauma activates would be a necessary precondition that would then allow community members to access and participate in other initiatives. This would be achieved not only in words, but also in actions. Local officials (and the trauma team, if in place) would co-ordinate the dissemination of accurate information (to combat gossip and rumours) through a community bulletin and/or website. This channel of information would also have an up-to-date resource list that people could access for various support services, announce public healing events, such as prayer services, memorial concerts, or vigils, and make known municipal-sponsored community rituals for mourning, such as a remembrance book displayed at city hall for individuals to sign. There was also the suggestion that the trauma team could act as a clearinghouse for suggestions from the public regarding any additional proposals that might serve to positively promote healing. In addition, municipalities could provide a variety of approved public expressions of remembrance (such as tree planting or setting up memorial park benches).

Participants believed that an appropriate display of grief leadership, behaviours and statements by key leaders that serve to facilitate healthy coping with loss (Fein & Isaacson, 2009), is an essential civic role. In confronting grief associated with community trauma, effective grief leaders can unify a community in mourning, appropriately guide people in ways of coping, and be symbolic representations of stability and direction.

### 4.2 *Creation of Safe Dialogic Spaces*

The second most common theme was the creation of dialogic spaces by municipal officials and other leaders for people to gather, mourn, share experiences, and reconnect. An important part of the communal healing process is having one's story validated and made part of the collective story. Participants proposed a variety of different kinds of spaces that corresponded to the needs of community members. From publicly-sponsored sharing circles, to school-based gatherings and family-friendly neighbourhood suppers, many opportunities for healing conversations and authentic connections should be offered to the community in a space that encourages the acceptance of diversity, fosters participation and trust, and cultivates respectful listening. Support materials, such as family discussion guides, could be borrowed from local libraries to be used by parents with their children. In cases of gendered or gang violence, facilitated discussion groups for men, women, youth, or other folx[2] directly affected by the trauma could be sponsored on an on-going basis. As well, participants recommended the creation of a permanent curated space where archived materials that documented people's experiences could be stored.

### 4.3 *Local Leadership Initiatives*

Local leaders have the potential to play a critical role in the recovery of communities after trauma. Every day they hear about how their friends, neighbours, and coworkers are doing, and understand the current emotions and needs of the people with whom they have direct contact. From instituting check-ins with employees or association members to see how people are doing, to sponsoring social activism projects to address the root cause of the trauma (like, for instance, lobbying for stricter gun regulations), local leaders can lead the community in recovery. Additionally, leaders can nurture and model the use of restorative practices and values that inspire healing, transformation, and empowerment (Wachtel & McCold, 2004) in their organisational milieus. As well as creating ripples of wellbeing, cooperation, and positive social connections that extend out to the community, the use of restorative approaches builds community capacity.

### 4.4 *Alternative Methods of Healing*

Participants advised that many non-stigmatising alternative methods of healing be available to community members. Many of these fell into the realm of expressive creative arts like the use of art, music, dance/movement, drama and playbuilding, poetry, and creative writing to process the trauma. The arts have been shown to be an effective tool in processing adversity, both in therapeutic and nontherapeutic contexts (Kuriansky, 2012; Mapp & Koch, 2004). Since art-making is a basic human behaviour (Dissanayake, 1995), it can provide individuals facing trauma with the opportunity for self-discovery and empowerment, and a context for meaning making through the creative process, as well as helping them develop new ways of expressing emotions, reduce anxiety and fatigue, increase emotional well-being, and support communication with family and friends.

### 4.5 *Support from Outside the Community*

The final theme concerned how doing good in ways big or small, not only feels good, but also does one good. Although affected communities can be overwhelmed with outsiders who undermine or marginalise local sources of support, members of neighbouring communities can lend a hand by offering secondary mutual support to combat compassion fatigue, the cost of caring for others in emotional pain (Figley, 1995), and burnout for those living, working, and leading in the affected community. Supporting others is exhausting and depleting work, so those who are leading healing efforts in the traumatised community need respite and care themselves. It also affords affected communities the opportunity to pay it forward, to be able to respond to one community's kindness by being kind to another community, lending their hard-won experience in the process.

## 5 Conclusion

This use of readers' theatre was a powerful tool for social engagement and municipal policy development. It successfully outlined community healing strategies crystallised around these five main themes from the point of view of residents. These strategies can foster community-wide posttraumatic growth from collective trauma. This growth could be seen in a transformed identity, as in *We are survivors-thrivers*, and an increase in the community's social capital, its resilience and generative coping mechanisms, and its capacity for hope in order to overcome adversity and to prevail with increased resources, support, competence, and connectedness.

### Notes

1 There is a vast body of literature that documents this trend. See Belliveau and Nichols (2017), Deloney and Graham (2003), (Feldman et al., 2013), Hundt et al. (2010), and (Nisker et al., 2006).

2 Folx, an alternative spelling of the word folks, specifically includes and highlights LGBTQ2+, gender non-conforming, and non-binary people thus acknowledging the violence perpetrated towards these communities.

### References

Belliveau, G. (2015). Research-based theatre and a/r/tography: Exploring arts-based educational research methodologies. *p-e-r-f-o-r-m-a-n-c-e, 2*(1–2). http://p-e-r-f-o-r-m-a-n-c-e.org/?p=1491

Belliveau, G., & Nichols, J. (2017). Audience responses to Contact!Unload: A Canadian research-based play about returning military veterans. *Cogent Arts & Humanities, 4*(1), art. 1351704. https://doi.org/10.1080/23311983.2017.1351704

Bleuer, J., Chin, M., & Sakamoto, I. (2018). Why theatre-based research works? Psychological theories from behind the curtain. *Qualitative Research in Psychology, 15*(2–3), 395–411. https://doi.org/10.1080/14780887.2018.1430734

Calhoun, L., & Tedeschi, R. (Eds.). (2006). *Handbook of posttraumatic growth: Research and practice*. Erlbaum.

Deloney, L., & Graham, C. (2003). Developments: Wit: Using drama to teach first-year medical students about empathy and compassion. *Teaching and Learning in Medicine, 15*, 247–251. https://doi.org/10.1207/S15328015TLM1504_06

Dissanayake, E. (1995). *Homo aestheticus*. University of Washington Press.

Donmoyer, R., & Donmoyer, J. (2008). Readers' theater as a data display strategy.In J. G. Knowles & A. Cole (Eds.), *Handbook of the arts in qualitative research: Perspectives, methodologies, examples, and issues* (pp. 209–224). Sage.

Erikson, K. (1976). Disaster at Buffalo Creek: Loss of communality at Buffalo Creek. *American Journal of Psychiatry, 133*, 302–305.

Fein, A., & Isaacson, N. (2009). Echoes of Columbine: The emotion work of leaders in school shooting sites. *American Behavioral Scientist, 52*(9), 1327–1346. https://doi.org/10.1177/0002764209332549

Feldman, S., Hopgood, A., & Dickins, M. (2013). Translating research findings into community based theatre: More than a dead man's wife. *Journal of Aging Studies, 27*(4), 476–486. http://dx.doi.org/10.1016/j.jaging.2013.03.007

Figley, C. (1995). Compassion fatigue as a secondary traumatic stress disorder: An overview. In C. Figley (Ed.), *Compassion fatigue: Coping with secondary stress disorder in those who treat the traumatized* (pp. 1–20). Brunner Mazel.

Hundt, G., Bryanston, C., Lowe, P., Cross, S., Sandall, J., & Spencer, K. (2010). Inside 'inside view': Reflections on stimulating debate and engagement through a multimedia live theatre production on the dilemmas and issues of pre-natal screening policy and practice. *Health Expectations, 14*, 1–9. https://doi:10.1111/j.1369-7625.2010.00597.x

Kaufman, M., & Members of the Tectonic Theatre Project. (2001). *The Laramie project*. Vintage.

Krueger, R., & Casey, M. A. (2009). *Focus groups: A practical guide for applied research* (4th ed.). Sage.

Kuriansky, J. (2012). Our communities: Healing after environmental disasters. In D. Nemeth, R. Hamilton, & J. Kuriansky (Eds.), *Living in an environmentally traumatized world: Healing ourselves and our planet* (pp. 141–167). Praeger.

Manyena, S., O'Brien, G., O'Keefe, P., & Rose, J. (2011). Disaster resilience: A bounce back or bounce forward ability? *Local Environment, 16*, 417–424. https://doi.org/10.1080/13549839.2011.583049

Mapp, I., & Koch, D. (2004). Creation of a group mural to promote healing following a mass trauma. In N. Webb (Ed.), *Mass trauma and violence* (pp. 100–119). Guilford Press.

Nisker, J., Martin, D., Bluhma, R., & Daar, A. (2006). Theatre as a public engagement tool for health-policy development. *Health Policy, 78*, 258–271. https://doi:10.1016/j.healthpol.2005.10.009

Raphael, B. (1986). *When disaster strikes: How individuals and communities cope with catastrophe.* Basic Books.

Reilly, R. C. (2011). "We knew her ..." Murder in a small town: A hybrid work in three voices. *Qualitative Inquiry, 17*(7), 599–601. https://doi:10.1177/1077800411413997

Saldaña, J. (1998). Ethical issues in an ethnographic performance text: The "dramatic impact" of "juicy stuff." *Research in Drama Education, 3*(2), 181–196. https://doi.org/10.1080/1356978980030205

Wachtel, T., & McCold, P. (2004, August). *From restorative justice to restorative practices: Expanding the paradigm.* Paper presented at the 5th International Conference on Conferencing and Circles, Vancouver, BC, Canada.

CHAPTER 6

# Lost in Transition

## *Brecht's Theatre as a Social Change Agent for Youth Empowerment in the Time of the Twentieth Anniversary of the Hong Kong Handover*

*Wai Luk Lo and Ka Lee Carrie Ho*

## 1 Introduction

Brecht's plays are not new to Hong Kong. Since *The Good Person of Setzuan* (1943), the earliest recorded Brecht production in 1966 (Lo, 1999), many of his plays are staged repeatedly by both professional and amateur theatre groups. His *The Caucasian Chalk Circle*, written in 1944 and premiered in 1948, the play on which we focus here, takes place in Georgia about a thousand years ago, but, in the Prologue, Brecht discusses a post-World War II dispute about the ownership of a valley between two groups of people who are living in the Union of Soviet Socialist Republics. The play advocates a new principle of ownership: the land should be managed by the people who can better develop it, regardless of whether they are the original inhabitants. The plot of the play is a celebration of the settlement of the dispute using this new principle.

The play was first staged in Hong Kong in 1977. Since then, many productions have followed. Perhaps this is because its theme echoes Hong Kongers' worry about their local political situation.

The production of this play in 2016 by Teen AIDS, an organisation focused on teenager AIDS advocacy, is the subject of this chapter. We discuss how this play was adapted and performed by a youth theatre group as the twentieth anniversary of the UK's returning Hong Kong's sovereignty to China in 1997 in what became called the handover. Their reinterpretation of the play focused on youth empowerment in the 21st century.

Since this organisation, of which most members are Christian, aspires to help members through arts education, besides offering social services, it runs Touch Theatre, a theatre group. Each year, it stages a play or a musical in a theatre with full costume and professional technicalities.

The annual drama production is a big event. Since the play has more than fifty characters, a production must recruit about a hundred participants as performers, and as front and backstage crew members. Their background diverse in including AIDS care advocates, church leaders, financial investment advisers, office workers, sales agents, youth workers, university students, teenagers,

 | DOI: 10.1163/9789004442870_006

and unemployed young people. Among the 100 participants, more than 30 had no previous theatre experience and some of them had emotional problems or were recovering their mental health.

The director of the play found that many Hong Kong citizens were saddened by the unsuccessful fight for the democratic reform of the political system in relation to the elections of the major government seats. In particular, the final resolution of the Umbrella Movement (26 September to 15 December 2014) with the clearance of the occupied areas of the demonstrators triggered a sense of loss among young people. Afterwards, they were haunted by confusion and helplessness; they saw no future for themselves.

For the director, theatre is a form of social practice, and that Brecht's play could become an agent of social change right then. Therefore, the objective of the production was to correlate *The Caucasian Chalk Circle* with the emotional aspects of Hong Kong's social situation. In order to encourage participants to live with hope, he refocused the story on the themes of righteousness, empathy, and courage.

Moreover, he insisted on a creative process that involved every member in the group. He adopted techniques of team building through group creativity. Regardless of the background, ability, and talent of the members, each one was treated as a valuable contributor to the production and to the interpretation of the play. Even before casting, he set up two basic principles regarding role assignment:

- Anyone who wanted to participate had a role in the production—performing, backstage, or front stage.
- Anyone who wanted to be on stage could take part in specific roles as a character, as part of the chorus, or as a member of a group.

These two principles implied a re-interpretation of the notion of empowerment.

## 2 Concepts of Empowerment

The driving element of the rehearsal process was empowerment. Empowerment is an idea that originated in the 1960s (Bartunek & Spreitzer, 2006). Since then, it has been adopted by practitioners in various fields and has become a conceptual tool in socio-cultural discourses. In the 21st century, empowerment is one of the essential operational strategies in social education. A general understanding of the term is that "empowerment aims at initiating the process of becoming stronger and being more confident, especially in controlling one's life and claiming one's rights" (Oxford English Dictionary, 2015).

Three types of empowerment are relevant here. Social Movement claims that changes come through an organised collective effort of problem-solving (McAdam, McCarthy, & Zald, 1996); Activist Theatre advocates the use of theatre as an agent of social change (Boal, 1979); while Youth Culture focuses on developing sociopolitical awareness in young people and enhancing their skills as agents of community change (Zimmerman, 1995, 2000).

In the Hong Kong Chinese community, the concept of empowerment in the social service community is usually viewed simply as a process that involves the participation of the clients in the planning of activities. This framework maintains the conventional power relationship of the authority of the service provider over the service recipient. Such an interpretation assumes a power hierarchy similar to that of the conventional parenting-style of authorisation; the one in power provides compassion and/or benefits to the other. This background led to a very delicate challenge to the directorial team during the rehearsals.

The host organisation's conventional arts education practices are quite didactic. It regards arts education as a kind of instruction from the one who knows to the one who does not know, or the giving by the one who processes to the one who does not process. With this background, therefore, there were very subtle negotiations on the interpretation of empowerment during the creative process between and among the members of the guest directorial team, the leaders of the organisation, and the participants.

To the director, empowerment is not merely the releasing of the power of the authority to the members. To avoid the trap of misinterpretation, the empowerment of this production emphasised facilitating the exploration of self-expression and presentation based on the understanding of Brecht's theory and his play; this was done by offering the young people a trusting environment in which to participate in the creative group process. Since every member observed what the others were trying, and anyone could join in and give feedback, this led to the development of their skills.

This idea of empowerment gave rise to the second challenge of the production. Given the diversity of the background of each participant, there were significant differences in their skills in acting, singing, movement, and communication. Additionally, members were not familiar with Brecht's theory, and their world views were different from his.

To tackle the challenges, the director adopted three significant strategies in the rehearsal:

- a group creative process
- creative empowerment
- a reflective exercise in which each member kept a journal or shared thoughts with members in a cell-group

## 3 Group Creative Process

The rehearsal of *The Caucasian Chalk Circle* began at the end of April 2016. The process combined performance training, dramaturgical studies, and team building.

Although there were casting sessions, these were arranged so that the director could get to know the ability of each of the participants, instead of his deciding on the cast from the start. After the casting sessions, the director started with script studies, combining them with group discussions on members' opinions about living in Hong Kong and about their interpretations of the play. He organised group theatre games and communication exercises for all participants.

The play was rehearsed without the cast having been determined. The play reading sessions and the initial blocking of selected scenes were conducted with different combinations and pairing of participants so that everyone had a chance to get to know the scenes and to experience playing different characters. At first, the rehearsals were workshops for adjusting and levelling up the acting skills of all the performers.

In this performance, the story was adopted collectively by all performers through four group rehearsals. The rehearsals were carried out according to Brecht's vision of Education Theatre. All performers were encouraged to participate actively in discussions and workshops ranging from script reading to scene rehearsals. Subsequent role assignments reinforced the process. All performers were more than just characters; they were also members of the chorus. They performed in group scenes, took part in recitals and songs, and some of them also participated in narration, music performances, and physical performances.

The rehearsals were conducted in a group ensemble fashion to enhance the team spirit. As a result, each participant actively observed the performance of others in the rehearsals and they all considered themselves an indispensable member of the group.

## 4 Creative Empowerment

To ensure that each participant was conscious of the fact that they shared the ownership of the production, the director decided to change the narration mode of the main story. In the original play, three singers narrate all the rhapsodic songs. In this rendition, the play was narrated in recitative rhythm by the entire company as chorus. It was complemented with three narrators who delivered the dramatic situation in a more naturalistic way. The realistic scene details were simplified to ensure the freedom of the unfolding of the dramatic action. This meant that each performer had the sense of being a member of a collective delivering a story. Such an arrangement echoed Brecht's Lehrstücke (teaching plays), such as, for example, *The Measures Taken* (premiered 1930) and *The Exception and the Rule* (circa 1930).

During the rehearsal process, the directorial team not only created an atmosphere of group participation with team spirit but also demonstrated to all the participants that their input contributed to the crucial part of the performance.

The creation of the new Prelude best illustrated effective empowerment through group creativity. The temperament of the socialist farmers in the original Prologue was quite difficult for members to enact with belief. After a group brainstorming session, it was decided to replace it with a theme song sung by the full company to express the members' genuine feeling of living in Hong Kong at that time.

In the first workshop, the director conducted some creative writing games for the members and facilitated the collective creation of the theme song. The first task required everyone to describe their emotions, which related to living in Hong Kong at that moment, in four ways by using adjectives, color, natural phenomena, and/or musical notes. Then, all these were shared. Immediately, the group's voice of anxiety and loss was apparent. The word "fog" was used very often by group members. The recognition of the prevailing sentiment inspired the creative spontaneity of some members. They improvised some tunes on the spot with some combinations of the words, and the creative spirit of the entire group flew upwards. A theme song sub-group was formed, and the work in progress was collectively tried and discussed in subsequent rehearsals. The final version of the lyrics of "Lost" were

> In a fog, confused, and lost, I can see no way out.
> In a fog, confused, and lost, (fearfully) moving on in the storm.
>
> The grey sky falls on me.
> I can't even see my fingers in the thick mist.
> There is not even a glimpse of light in the unbreakable mist.
>
> No matter how hard I try, there is no direction.
> Who can tell me where the exit is?
> Who can hear my heartbeat screaming?!

The Prelude[1] acted as a process of cognitive provocation in the performers. It gave them the sense of living in Hong Kong at that particular moment. The main body of the play, then, became a way for the group to discover how to change the world into a place fit for people to live in.

## 5 Conscious Embodiment of Brecht's Aesthetics

In producing a play by Brecht, we need to do it in a Brechtian way. Therefore, in this production creative empowerment is not only an operational strategy, it has an aesthetic dimension.

Brecht's theory was explained during the workshops, but, during the rehearsals, the director also led the group members in the development of some ways of character presentation, interaction, and mise-en-scene that illustrated their understanding of Brecht's theory. This strategy is one of conscious embodiment in its allowing the company to discover themselves while they are trying to employ techniques of Brechtian theatre during the rehearsals. Members gained self-confidence by getting positive feedback from others, so the process itself contributed to the changes in the company.

As early as 1930, Brecht put forward his idea of epic theatre in contrast to dramatic theatre (Willett, 1964/1974). Brecht continued to develop his theory, and he tried out various techniques. In 1935, he had the experience in Moscow of watching the performance of Mei Lan Fang (梅蘭芳, 1894–1961). The Chinese operatic master's theatrical techniques struck him. In particular, he reflected on the simultaneous acting out of a particular character and performing the role of the narrator, and came up with a term, Verfremdungseffekt (Alienation Effect) that became the core of his theory. Brecht used this for the first time in 1936 in an article on the alienation effect of Chinese performance as Willett (1964/1974) has reminded us.

Brecht's theoretical illumination came with his appreciation of the embodiment of individual self-alienation performative acts. This production, with the objective of youth empowerment, illustrated Brechtian theatre primarily with three essential Brechtian aesthetic principles and techniques, namely, verfremdungseffekt, historicisation, and gestus.

### 5.1 *Verfremdungseffekt* (*Alienation Effect*)

According to Brecht (1964), the core of the Alienation Effect is the non-existence of the "fourth wall" (p. 91). The actors can "speak directly" to the audience and "dissociate themselves from their roles" in the play by observing and commenting on their performance before the audience (He, 2019, p. 55). The breaking of the fourth wall results in the "abolishing [of] the illusion of life." When the actor "admits [the character's] fictionality" (He, 2019, p. 56), the character will then become a symbol with a symbolic meaning, so "sympathies will not be engaged" in the members of the audience (Wixson, 1972/2016, p. 113).

"Every era has to re-explore the concept of 'alienation effect'" (Lo, 1999, p. 13). In this production, each performer took on at least two characters—the Hong Kong citizen in the prologue and the character in *The Caucasian Chalk Circle*. They also participated in narratives, music performances, and physical performances[2] by acting as chorus members, songwriters, musicians, and members of the stage crew.

### 5.2 *Historicisation*

Brecht said that "the spectator must come to grip with things" (quoted in Willett, 1964/1974, p. 23) so how can his aesthetic idea of Alienation Effect be upheld? The answer is that he complements his dramatic practice with the idea of historicisation. This production used some raps that imitate contemporary western music, Cantonese operatic style rhythmic recitative verses (*shubailan* 數白欖), and Chinese fishermen folk song (*xian shui ge* 咸水歌) to convey the feeling of old Hong Kong culture and customs. This arrangement was done not only to fulfil the play's Brechtian musical narration but also served as a consideration of local Hong Kong theatre aesthetics (Lo, 1999). We successfully created the sense of a remote local culture that was not so familiar but was, at the same time, intelligible.

### 5.3 *Gestus (Characterisation/Action)*

Brecht's characterisation focuses on the Didactic Drama: "the audience is forced to take a critical role" (Wixson, 1972/2016, p. 113). With the "scientific acting" (p. 117) technique, it is demanded of actors that they portray the character consciously with the ideological conscience pointed to by the playwright. During the rehearsals, quite some time was spent to ensure that the performers carried with them the required social attitudes in dramatic situations.

## 6 Exploration of the Theme

After being equipped with the embodiment of Brechtian aesthetics, the company was engaged in the exploration of the theme of *The Caucasian Chalk Circle*.

With the failure of the Umbrella Movement in 2014, Hong Kong citizens suffered a great sense of loss in this large-scale social protest. The director felt strongly that the play was asking an essential question: "In the time of turmoil, what do we care about the most? What is the most important thing to us?" (Lo, 2016).

All the characters in this play answered the questions with their actions: the wife of the Grand Duke cares about her clothing, most characters care about their lives, Simon cares about love and duty, but his lover Grusha cares about an innocent life, that of the baby Michael. By pointing this out to all performers and asking them to create gestures and attitudes to illustrate the standpoints of the characters, to show what they were caring most about in different dramatic situations, the flow of the play was full of gestus. This process was an empowerment, as well as a salute to Brecht's dramatic aesthetics.

Knowing what we care about in the time of turmoil is one thing, but sustaining the original determination is another. Therefore, compassion must be charged with courage. Everybody has compassion, but most people will act like the middle-aged peasant lady in Act II. She has a moment of compassion, but she collapses when she is facing the iron shirt soldiers. However, Grusha is kind-hearted and cannot tolerate throwing aside the baby. Although, out of selfish motivation, she has momentarily thought of abandoning the child, she cannot stand the test of her conscience, and her inner voice urges her to admit the responsibility (and its consequences) of carrying along with her this innocent life. She decides to live and die with the child. With him, Grusha becomes courageous. She dares to stun the soldiers, challenges the elite, and even the superior judge.

Only one performer acted as the character Grusha, but we arranged to have all the members of the group come out on stage at the end of Act II to sing the song, "Live and Die Together."

> A single route, a single life;
> Child, do you know how deep the cliff is?
> The broken bridge will break anytime,
> Which route should I go?
> Who can choose? (It's not up to you!)
> Lean on me if the route is too far to you.

By letting the entire company sing the inner voice of Grusha, all members experienced a moment of determination. This moment had a subjectivity that combined righteousness, empathy, and courage.

## 7 Conclusion

The production demonstrated a newly interpreted definition of empowerment that emphasised the facilitation of the exploration of self-expression and presentation concerning the particular context. The rehearsal process proved that group creativity and creative empowerment are valuable strategies to use among the members of a group of people of diversified background.

With the 6 workshops and 200 hours of rehearsals, more than 30 novice youth performers were trained, and the 100 members re-adapted the script to fit a Hong Kong context with collective effort.

The creative process and the outcome proved to all participants that all of them were significant in this production since a total of 18,000 words of thoughtfully written post-performance reflective journals by 32 participants were received and shared. The production empowered a group of young people through arts-based experiences to deal with their personal and social anxiety about the uncertainty of life in Hong Kong. This methodology may well be applied to other groups in other contexts with some appropriate adjustments.

## Notes

1 See the Prelude of the production in the promotion video, https://www.youtube.com/watch?v=FGGegitlKzM

2 In Act III, performers became snow; they employed body movement to suggest snow melting in spring

## References

Bartunek, J. M., & Spreitzer, G. M. (2006). The interdisciplinary career of a popular construct used in management empowerment in the late 20th century. *Journal of Management Inquiry, 15*(3), 255–273.

Boal, A. (1979). *Theatre of the oppressed*. Pluto Press.

Brecht, B. (1947). *The Caucasian chalk circle* (E. Bentley & M. Bentley, Trans.). University of Minnesota Press. (Original work published 1944)

Brecht, B. (1948). *The good man of Setzuan* (E. Bentley, Trans). University of Minnesota Press. (Original work published 1943)

Brecht, B. (1964). Alienation effects in Chinese acting. In J. Willett (Ed. & Trans.), *Brecht on theatre*. Hill & Wang.

He, W. H. (2019). Bertolt Brecht's theatrical concept of alienation effect and the Chinese application and transformation. *Neohelicon, 46*, 53–67. https://doi.org/10.1007/s11059-018-0468-3

Lo, W. L. (1999). 我的名字不是布莱希特: 香港布萊希特演出及研究 [Bertolt Brecht in Hong Kong]. In J. Yeung & W. L. Lo (Eds.), *My name is not Bertolt Brecht: Performance and research on Bertolt Brecht in Hong Kong* (pp. 15–55). International Association of Theatre Critics (Hong Kong).

Lo, W. L. (2016). The director's notes. In *The Caucasian chalk circle programme* (pp. 3–4). Touch Theatre.

McAdam, D., McCarthy, J. D., & Zald, M. N. (1996). Introduction: Opportunities, mobilizing structures, and framing processes—toward a synthetic, comparative perspective on social movements. In D. McAdam, J. D. McCarthy, & M. N. Zald (Eds.), *Comparative perspectives on social movements: Political opportunities, mobilizing structures, and cultural framings* (1st ed., pp. 1–20). Cambridge University Press.

Willett, J. (Ed. & Trans.). (1974). *Brecht on theatre*. Eyre Methuen. (Original work published 1964)

Wixson Jr., D. C. (2016). The dramatic techniques of Thornton Wilder and Bertolt Brecht: A study in comparison. *Modern Drama, 15*(2), 112–124. https://moderndrama.utpjournals.press/doi/10.3138/md.15.2.112 (Original work published 1972)

Zimmerman, M. A. (1995). Psychological empowerment: Issues and illustrations. *American Journal of Community Psychology, 23*(5), 581–599.

Zimmerman, M. A. (2000). Empowerment theory: Psychological, organisational, and community levels of analysis. In J. Rappaport & E. Seidman (Eds.), *Handbook of community psychology* (pp. 43–63). Kluwer Academic/Plen.

CHAPTER 7

# Making Stone Soup

## *Arts-Based Organisational Interventions and Participants' Communication, Teamwork, and Sense of Wellbeing*

*Mariam Ugarte and Warren Linds*

## 1 Introduction

As a nurse and health care teacher, I (Mariam) am passionate about creating safe spaces that promote empowerment and allow people, especially women, to reach their potential. In 2016, when I returned to University to complete a master's program in Human Systems Intervention (HSI) I could engage with this passion since the fieldwork component requires students to work with a client on an organisational development project. This led me to an NGO, Rural Development Trust (RDT) Hospital, in Kalyandurg, Andhra Pradesh, India, where I had worked as a volunteer to update labor and delivery room nurses. The goals and ethics of RDT are to improve the lives of women and children living in extreme poverty; working with them matched the expectations and requirements of the HSI program to "enable the client system to catalyze its own learning and renewal" (Taylor, de Guerre, Gavin, & Kass, 2002, p. 361). The hospital administrator's aim was to improve nursing retention.

## 2 The Project

This project took place between July and December, 2016. Participants included three head nurses, twenty-three labor and delivery room and antenatal nurses and ten maternity doctors (two of whom were medical administrators). Most nurses had one to five, while three had ten or more, years of experience.

My goal was to improve communication among, and between, all levels of staff, to improve participation and thus empower the nurses. I used arts-based organisational interventions based on participatory action research methods to help improve communication and foster a feeling of wellbeing.

I began with interviews with each nurse. These revealed how difficult it was to express their opinions. Their stock answers were either silence or "perfect, no problems, very happy." They seemed afraid to talk. Field observations during and outside of work hours revealed extreme deference shown towards doctors

 | DOI: 0.1163/9789004442870_007

and administrators. The behavior was likely influenced by deep-rooted cultural, socio-economic, political, historical, and religious norms. These nurses, all women, came from rural areas and belonged to the lower castes of Indian society. Freire (1996) described the effect of internalising perceptions of how one is thought of and how those in authority treat others. If these ways of seeing and behaving towards someone are judgmental, the person believes that she[1] is undeserving or unworthy of respect. This is why the nurses were surprised when I requested their input. There was a lack of communication both among nurses and between them and their supervisors. There were pleasantries and the exchange of basic information, but we were able to probe deeper as more questions were asked.

## 3 The Role of Culture

It was important for me to consider the role of culture and its effect on behaviour in planning appropriate interventions. According to Hofstede and Hofstede's (2005) framework of cross-cultural communication, certain societies (in this case, of Andhra Pradesh), accept that power is unequally distributed between superiors and subordinates. They refer to this as "power distance" (p. 26). It is no wonder that even I, as a facilitator, was treated with extreme deference.

While interviewing these nurses, I became immersed in the "culture of silence" (Freire, 1996, p. 13) and confronted by many interwoven difficulties ranging from cultural oppression to the absence of a nursing union. I wanted to facilitate a birthing process for them into a new reality in spite of their history of oppression.

## 4 Relationality

A relational approach to working with organisations requires paying attention to "the intersubjective and interdependent nature of organizational life" (Bradbury & Lichtenstein, 2000, p. 551). Interactions between and among members of the system are as important, or perhaps more so, than the actions of individual members. I decided to connect with the nurses by organising two field trips to a Hindu temple and a nearby lake. This brought us closer and helped break down some of the initial communication barriers.

The nurses were more comfortable and forthcoming in a group. The field trips aroused the interest of the doctors who wondered why they were not included. Their sudden interest in the project made the nurses feel important.

When workers are valued and their contributions encouraged and recognised the result is increased fulfillment and commitment. Meyer (2010) has described the possibilities of improvement, transformation, and growth in a space that is safe, joyful, and collaborative. Job satisfaction and retention increase, as does organisational success in this positive environment.

An important component of this project was getting together, sharing a meal, and talking to each other. Eventually, more trust emerged, and participants began to share their stories and talk about what mattered to them. As Block (2011) has stated, "the future is created one room at a time, one gathering at a time. Each gathering needs to become an example of the future we want to create" (p. 93).

## 5 Why Art and Play

Arts-based interventions take participants into an expressive and sense-making journey that appeals to the senses and emotions, enabling participants to collaborate in new ways. These approaches cut through cultural and religious barriers, are non-threatening, bring out the inner child, and leave no place for hierarchy (West, Hoff, & Carlsson, 2017). An added kinesthetic element such as improvisation provides a more holistic experience because it engages the body as well as the brain (Kolb, 1984; Dewey 1916/2011; Jensen, 2013).

Play is often associated with the cultural development of children. Vygotsky (1978) noted that "play contains all the developmental tendencies in a condensed form; in play, it is as though the child were trying to jump above the level of his 'normal behavior' and serves as a 'zone of proximal development'" (p. 70). By focusing on imagination and interpersonal connection, play and performance create opportunities (Lobman, 2015.) Rieber, Smith, and Noah (1988) and Goldmintz and Schaefer (2007) note play is also vital to lifelong learning in adults. Meyer (2010), an organisational development consultant, found that participants in her "playshops" describe the playspace co-created for improvisation as "energizing, free from judgment, and a place where they could be themselves" (p. xiii).

Drawing from Hunter's (2008) work with refugee youth, I knew that theatre games serve to create what can be called a safe enough space to try out new relationships. This space is a process and a place in which to encounter risk and messiness. It is "less about prescribing conditions and more about generating questions" (p. 19) as participants are invited to collaborate, risk, and explore in the name of expanding creative and imaginative possibilities.

I had been inspired by my courses at *Improv Montreal*[2] where I discovered theatre games and communication methods that developed my observational skills. I learned to be present in the moment, hold space for others, and relinquish control so others might be heard. The combination of communication, creativity, and collaboration are three essential qualities that teams need to thrive in today's world as Leonard and Yorton (2015) have reminded us. With this in mind and recognising the fast-paced working conditions of the nurses with their enormous patient load, I created an inviting environment for play. I used dialogue, improvisation, metaphors, storytelling, collective painting, and puppet making. To respond to the dynamic of the group as it changed in situ, I continually designed and re-designed improvisational games every day. This enabled the creation of a more dynamic, playful, and authentic environment one step at a time.

## 6 Dialogic Circles

We began and ended every activity session with a sharing circle where a safe container emerged, a place where "effective processes can unfold" (Bushe, 2010, p. 10). Our conversations and activities took place in an atmosphere of trust; respect for each other's comments and opinions was fostered. No one was rushed or forced to speak. When someone shared something difficult to express, they were thanked and praised for their courage. This served to model positive communication.

Three different groups with twenty-six nurses from two different shifts attended all sessions four times a week. Discussions began with a question from the facilitator. We passed a mala (a string of Hindu prayer beads) from person to person. The person with the mala could choose to speak or pass it on.

## 7 Improvisation

Friis and Larsen (2006) use improvisational theatre with organisations. They argue that in improvisation no one can rely on carefully planned agendas but must take risks to respond spontaneously to each other, so "people are able to recognize themselves, each other and their work in new ways" (p. 17). Its main principle of "Yes, And" (rather than "Yes, But") justifies and builds on the contribution of another. It encourages active listening, participation, and mindfulness, and it promotes a safe environment for risk-taking while minimising self-consciousness. This approach emphasises that failure is part of life and making mistakes is essential to success. (Spolin in Leonard & Yorton, 2015).

Improvisation activities consisted of many short and fast-moving theatre games during which participants spontaneously created words and gestures.

I also briefed the translator on the process and its importance. She quickly became a passionate participant.

Initially, the nurses were very shy. However, they began to understand the concept of "Yes, And" and became truly engaged. Nurses stated that they were using the concept both at work and in their private lives and used it to discuss and solve problems with the doctors. One nurse commented that she was teaching it to her neighbor's children, thus sharing this tool with her community; it was at those moments that I felt change had begun.

## 8 Storytelling

One does not need to be articulate and/or highly educated to use and benefit from imaginative tools such as metaphors and storybooks. In a systematic review of arts-based interventions in nursing Meyer (2012) found that benefits included "empowerment, building social supports, providing distraction, and promoting the expression of emotions" (p. 33). She distinguishes between the arts as a tool of therapy with healing as an end product and arts-based interventions that are a process of "creating art that appears to be healing" (p. 7). Many artistic forms have been used in health care for the past sixty years to help people heal from trauma and loss and have probably been used for hundreds of years informally by people all over the world (Malchiodi, 2016). For example, Walsh, Chang, Schmidt, and Yoepp (2005) found that engaging in four creative arts interventions in a nursing classroom lowered stress, reduced anxiety, and engendered positive emotions among the students.

Metaphors lay the groundwork for storytelling. As Baskin (2005) explains, we use the wisdom gained from stories to make decisions in our daily lives. Participants read a different (and translated) storybook left on each unit every week.

I used *Stone Soup* (Muth, 2003) to demonstrate how goals are achieved through teamwork. A delicious soup, which began with only boiling water and a stone, was made when the inhabitants of an entire village gave small individual contributions like a carrot, salt, and so on. It highlights how a simple creative activity helped rebuild the community.

> Something magical began to happen among the villagers. As each person opened their heart to give, the next person gave even more. And as this happened, the soup grew richer and smelled more delicious. (p. 21)

An analogy offered by one of the nurses was how easy it is to break one stick but how much more difficult it is to break a bundle of sticks.

## 9 Painting

Before the collective painting activity, I emphasised that the quality of the art work was not as important as their attempt to express themselves through art. Their paintings would show their thoughts on the portion of the large sheet of paper in front of them. I played a recording of traditional Indian music without lyrics while each person painted silently. When the music stopped, participants moved to the next spot in clockwise order and added to the painting in front of them, without changing, erasing, or destroying the previous person's contribution. At the completion of the painting, every member of each group described what they saw. All the paintings were similar in representing hospital scenes with mothers and babies but each person's interpretation was unique. This activity exposed the nurses to various forms of self-expression, preparing them for the next exercise, the puppet show.

## 10 We Make Puppets

Puppet making has a long tradition in India, first mentioned in the Mahabharata as early as the 9th century BCE (Autiero, 2018). It was used successfully by the founder of RDT during its origins to motivate people to participate and build community. Kroger and Nupponen (2019) have identified the potential uses of puppets as pedagogical tools for

- communication,
- supporting positive classroom climate,
- enhancing creativity,
- fostering co-operation in and integration into a group, and
- changing attitudes (p. 399).

As the nurses made their paper bag puppets, I explained that they could use them to talk in the third person about things that were on their minds. I suggested they begin by introducing themselves through their puppets. We then made rod puppets (made with three sticks, two for the arms and one to hold the head) to practice role-playing in preparation for a final puppet show. One of the issues that emerged was the use and abuse of power. This was a huge breakthrough. They were finally able to bring up a repressed issue through the voice of their puppets. As Block (2008) has explained, signs of resistance in the system (in this case, silence), include the client expressing ambiguity and/or fear about finally acknowledging that which was hidden, and facing the fact that they may be contributing to the problem. Even more difficult are the questions that may follow this realisation.

- What can I do now and how?

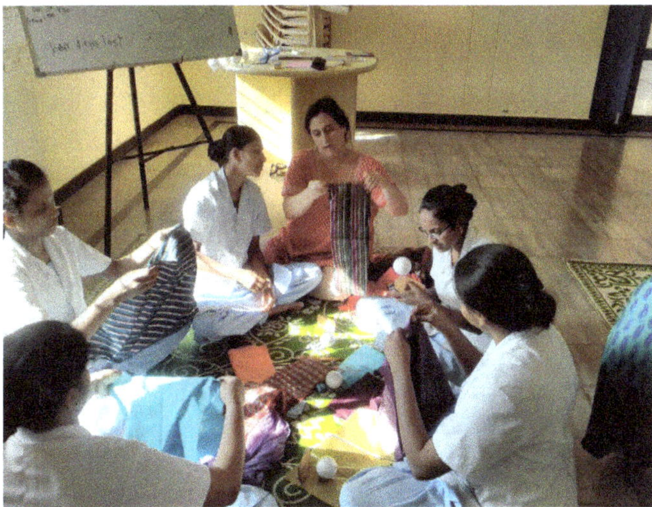

FIGURE 7.1 Making rod puppets

- Will it change anything?
- How will it affect me? Is it worth the effort?

## 11 The Doctors Join In

The doctors became progressively more curious and even slightly envious that they were not being included in this project. I invited them and the medical administrators to become part of it, and, hence, part of the solution. To this end, they were included in some of the facilitation activities, participating separately from the nurses in improv, dialogue, storytelling, collective painting, and world café (a structured process of group discussion). The final activity, in which nurses and doctors worked together in silence to create drawings of mandalas was evidence of improved teamwork.

## 12 Outcomes

The participants noticed changes in themselves.
- I learned to be strong and how to talk to others.
- I know all the names from LR now before I only knew the names of where I work.
- With the activities, we learned more how to work together.
- You listen and today because of you, we solved a problem, the doctors are listening more and we had a problem and we are all the same and so they listened.

## 13 Follow-up

As follow-up, the unit and I arranged to meet monthly on Skype. In order to accommodate everyone since most participants were interested, we formed three groups, two of nurses, and one of doctors. I held eighteen Skype sessions over eight months. Nurses participated so eagerly that sessions lasted at least two hours. One result was the decision that each person would share her strongest ability with a colleague, and report to the group on how it went. They were learning from each other and interacting in a more meaningful way. Towards the end of the process, the nurses started inviting one or two doctors to their own meetings and the conversation between them became more fluid and dynamic.

## 14 Reflection

In the beginning, I felt that I faced the weight of hundreds of years of tradition and submission. However, I reminded myself that my role was not to give solutions but to accompany the participants on their journey, help them notice, and let them create a safe environment in which to start communicating.

- Would we be able to cross the huge cultural, language, and religious barriers between us?
- Would we succeed in understanding each other?
- What would we learn on the journey?

Overall, I felt equipped with a tool kit of arts-based interventions. Malchiodi points out, "Art engages our senses in ways that words cannot" (2016, n.p.). For every challenge, some form of art played a role. Play and laughter helped overcome their silence; Improvisation made them forget their shyness; puppets and role-playing enabled them to find their voices and allowed them to speak of power, which, as women and nurses, they sorely lacked. They also found their voices through storybook analogies and drawing which at first seemed unrelated to their work, but ultimately led to talking about it. Any art method that is appropriate to the culture in which one is immersed can be used, thus becoming a medium resembling a form of meditation. Stroke by stroke participants got closer to their emotions, to their true selves, and change began to happen.

## 15 Conclusion

> Artistic inquiry … typically starts with the realization that you cannot define the final outcome where you are planning … Most meaningful

> insights often come by surprise, unexpectedly, and even against the will of the creator. (McNiff, 2008, p. 40)

My experience with this project seems to parallel the events in Stone Soup. Our soup making became a deep arts-based process during which collaboration and community building emerged. Through many arts-based interventions we arrived at a place of collaborative work and trust. The journey continued through our Skype calls. As we have shown, arts-based interventions are important tools for social change because of their inclusiveness, versatility, effectiveness, and accessibility.

## Notes

1 I use "she" to represent both females and males.
2 An organisation that conducts workshops to improve team dynamics through improvisation theatre techniques.

## References

Autiero, S. (2018). *An introduction to Indian puppetry.* https://www.sahapedia.org/introduction-indian-puppetry

Baskin, C. (2005). Storytelling circles: Reflections of Aboriginal protocols in research. *Canadian Social Work Review/Revue canadienne de service social, 22*(2), 171–187. www.jstor.org/stable/41669834

Block, P. (2008). *Flawless consulting: A guide to getting your expertise used* (3rd ed.). Pfeiffer.

Bradbury, H., & Lichtenstein, B. M. (2000). Relationality in organization research: Exploring the space between. *Organization Science, 11*(5), 551–564. www.jstor.org/stable/2640345

Bushe, G. R. (2010). Being the container in dialogic OD. *Practising Social Change,* 2, 10–15.

Dewey, J. (2011). *Democracy and education.* Simon and Brown. (Original work published 1916)

Freire, P. (1996). *Pedagogy of the oppressed* (2nd ed.). Penguin Books.

Friis, P., & Larsen, H. (2006). Theatre, improvisation and social change. In P. Shaw & R. Stacey (Eds.), *Experiencing risk, spontaneity and Improvisation in organizational change: Working live* (pp. 19–43). Routledge.

Gilmand, P. (1992). *Something from nothing.* Scholastic Canada.

Goldmintz, Y., & Schaefer, G. E. (2007). Why play matters to adults. *Psychology and Education: An Interdisciplinary Journal, 44*(1), 12–25.

Hofstede, G., & Hofstede, G. J. (2005). *Cultures and organizations: Software of the mind* (2nd ed.). McGraw Hill.

Hunter, M. A. (2008). Cultivating the art of safe space. *Research in Drama Education: The Journal of Applied Theatre and Performance, 13*(1), 5–21. https://doi.org/10.1080/13569780701825195

Jensen, A. (2013). Beyond the borders: The use of art participation for the promotion of health and well-being in Britain and Denmark. *Arts & Health, 5*(3), 204–215 https://doi.org/10.1080/17533015.2013.817448

Kolb, D. (1984). *Experiential learning: Experience as the source of learning and development.* Prentice-Hall.

Kroger, T., & Nupponen, A. M. (2019). Puppet as a pedagogical tool: A literature review. *International Electronic Journal of Elementary Education, 11*(4), 393–401. https://www.iejee.com/index.php/IEJEE/article/view/688

Leonard, K., & Yorton, T. (2015). *Yes, and: How improvisation reverses "no, but" thinking and improves creativity and collaboration: Lessons from the second city.* HarperCollins Publishers.

Lobman, C. (2015). Performance, theater, and improvisation: Bringing play and development into new arenas. In J. Johnson, S. Eberle, T. Hendricks, & D. Kuschner (Eds.), *The handbook of the study of play* (Vol. 2, pp. 349–363). Rowman & Littlefield.

Malchiodi, C. (2016). *Art therapy: Changing the game, one image at a time.* https://youtube.com/watch?v=HJHYZDN4DFo

McNiff, S. (2008). Arts-based research. In J. G. Knowles & A. L. Cole (Eds.), *Handbook of the arts in qualitative research* (pp. 29–40). Sage Publications.

Meyer, A. A. (2012). Perceived benefits of art-based interventions and nursing implications: A systematic review. *Antonian Scholars Honors Program*. 18. https://sophia.stkate.edu/shas_honors/18

Meyer, P. (2010). *From work place to playspace: Innovating, learning, and changing through dynamic engagement.* Jossey-Bass.

Muth, J. J. (2003). *Stone soup.* Scholastic Press.

Rieber, L. P., Smith, L., & Noah, D. (1998). The value of serious play. *Educational Technology, 38*(6), 29–37. http://lrieber.coe.uga.edu/valueofplay.html

Taylor, M., de Guerre, D., Gavin, J., & Kass, R. (2002). Graduate leadership education for dynamic human systems. *Management Learning, 33*(3), 349–369. https://doi.org/10.1177/1350507602333004

Vygotsky, L. S. (1978). *Mind in society: The development of higher psychological processes.* Harvard University Press.

Walsh, S. M., Chang, C., Schmidt, L. A., & Yoepp, J. H. (2005). Lowering stress while teaching research: A creative arts intervention in the classroom. *Journal of Nursing Education, 44*(7), 330–333.

West, S., Hoff, E., & Carlsson, I. (2017). Enhancing team creativity with playful improvisation theater: A controlled intervention field study. *International Journal of Play, 6*(3) 283–293. https://doi.org/10.1080/21594937.2017.1383000

CHAPTER 8

# Visions of Hope in Education

## *Fostering Student Teachers' Identities of Becoming Agents of Change through a Photo Competition and Exhibition*

*Avivit M. Cherrington*

## 1 Transformation in Teacher Education Programmes

Global calls for the restructuring and re-visioning of education systems to make them more relevant and responsive to current issues and realities have increased in urgency. In South Africa, where socio-political ideologies were intentionally woven into oppressive education systems to dehumanise people designated non-white, the challenge to design a quality education for all carries immense weight. Although giant steps have been taken towards ensuring equitable access to education and to decolonise curricula that are now more inclusive of the country's diversity, concerns remain in relation to the slow progress towards substantial educational change. The country's youth, born into a democratic and free nation with the promise of equal opportunities for social and economic wellbeing, have re-ignited questions about the purpose and nature of education reforms.

Raising these questions has prompted further calls for reforms in higher education that shift current theoretical foundations and practices towards capacitating students as agents of change and social justice. However, simply theorising about the possibility for change does not necessarily lead to agentic involvement in bringing about such change. For active, sustainable transformation to occur I argue that people within that system must become agents of their own development. Central to educational change is the need to assert the transformative potential of empowering student voice and participation to effectively advance agency, inclusion, and democratic thinking (McLeod, 2011). But the notions of voice and power in participatory research are highly contested. For McLeod (2011), this goes beyond simply having an opportunity to speak: "Voice can be a code word for representing difference, or connote a democratic politics of participation and inclusion, or be the expression of an essentialized group identity … It has methodological and pedagogical dimensions and is rarely—if ever—simply a matter of creating opportunities for unfettered expression" (p. 181).

 | DOI: 10.1163/9789004442870_008

To gain more insight into this notion, I initiated a three-year research project[1] in collaboration with a cohort of student teachers to explore the question of how a critical participatory visual methodology, engaging with student teachers on the notion of hope in education, might mobilise transformative actions in the Faculty of Education.

## 2 Hope and Change in Education

Both hope and education can be understood as processes of becoming, and both entail having a reflective understanding of the world and one's place in it. Although the concept of hope has been frequently linked to educational outcomes, especially in relation to the pursuit of goals, there is still a paucity of literature expounding on the agentic and collective value of operationalising it in teacher education programmes. Schooling and education are often considered necessary tools for promoting collective wellbeing and empowering democratic citizenship aimed at creating a just society. This requires teachers who are able, willing, and motivated to lead the country's agenda that sees education as a nation-building strategy. However, according to Bantwini and Letseka (2016), the excessive changes in curriculum and educational restructuring since 1994 have instead eroded teachers' hope and enthusiasm; many reveal feelings of "professional identity bankruptcy" (p. 34) in having lost a sense of belonging and attachment to their profession. They recommend that for successful education reform teachers should be given opportunities to develop a shared vision for such transformation. I argue that to act on that vision, teachers need to be empowered both professionally and personally to believe in the possibilities of change.

Collective hope, or democratic activist hope, is fostered when a group of people with a shared sense of commitment create a common vision for a better future and then are determined to make it happen (Cherrington, 2018; Hytten, 2019). To motivate this level of hope in anyone, three conditions are necessary: creating shared experiences; igniting social imagination; and advocating for critical action. Drawing on the conceptualisation of hope as a way of becoming, and the transformative potential of having voice, interwoven into participatory arts-based methods for engaging student teachers, in this chapter I invite the reader to consider the value and potential of arts-based research and public engagement for creating opportunities for collective creativity, critical self-reflection, and inviting possibilities for social change.

## 3 'Hope in Education' Photo Competition and Exhibition

According to Hytten (2019),

> If we believe in an activist notion of hope—as a verb, an activity, and a habit—one of the tasks ahead of us is to figure out how to best cultivate a coordinated set of actions and ways of being that support enduring democratic hopefulness. (p. 13)

Activating such a democratic hope to disrupt existing divisions and create a sense of belonging and community requires spaces for storytelling, creativity and mindfulness as Hytten (2019) has reminded us. In 2017, I initiated a pilot research project in the Faculty of Education to engage with student teachers through multiple hope-enhancing arts-based activities to encourage reflective thinking and conversations about hope and transformation in education. In the first year, I recruited a cohort of second-year education students to the project and engaged in numerous group workshops to explore the concept of hope in education. The following year seven members were able to continue and became co-researchers, calling themselves the Hopeful Vision Gang. They initiated a Facebook page and planned various activities in the faculty to recruit and motivate fellow students' participation and collaboration (Cherrington, 2018).

One such activity, the Hope in Education Competition, sought to engage critically with student teachers about the issue of possibilities for change in education. A faculty-wide email advertised the competition and encouraged education students to submit original photographs representing what the notion of Hope in Education meant to them. Fourteen images were selected, printed in colour on A4 paper, laminated, and exhibited in a busy hallway in the faculty for a week (see Figure 8.1). A voting box was made available for students to vote for their favourite image. The photographs were also loaded onto the Hopeful Vision Gang's Facebook page encouraging visitors[2] to like and share the images they preferred. Once the votes were counted various prizes were awarded at an open prize-giving session held during lunch break for *Most Voted For, Most Liked on Facebook*, and *Most Talked About* pictures. Following Mitchell, De Lange, and Moletsane (2017) critical audience engagement was facilitated through informal interviews with any students who had stopped to view the exhibition. While only education students were permitted to enter the competition, the voting and audience interviews were open to all university students. The co-researchers transcribed their own audience interviews and included a reflection on their experience of the activity. A workshop retreat was held at the end of the year to collate all the data from this activity and compile a report with recommendations that emerged.

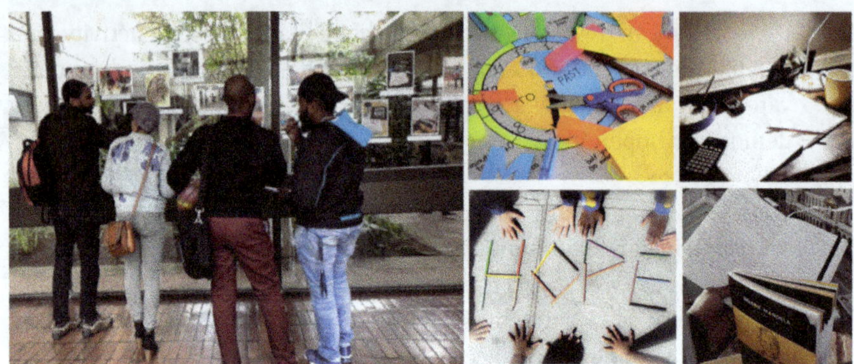


FIGURE 8.1 Students engaging with images exhibited and a montage of some of the images representing hope in education

## 4 Re-Imagining Ourselves as Teachers Who Are Agents of Hope and Change

For the purpose of this chapter, four of the co-researchers[3] (Cindy Lee; Thembeka Getyengana, Simanyene Makhontso; and Solomon Ngaleka) and I met to reflect on how our engagement might have contributed towards our understanding of arts-based inquiry for social change. The generated data was subsequently re-read through the lens of Hytten's (2019) conceptualisation of activist democratic hope to deepen our understanding of how using an arts-based method to engage in public dialogue with the students might have enabled possibilities for social change. Some of the comments inserted in the discussion below were taken verbatim from the audience engagement interviews while others are personal comments and reflections provided by the co-researchers during the re-analysis discussion.

### 4.1 *Creating Shared Experiences*

The students viewing the photo exhibition seemed pleased that they could relate to many of the images presented by their peers, commenting that it made them feel that their personal experiences of hope in education were not isolated but shared. Solomon, reflecting on a student's response when he was asked what he liked about the images, told us, "He says that it's a reality he can relate to, and many more students can also relate to them." Another student viewing the exhibition noted that looking at all the images reminded him of "where we come from and where we are going" as role-payers in the country's education.

Cindy, noting a common thread in her interviews, commented that for some students the photos affirmed their belief that as a teacher one should always be hopeful. A student explained that seeing other students' images of hope reminded her of why she chose this profession: "For me it's just that hope will always be there. That is actually why I decided to study education, because I have hope in the future of the youth." Other students, according to Simanyene, reflected that looking at the photographs made them acknowledge and appreciate the diversity of learners with whom they will engage as teachers and that everyone experiences hope in a unique way. It seems that engaging with fellow students' personal experiences of the challenges they face to become teachers (as represented in the photographs) fostered a sense of belonging and inclusivity. It offered insight and understanding that, despite their differences, there was a shared commitment to the goal of becoming teachers as agents of change.

We reflected that the students quite enjoyed the fun and non-intimidating nature of the activity. According to Simanyene, "Most people are not good at expressing their views especially in a group of people. Using images gave everyone an opportunity to sit back and critically think and reflect on themselves." Thembeka added that it was the creative aspect of the engagement that invited thought-provoking conversations. She admitted that as students they are so used to answering questions or filling out questionnaires that it has become routine but expressing an idea through an image and then having the opportunity to think about and relate to other people's photos allowed more creativity.

### 4.2 *Igniting Social Imaginations*

For some students viewing the photos and listening to other students' perspectives offered an opportunity to reflect on how they saw themselves as responsive and adaptive teachers. An interesting observation was that although as student teachers they were very aware of the challenges of education and the problems many schools face, looking at the photographs and talking about their own hope as future teachers made them realise that change is possible; this lifted their spirits. Simanyene recalled that an education student had brought along a friend who was from another faculty to see the exhibition. The visitor seemed very impressed and felt that it was important for future teachers to familiarise themselves with the realities of the workplaces into which they will be going. Simanyene wrote, "He also concluded that he is fascinated by the fact that we as young people are able to take a stand and spread hope onto others, and that shows that the country's future is indeed in good hands."

When they were visiting the exhibition, students were informed that the display was aimed at building the faculty's vision to promote teachers who are agents of hope and change. This led one student to say, "Yes, now I can see the vision and I want to be a part of it. I can do whatever is necessary to be part of it which include me studying and being involved in community projects."

### 4.3 *Advocating for Critical Action*

This condition for democratic hope was the most complex on which to reflect. While we could all provide examples of the excitement and determination of the students to enact hope, we had no way of knowing whether this was actualised in any way. Thembeka believed the activity had stimulated students to think more about ways of incorporating hope into their teaching and learning practices.

> It made them aware of the importance of hope in education and their role in making sure there is hope in education. I think it also made it clear to what is hope and ideas of how to implement hope activities as prospective hope agents. An experience that confirmed this was when I was working in class and my group insisted that we include a hopeful approach in the solutions to our research assignment.

Solomon noted in his reflection that many of the students believed that there is definitely hope in the faculty, but "looking at the photographs and talking about it made them realise that it's always possible to create more hope … and that it helps to remember that it starts with creating hope within ourselves." He therefore felt confident that when given an opportunity to practice during the school-based learning aspect of the programme they would enact hope, because "then they will have a chance to become better versions of themselves [and] that sends a huge hopeful message out." Therefore, they could be agents of hope and change. We also noted that many of the students who came from poor schools believed they could be agents of hope and change by being positive role models for others. As one of Cindy's interviewees said,

> I'm going to make an example of me because I'm not coming from the model C schools, I come from the rural areas. So, they will see that one day we each can contribute something to have a better future.

There was no doubt that the students who engaged with the exhibition enjoyed the activity and wanted more opportunities to have the faculty engage with them, especially if it involved them in decision-making and meaningful dialogue and not only in evaluations and feedback. According to Simanyene, the activity piqued other students' interest. She said that she received many queries from her peers asking to be involved the next time a hope activity was being planned. She noted, "It did stimulate other students' interest because most of students are so keen to join the project and keep it going. They cannot wait to take part on the next activity of hope."

Although the reflections on being teachers as agents of hope and change seemed more focused on how they would practice their teaching in schools, there was an underlying sense that learning to be hopeful starts with the self and should be emphasised more in the faculty's offering.

## 5 How Might Hope-Enhancing Arts-Based Methods Foster Student-Led Possibilities for Critical Thinking and Social Change in Teacher Education?

The students' engagement in re-imagining possibilities for hope in education, and then reflecting on the role that they as future teachers could play in actively shaping this vision, represents a liminal space in their journey of becoming teachers as agents of change. This threshold in the process of becoming further resonates with Salazar's (2013) notion of reflective praxis creating a "not yet" space in which individuals can "relentlessly strive for humanization, liberation, and transformation in education and society" (p. 375). Further, it can be argued that the activity was able to inspire democratic hope as described by Hytten (2019) in that the three necessary conditions of creating shared experiences, igniting social imagination, and advocating for critical action were all demonstrated in some way in the students' engagement with, and responses to, this activity.

Another emerging quality of the engagement was the students' enthusiasm in participating and engaging in critical discussions. This relates to emerging debates around the transformative aspect of recognising voice-as-right and voice-as-participation, especially its significance as a strategy for building democratic and responsive practices in higher education (McLeod, 2011). As Kirshner (2015) has noted, in educational contexts collective agency can be demonstrated when people come together to resist and "dismantle barriers to their education or to forge new educational pathways that did not exist before" (p. 25). Thus, if students in higher education are seen to be the future innovators and designers of a better and more just world they must be given more opportunities to "talk about challenges in their everyday lives, examine root causes on inequality, and take action, broadly defined, about issues that affect them" (Kirshner, 2015, p. 25). As Roux and Becker (2016) state bluntly, "Students neither lack the capacity for speech, nor are they producing noise" (p. 137).

Learning occurs beyond the classroom and the values that universities seek to develop in students, such as diversity, a commitment to social justice, and the ability to think critically can be enacted and experienced by providing opportunities to open dialogue and share experiences of hope. In using arts-based methods framed by a critical participatory design, this activity gave ownership of voice and representation to students. Adding the audience engagement component allowed for multiple opportunities to make meaning as the audience became actively involved with the images and those who created them as Mitchell et al. (2017) have pointed out.

## 6 Implications and Conclusion

How we re-story our past and imagined future matters significantly (Hytten, 2019). Education can truly begin to be transformative, and in turn transformed, only when student teachers are encouraged to shift their intellectual worldviews and ways of engaging with the world around them (Sayed, Motala, & Hoffman, 2017). Democratic hope and action are "inextricably related and mutually reinforcing" (Hytten, 2019, p. 12), so, merging hope-enhancing prompts with an arts-based method provoked the students' imaginations in offering them a shared and amicable space in which to reflect on what they can do to cultivate hope as part of their emerging identities as agents of change. It appears that reflecting on their own as well as their fellow students' visions of hope in education moved the students' conceptualisations of what *is* currently, to what *could be*. This shift in their recognition of possibilities for change re-ignited their passion in teaching and their determination to be agents of change. The students' reflections on their goal of becoming teachers who are agents of hope and change evoke political sociologist Schaar's (1981) position on citizen participation in the "modern state" in which

> the future is not some place we are going to, but one we are creating. The paths are not to be found, but made, and the activity of making them, changes both the maker and the destination. (p. 321)

Since this engagement described above was limited to a once-off activity, we are unable to say, with confidence, that it produced meaningful social change (or activism towards it) within the faculty or outside of it. However, it did offer some indication of its potential to do so. Perhaps if this activity were an annual event that could encourage and sustain more students and offer greater audience reach, or if it were embedded in some way within the curriculum, reinforced through the service-learning component or in a community-engagement project, the critical action component would emerge more strongly. Such options would provide valuable foci for future research.

In this chapter, I highlight the relevance of using a photo competition and exhibition on the topic of Hope in Education as a transformative tool to enhance critical reflection and dialogic engagement aimed at helping to shape students' identities as becoming-teachers who are agents of hope and change. I hope that the discussions presented here will open further conversations on ways of using arts-based research to cultivate and sustain hope as an activist orientation in education contexts to mobilise possibilities for change.

## Notes

1 The project, positioned in the Faculty of Education of a public university, focused mostly on generating knowledge and engagement with registered student teachers. However, the various public aspects of this project involved students from other faculties who were in some way associated with education students.
2 The HopeVision Facebook page was a public page and it was evident that the students who participated in the competition invited friends who were not associated with the faculty to follow the page and like the photographs.
3 The co-researchers, who played a key role in conceptualising, planning, generating data, and analysing the 'Hope in Education' competition and exhibition wish to be fully acknowledged by name in this chapter.

## References

Bantwini, B. D., & Letseka, M. (2016). South African teachers caught betweennation building and global demands: Is there a way out/forward? *Educational Studies, 52*(4), 329–345. https://doi.org/10.1080/00131946.2016.1190366

Cherrington, A. M. (2018). Research as hope-intervention: Mobilising hope in a South African higher education context. *Journal of Community Psychology, 46*, 502–514.

Hytten, K. (2019). Cultivating democratic hope in dark times: Strategies for action. *Education and Culture, 35*(1), 3–28.

Kirshner, B. (2015). *Youth activism in an era of education inequality*. New York University Press.

McLeod, J. (2011). Student voice and the politics of listening in higher education. *Critical Studies in Education, 52*(2), 179–189. https:/doi.org/10.1080/17508487.2011.572830

Mitchell, C., De Lange, N., & Moletsane, R. (2017). *Participatory visual methodologies. Social change, community and policy*. Sage Publications.

Roux, C., & Becker, A. (2016). Humanising higher education in South Africa through dialogue as praxis. *Educational Research for Social Change, 5*(1), 131–143. https:/doi.org/10,17159.2221-4070/2016/v5i1a8

Salazar, M. (2013). A humanizing pedagogy: Reinventing the principles and practices of education as a journey towards liberation. *Review of Research in Education, 37*, 121–148. https:/doi.org/10.3102/0091732X12464032

Sayed, S., Motala, S., & Hoffman, N. (2017). Decolonising initial teacher education in South African universities: More than an event. *Journal of Education, 68*, 60–91.

Schaar, J. H. (1981). *Legitimacy in the modern state*. Transaction Publishers.

CHAPTER 9

# Empty Jars

## *Using Memoration to Confront the Settler Colonial Project through Arts-Based Research*

*Deanna Del Vecchio*

## 1 Positionality in Art for Social Change

My grandmother's cantina was a mysterious place, dim even when illuminated by the bare lightbulb that hung from the ceiling, gently swinging. A small room tucked into the far corner of the basement, its plywood shelves supported row upon row of jars, lined up tightly. Most were earthy red or green in color, depending on their contents. All bore labels, which were decipherable only through guesswork and inference. Written in my grandmother's shaky handwriting, in a mix of Italian and misspelled English, the labels provided clues rather than descriptions of the jars' contents. The creation and preparation of food was a central theme in my grandmother's life—a source of self-sufficiency and a sign of care.

As a white settler reading Indigenous feminist scholars (Eve Tuck and Karyn Recollet among others), I am increasingly compelled to address my positionality in my work, and increasingly confused about how to do this responsibly. Focusing on personal entanglements with settler colonialism is a way of considering my own responsibilities in the system. In this chapter, I draw on arts-based research and critical scholarship to add nuance to the nostalgia that often permeates settler histories by exploring my personal and family history of cultural practices around preserving food. My experience with art as an agent for social change has so far been centered on community arts and participatory methodologies; I am interested in how personal reflection through art-making can complement community projects by addressing the personal change required for broader social change.

I created a photograph series (Figure 9.1) to play with the notion of preservation through an alternative way of viewing my grandmother's canning jars. Their preserving function, which was once literal (conserving food for the winter) is now figurative (keeping memories that she can no longer articulate because of dementia). Benjamin (1968) referred to photographs as both a cult of remembrance and as historical evidence. This photograph series is my attempt to unite these two elements in a critique of white settler societal

 | DOI: 10.1163/9789004442870_009

norms in Canada. I begin by describing the photograph series, followed by an overview of memoration (Decter, 2016) as methodology. In the analysis, I explore how government policy and cultural practices bolster settler claims to land through a discussion of multiculturalism, settler relationships to land, and the uncertainty of settler roles in Indigenous futurities.

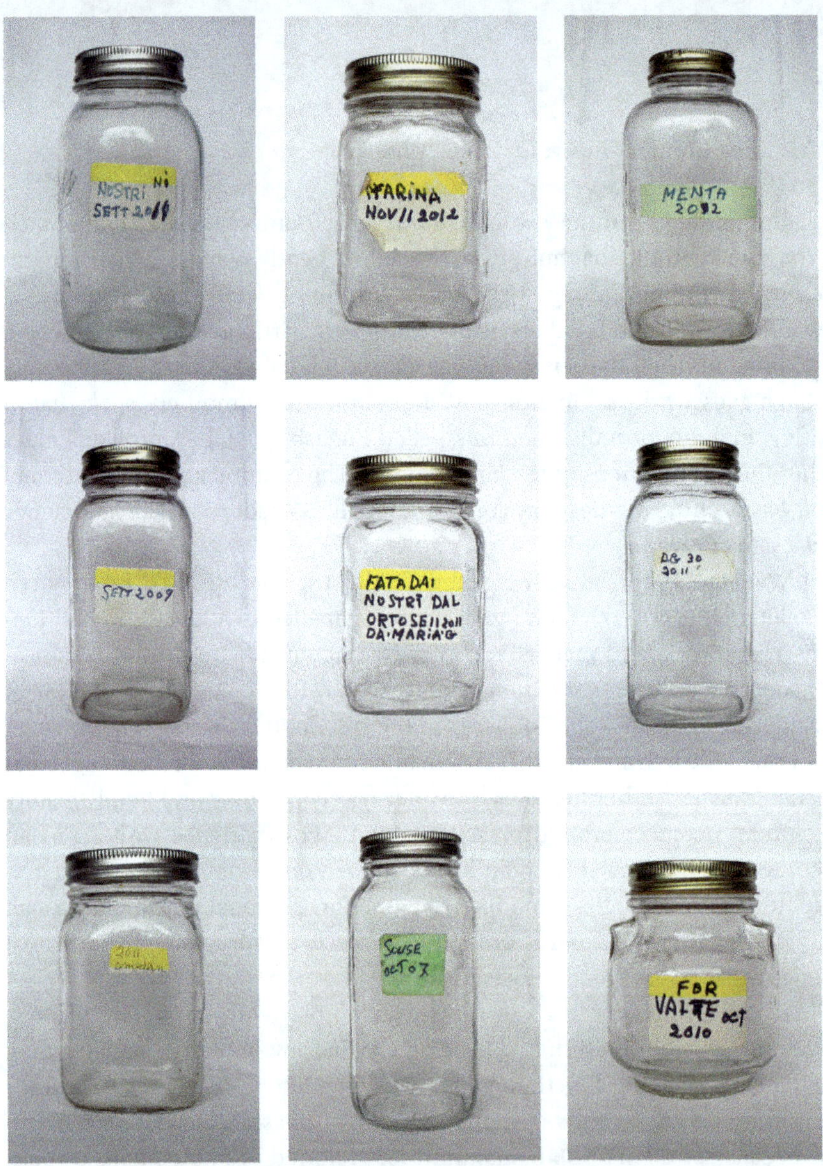


FIGURE 9.1 "Typology of Preserves." (Photograph by D. Del Vecchio, 2015, retrieved from https://typologyofpreserves.tumblr.com/)

## 2 Typology of Preserves

As forms of symbolic work (Willis, 1990), the jars and, in particular, their labels, expose nuances of literacy, language, and cultural practice. With her minimal formal education, my grandmother's writing skills in her mother tongue were limited. After moving to Canada, she took every opportunity to practice speaking, reading, and writing in English. Reading through the labels one by one, I glean a picture of her life through the details she deemed worthy of recording. Some simply indicate the date ("Sept. 2011"), and some specify the contents ("sauce"). Some contain more descriptive information ("last of the garden," "made from ours from the garden Sept. 2011 from Marina G."). Others include names: hers, to indicate that she produced it ("Marina Nov. 11 2012"), or those of the friends or family who would be receiving it ("For Walter Oct. 2010"). As remnants of daily life, they are a reminder of her priorities.

I documented these remnants by creating a typology. I made photographs of nine jars and arranged them in a three-by-three grid (see Figure 9.1). The layout is intended to mimic Bernd and Hilla Becher's photographs of old industrial structures. The Bechers documented commonplace subject matter in a way that highlighted its significance. The buildings they photographed "were somewhat unspectacular and primarily determined by their function; yet they are not only testaments to technical and economic achievements but also reveal key aspects of the zeitgeist of an entire epoch" (Lange, 2007). The Bechers used the typology as a creative element to organise and present their work. By emphasising the form of industrial structures, they separated unremarkable buildings from their functions and allowed the viewer to see them in a new way. Moreover, documentation of the tools of industrialisation hints at the impact of global capitalism and settler colonialism. I applied this treatment to the canning jars in order to consider the themes they represent. Beyond their mundane presence and ubiquity in my grandmother's kitchen, they symbolise self-sufficiency and land use practices.

## 3 Methodology

Artist/scholar Decter's methodology of memoration, "an evolving set of theoretical and aesthetic provocations directed at destabilizing white settler dominance as it is entrenched in the landscape of everyday Canadian life," (2016) is an ideal framework for analysis of my "Typology of Preserves"—in line with my intention to use the creative process to unsettle the settler colonial project and responsibly engage with Indigenous visual methodologies and theorisations of land and place (Tuck & McKenzie, 2015; Goeman, 2013; Kermoal & Altamirano-Jiménez, 2015). Memoration offers a possibility for using arts-based research to examine this subject matter critically while watching out for settler moves to innocence (Tuck & Yang, 2012). Its name refers to an activation of the personal (memory) and the collective impulse to recall (commemoration). Developed through Decter's own artistic and academic practice, memoration is intended to be a flexible methodology, "an evolving set of theoretical and aesthetic provocations directed at destabilizing white settler dominance as it is entrenched in the landscape of everyday Canadian life" (2018, p. ii). Incorporating reflection on the past and present as well as attention to the future, it involves disrupting romantic notions of settler roles and histories. Decter created memoration to apply to the artistic practice itself, but since the methodology is adaptable and content-driven, it is also applicable as a methodology for analysis, as I use it here.

What draws me to memoration as a methodology is Decter's goal of paying critical attention to her positionality and not glossing over concerns about white settlers addressing these topics. She acknowledges the limitations of engaging from a white settler position, while at the same time recognising personal and generational accountability and responsibility. Decentering whiteness as a white scholar/artist is a fraught project, in some ways a catch-22 situation: how does one acknowledge whiteness without recentering it? Decter discards the goal of mastery and/or redemption and is, rather, open to encountering unfamiliar ontological and epistemological concepts that one may not be able to fully comprehend fully. It is crucial to acknowledge the risk that self-reflection might center my own whiteness and reinforce the colonial project. Here, I apply memoration through three threads of analysis, connecting "Typology of Preserves" to multicultural narratives in Canada, settler relationships to land, and the uncertainty of settler roles in Indigenous futurities.

## 4 Analysis

### 4.1 *Multicultural Narratives*

Multiculturalism is entrenched in the Canadian imaginary as well as its institutions. The Canadian government first toyed with the notion of multiculturalism in the 1960s, with Prime Minister Lester Pearson's assertion that "Canada is now a multiracial society" (quoted in Mann, 2012, p. 487). By 1971, multiculturalism had shifted from a philosophy to a policy ushered in by then Prime Minister Pierre Trudeau. Institutionalised multiculturalism activated a warm and fuzzy idea of diversity that glosses over the particular struggles of racialised immigrants and aims to envelop Indigenous peoples under the so-called ethnic umbrella, attempting to remove their claims to this land as its original inhabitants since time immemorial as Grande (2004) has reminded us. Multicultural policy trickles down to the systems that shape our daily lives in Canada, including our education systems, working to subsume the other into the whitestream as a way of taming it (Tuck & Gaztambide-Fernández, 2013).

The years during which my family was settling in Toronto coincided with the emergence of multiculturalism. Close to 500,000 Italians left Italy for Canada between 1946 and 1972, seeking better living conditions and financial stability in the years after World War II. The city of Toronto received a large number of these immigrants. The jars I photographed represent the Italian immigrant cultural practice of canning tomatoes at the end of summer, a practice often maintained in Toronto in the rocky "transition from rural peasant to urban proletariat" (Lallani, 2018, p. 410). Italians who were part of the early-20th century wave of immigration were considered inferior to northern Europeans and Anglo-Saxons, but this changed in the post-war period (see Luconi, 2011). Now under the umbrella of whiteness, Italians were embraced through the multicultural policies that enforced the normative Canadian identity as white and enveloped immigrant narratives of hard work and sacrifice into notions of Canadianness.

Multiculturalism is based on a value system that positions white settlers as the intended beneficiaries of settler colonialism. It glorifies cultural practices from the supposedly "right" kind of immigrant and removes these practices from their historical contexts in order to envelop them in the patchwork of ethnic identities that make up the Canadian imaginary. Canada's shift from cultural assimilation to cultural pluralism operates on a logic of containment, the notion that "the removal of ethnicity's threatening features [could] transform it into a form of entertainment by which Canada could promote its cultural diversity" (Lallani, 2018, p. 415).

## 4.2 *Settler Relationships to Land*

As containers for produce my grandmother grew in her backyard vegetable garden, the jars represent her relationship to land and the transfer of land-use habits from another place. As white settler artist Sandra Semchuk has written, "We wrote our names on the land with the seeds we brought … we were complicit in creating the echoes of the old violences here in the new country" (Semchuk, Nicholas, & Jimmy, 2011, p. 63). The jars are containers for products my grandmother grew on the land from seeds she brought from her family's farm in Italy. She and my grandfather had a singular goal in their new country—land ownership. Owning a home was the mark of success, and they painstakingly saved money for years to do so. Their claim to land was based on integration into the norms of settler society through hard work. The neat geometric lines of their garden, and on a macro level, of the photographs in a grid, mimic the straight lines used to parcel out Indigenous land to settlers in the 19th century. This is a microcosm of the western notion that land needs to be used in a certain way in order to be claimed, based on John Locke's labour theory of property (Locke, 1690/1948) and invoked in *terra nullius*. As a "mechanism of spatial ordering" (Rose-Redwood, 2008), the grid has a history as a tool of colonisation: it is linked to notions of property (Blomley, 2003) and used to control populations from a distance (Stanislawski, 1946).

Indigenous scholars have written that struggles for sovereignty are ultimately about land (Tuck & Yang, 2012). The settler colonial government's tactic is to distract attention from their theft of Indigenous land by treating it as a resource to be bought and used. Indigenous nations, however, view land as a relation, an other-than-human relative to whom one is responsible, and this forecloses the notion of land ownership. In this way, my family's normative settler goal of buying a house perpetuated the imposition of a western land use system on Indigenous land. Through the narrative of bootstrap immigration, settler colonial societies cover their tracks, disseminating their own narrative of hardworking newcomers to hide the fact that they are founded on the theft of land and violence towards its original inhabitants (Tuck & Gaztambide-Fernández, 2013). My family's use of the land was and is part of the settler colonial government's new story about land use. We were and continue to be complicit in Indigenous erasure. My grandmother's gardening and canning practices were lauded and respected as ideal examples of cultural pluralism, while the fact that it was stolen land she worked hard to purchase and cultivate was obscured and absent from the narrative.

### 4.3 *Uncertainty of Settler Futurities*

Finally, the emptiness of the jars represents the willingness to embrace uncertainty that is required of white settlers in order to truly support decolonisation and Indigenous sovereignty, because decolonisation should be accountable to Indigenous futurity, not that of the settler state (Tuck & Yang, 2012). The term futurity refers to specific practices that anticipate the future and make it knowable (Baldwin, 2012). According to Cree scholar Recollet (2016), futurity is a project "whereby we imagine future worlds, relationships and actions" (p. 93) and "refutes settler colonial fantasies of Indigenous disappearance and erasure" (p. 96). Eve Tuck and Rubén Gaztambide-Fernández (2013) have written about settler futurities in their article about settler colonialism and the field of curriculum studies. As they have explained, settler futurity involves the integration of Indigenous peoples into the nation-state under the guise of multiculturalism. Indigenous futurity overturns settler worldviews and systems of power, although it does not rule out that settlers might still inhabit Indigenous land. These authors have observed that in curriculum studies, "the future of the settler is ensured by the absorption of any and all critiques that pose a challenge to white supremacy, and the replacement of anyone who dares to speak against ongoing colonization" (p. 73). In this process, white scholars take over the spaces created by multiculturalism and critical race theory scholarship, thus reinscribing the harm of racism and colonialism. In "Typology of Preserves," the idea of settler uncertainty is represented by labeled jars that do not contain what their labels claim they do, since they are, in fact, empty. The unease of unmet expectations is a harbinger of the settler attitude that is required for Indigenous futurities. Part of the work of white settlers is to learn to sit with the discomfort that surfaces when acknowledging personal and ancestral complicity in settler colonialism.

Indigenous land reclamation requires an overturning of the "current power paradigms of simultaneous dispossession and containment and [the] political, sociological, and ideological prescriptions that produce them and ensure settler futures" (Bang et al., 2014, p. 50). As Tuck and Gaztambide-Fernández (2013) assert, the necessary shifts in knowledge systems and world-making that are required for Indigenous sovereignty cannot be accomplished while attending to and assuaging settler anxieties about the future. While they were talking about curriculum studies in education research, their analysis is applicable beyond that context. We need to be able to sit with uncertainty in order to support Indigenous scholars' refusal to accommodate the settler. It is crucial that settler scholars hold each other accountable when we "invade emergent work by requiring it to comfort [our] dis-ease" (Tuck & Gaztambide-Fernández, 2013, p. 86).

## 5 Canning in Hipsterdom

Every year towards the end of summer, I haul out my giant black-and-white speckled canning pot and gather up jars and lids. Canning has become an annual practice of mine for a decade, sometimes with a group of friends, sometimes on my own. Along with knitting, farm to table restaurants, and barbershops, it falls squarely within the (white) hipster trend of bringing back traditional practices, reified as authentic. My grandmother's writing on the jars' labels is a prime example of an artifact that would be glorified under the umbrella of authenticity. While Mason jars can be easily shipped to one's doorstep via Amazon, the jars in "Typology of Preserves" are clearly of another, authentic provenance. As I continue the traditional practices of my grandmother on land that we are both newly in relation to, I try to stay on the lookout for traps of nostalgia. It is easy to slip into sentimentality and reify the immigrant experience via cultural practices that Paul Willis (1990) would call symbolic work: the use of "symbolic resources and raw materials … to produce meanings" (p. 9). Symbolic work involves the production of identities in relation to time and place (Hall & Thomson, 2010), making it important ground for critical reflection in the context of settler societies. Thinking critically about my own canning practice is a way to bring this analysis into the present and implicate myself as I critique the invisibilised side of the cherished things we know about Canada, working towards undoing rather than just understanding (Ahmed, 2012).

It is hard to resist romanticised views of family history, to ask the question Whiteness Studies scholar Fiona Nicoll (2002) says all white people should ask themselves: "What is it we know but refuse to tell?" (n. p.). Warm sepia-toned memories of loved ones beckon, encouraged via the settler narratives many of us were raised with in the Canadian nation-state. Paulette Regan, scholar and former research director of Canada's Truth and Reconciliation Commission, has emphasised that the settler's task is one of critical reflection and personal unsettling (2010). This chapter is my attempt to take up that task, a call to action for settler arts-based researchers and community-based artists to undertake critical reflection of their creative and cultural practices through the lens of settler colonialism. I have used my practices of canning and photography to disrupt romanticised notions of my grandmother's gardening and kitchen practices, which evoke strong feelings and memories, by applying memoration as a way of unearthing the settler narratives tucked away within them. I am still left wondering if it is possible to at once honor one's heritage *and* acknowledge one's role in perpetuating settler colonialism.

## References

Ahmed, S. (2012). *On being included: Racism and diversity in institutional life*. Duke University Press.

Baldwin, A. (2012). Whiteness and futurity: Toward a research agenda. *Progress in human Geography, 36*(2), 172 187. https://doi.org/10.1177/0309132511414603

Bang, M., Curley, L., Kessel, A., Marin, A., Suzukovich, E. S., & Strack, G. (2014). Muskrat theories, tobacco in the streets, and living Chicago as Indigenous land. *Environmental Education Research, 20*(1), 37–55. https://doi.org/10.1080/13504622.2013.865113

Becher, B., & Becher, H. (Photographers). (1972–2009). *Water towers.* Tate.

Benjamin, W. (1968). The work of art in the age of mechanical reproduction.In H. Arendt (Ed.), *Illuminations* (pp. 217–251). Schocken Books.

Blomley, N. (2003). Law, property, and the geography of violence: The frontier, the survey, and the grid. *Annals of the Association of American Geographers, 93*(1),121–141. https://doi.org/10.1111/1467-8306.93109

Decter, L. (2016). Moving unsettlement: Excursions into public and pedagogical memory.*Journal of Critical Race Inquiry, 3*(2), 35–60. https://doi.org/10.24908/jcri.v3i1.5976

Decter, L. (2018). *Performing memoration: Integrative artistic strategies for unsettling from a white settler perspective* (Unpublished doctoral dissertation). Queen's University.

Goeman, M. (2013). *Mark my words: Native women mapping our nations*. University of Minnesota Press.

Grande, S. (2004). *Red pedagogy: Native American social and political thought.* Rowman & Littlefield.

Hall, C., & Thomson, P. (2010). Grounded literacies: The power of listening to, telling and performing community stories. *Literacy, 44*(2), 69–75. 10.1111/j.1741-4369.2010.00553.x

Kermoal, N., & Altamirano-Jiménez, I. (2015). *Living on the land: Indigenous women's understanding of place*. AU Press.

Lallani, S. (2018). The culinary gender binary in an era of multiculturalism: Foodwork in Toronto's late postwar Italian immigrant community. *Journal of Family History, 43*(4), 409–424. 10.1177/0363199018787561

Lange, S. (2007). *Bernd and Hilla Becher: Life and work*. Cambridge, MA: MIT Press.

Locke, J. (1948). *The second treatise of civil government and a letter concerning toleration*. B. Blackwell. (Original work published 1690)

Luconi, S. (2011). Discrimination and identity construction: The case of Italian immigrants and their offspring in the USA.*Journal of Intercultural Studies, 32*(3), 293–307. https://doi.org/10.1080/07256868.2011.565739

Mann, J. (2012). The introduction of multiculturalism in Canada and Australia, 1960s–1970s. *Nations and Nationalism, 18*(3), 483–503. https://doi.org/10.1111/j.1469-8129.2012.00553.x

Nicoll, F. (2002). Defacing Terra Nullius and facing the public secret of indigenous sovereignty in Australia. *Borderlands, 1*(2). http://www.borderlands.net.au/vol1no2_2002/nicoll_defacing.html

Recollet, K. (2015). Glyphing decolonial love through urban flash mobbing and *Walking with our Sisters. Curriculum Inquiry, 45*(1), 129–145. https://doi.org/10.1080/03626784.2014.995060

Regan, P. (2010). *Unsettling the settler within: Indian residential schools, truth telling, and reconciliation in Canada*. University of British Columbia Press.

Rose-Redwood, R. (2008). Genealogies of the grid: Revisiting Stanislawski's search for the origin of the grid-pttern yown. *Geographical Review, 98*(1), 42–58. https://doi.org/10.1111/j.1931-0846.2008.tb00287.x

Semchuk, S., Nicholas, J., & Jimmy, E. (2011). 'On loan': Thoughts on stolen strength, seeds of lubestrok, seeds of truth, seeds of reconciliation. In A. Mathur, J. Dewar, & M. DeGagne (Eds.), *Cultivating Canada: Reconciliation through the lens of cultural diversity* (pp. 53–68). Aboriginal Healing Foundation.

Stanislawski, D. (1946). The origin and spread of the grid-pattern town. *Geographical Review, 36*(1), 105–120.

Tuck, E., & Gaztambide-Fernández, R. (2013). Curriculum, replacement, and settler futurity. *Journal of Curriculum Theorizing, 29*(1), 72–89.

Tuck, E., & McKenzie, M. (2015). *Place in research: Theory, methodology, and methods.* Routledge, Taylor & Francis.

Tuck, E., & Yang, K. W. (2012). Decolonization is not a metaphor. *Decolonization: Indigeneity, Education & Society, 1*(1), 1–40.

Willis, P. (1990). *Common culture: Symbolic work at play in the everyday cultures of the young*. Open University Press.

# PART 2

## *Collaborations*

CHAPTER 10

# Walking with Wonder

## *Attunement to the Senses and Relationality in Photographic Inquiry*

*Amélie Lemieux and Boyd White*

## 1 Introduction

In this chapter we invite reader reflections on walking as a private, yet relational artful practice that may foster public educational change and growth. Although we teach and practice our walking routines in different cities (Amélie Lemieux in Halifax and Boyd White in Montreal) we take mutual inspiration from land artist Richard Long. Long's artistic practice since the 1960s has involved mostly solitary walks, recorded photographically, across isolated territories. He regards these walks, which have inspired his reflections on place, space, and time and human↔nature intra-actions, as sculptures, although the works consist of "minimally invasive marks on the landscape."[1] Unlike Long, we do not deliberately alter our landscapes, even minimally, with the exception of leaving our footprints and our breath-induced carbon imprint. Instead, through the lens of post-intentional phenomenological hermeneutics (Van Manen, 2014; White & Lemieux, 2017), we interrogate our intra-actions with time and place to engage in conversations, first with ourselves in internal dialogue and interrogation, then with each other, and ultimately, we hope, with the wider academic community. On our walks we sometimes, although not always, bring our cameras. We do not always want to experience our worlds through a camera lens, nor do we want to troubleshoot angles, lighting, landscapes, filters, and so on. Cameras, like any tool, present a set of limitations as well as opportunities. One limitation is the narrowing of experience to that seen through the camera lens. As Triggs, Irwin, and Leggo (2014) have reminded us, "Seeing depends on fusions between vision and other senses, especially touch and hearing, all of which must be indexed to movement" (p. 29). Nonetheless, while our walking rituals are definitely about seeing in the full sense of that term, sometimes the restrictive lens of a camera can heighten a focus and act as a springboard to further work in considering art as a tool for social change. In our case, we have found that our photographs have sometimes assisted our private interrogations. For instance, I, Boyd, recently assigned self-portrait monoprints to my studio class. To demonstrate the process, I took a high contrast photograph on

 | DOI: 10.1163/9789004442870_010

my iPad. My advanced age shows clearly. In looking at the image, I could not help but be reminded of my genetic inheritances.

Shaving.
In the mirror
my father
stares back.

Photographs, as Mills, Comber, and Kelly (2013) noted, can help "account for the inextricable interrelationships between place and the sensing body" (p. 25). We continue to seek those experiences through ekphrasis, building on previous work we have done (White, 2014; White & Lemieux, 2017) as the above example illustrates. We strive for intersectionality between and among photography, art, poetry, film, social change, and, now, walking. Such relationality in walking methodologies, Fairchild (2019) observed, allows for "expansive visions of the human subject in relation with non-human materiality, rather than … flatten[ing] and disavow[ing] the human" (n.p.). In this new research venture, we wanted to sense how engaging in walking methodologies (Springgay & Truman, 2017, 2019) and photographic inquiry (Sontag, 1977) can both augment and document such experiences. These rituals guide us towards shared intersections of pathways to reflections on walking and education (Triggs, Irwin, & Leggo, 2014). Walking methodologies have been theorised around embodiment as lived experience (Jung, 2014; Springgay & Truman, 2017) and as an ethos of walking with (Springgay & Truman, 2019), more specifically with each other, our cameras, our intra-actions, our perceptions and values, and nature.

To write this chapter, we decided that we needed to have at least one walk together. Amélie came to Montréal and we visited Westmount's Summit Park,[2] which is a 23.087-hectare (57.05 acres) bird and wildflower sanctuary that overlooks the urban landscape below (see Figure 10.3). What follows are our respective reflections on the excursion, which took the better part of a warm spring afternoon.

## 2 Camera as Third Agent

Amélie: The complexities inherent in a seemingly uncomplicated afternoon walk dominated our conversations as we walked through the park considering how settlers colonised this land and transformed it into a park replete with regulations. A current notice board informs walkers about nature—different tree species, delicate plants, and endangered birds—and the problematic nature of (taking) pictures (Elliott, 2019) in a colonial Western world, walking in restricted areas near nesting birds, and the like. So, too, we had to consider our photographing in that light. We tried to be aware of our responsibilities to the park as we went along the trails. Springgay and Truman (2019) remind us of our accountability to nature since our actions, conscious or otherwise, continue to shape the trails we walk on. My finger, barely noticeable on the bottom left of the picture (Figure 10.1), is almost intentional; I relied on the tree for balance as I was crouching. My instinctive reaction also hints at the human interactions with this land that may affect nature in considerable ways. For example, what if I had not used the tree for support and fallen among the flowers?

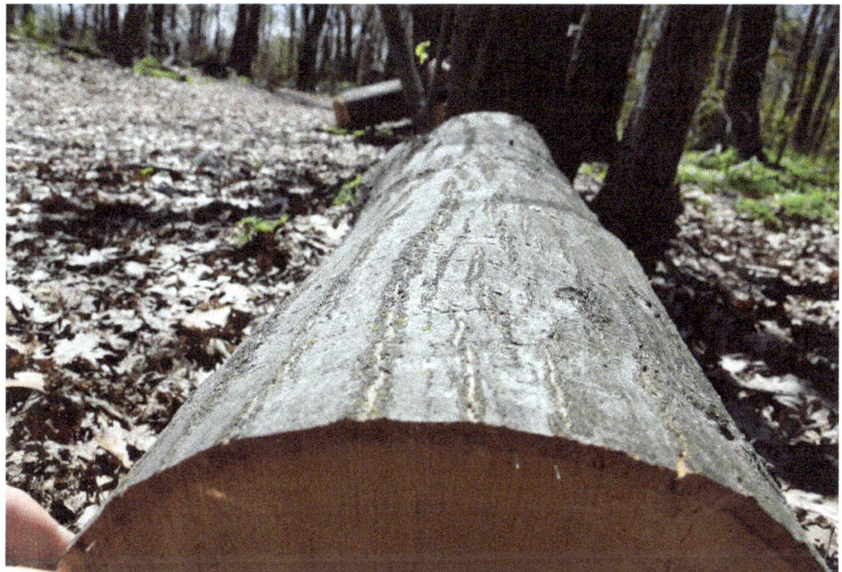

FIGURE 10.1 Photographing a tree log

We entered many comfortable silences that slowly transformed into wonderment, listening to our footsteps, feeling the soil under our soles, thinking with nature and each other. From these moments came pauses, camera adjustments, crouching to observe the shades of green more closely, attuning to wooden textures, and touching the trail. First and foremost, we delved into our sensed perceptions as a first step to knowledge (Grosz, 2017). As a second step, we reflected on the inter-relatedness of those perceptions through camera play as we intuitively walked in the park. In other words, we contemplated walking as first agent of this event, and relationality (being-with) as a second agent. The camera became a third agent, one that filtered and altered our experiences of walking. And since we both walked with our own cameras, we could photograph each other taking pictures and engaging with the environment. In Figure 10.2, I, Amélie, felt compelled to take a snapshot of Boyd as he was himself engaging with wood branches. The camera, as third agent, is entangled in a mise-en-abîme—fluctuating between passive↔active states of action.

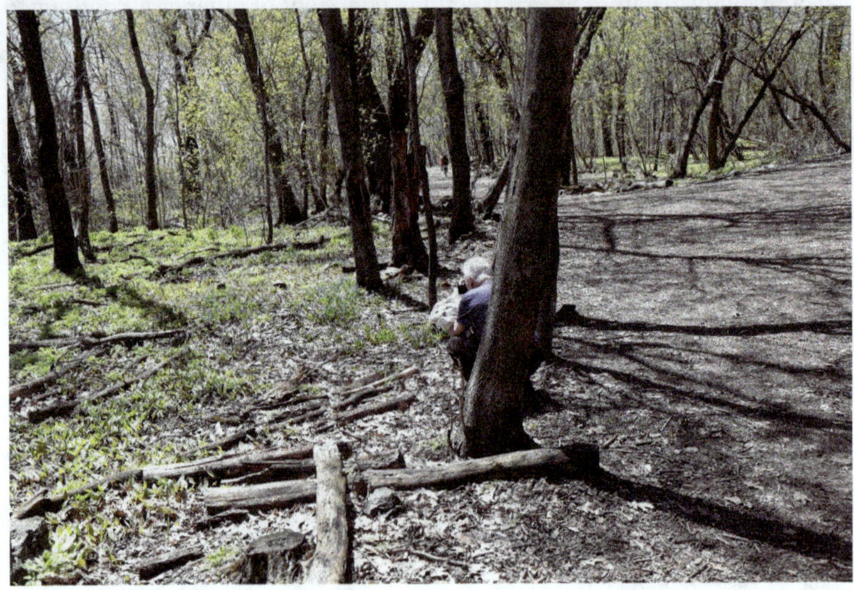

FIGURE 10.2 Camera as third agent

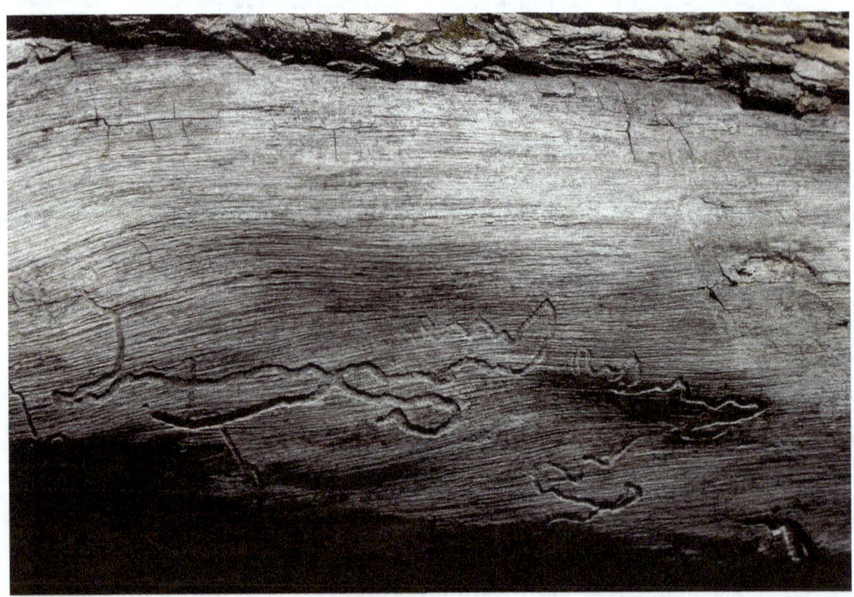

FIGURE 10.3 Log pathways, ruptures, and forces

Boyd: The insect trails (termites?, ants?) provide a visual metaphor for the somewhat erratic and not quite predictable nature of my life's journey. Alternatively, the undulating parallel lines that texture the length of the log suggest forces that have taken me in a fairly consistent directions; the thin cracks in the surface of the log, especially toward the top of the photograph, hint at ruptures in the general trajectory. But my walks are not just metaphoric. I am a walker in the most physical sense of the word. And while I was not aware of the possibility that walking could be a form of art until my introduction to Haas's 1989 film, *Stones and Flies: Richard Long in the Sahara*, that introduction made me aware of my own ambulatory inclinations, really an extended peregrination. My walks span almost eighty years, over fifty of them as an educator, first in public schools, then in a Faculty of Education. While each walk is fixed in a time and place, the walks are not separate; they are entangled. Each one contains echoes of previous ones and suggests ones to follow. In the film just mentioned, Richard Long expresses similar thoughts. "With each new walk I carry with me the memory and experience of all the others … [The] different contexts … sort of add up and have another meaning on top of each" (Haas, 1989, n.p.). Like Long, I find that the simple act of walking heightens my senses while at the same time narrows my focus. I let go of everyday duties and chores. Walking restores my sense of self and releases me from what Long has referred to as "the chaos of the normal world" (n.p.). I (Boyd) wrote the following ekphrastic poem to accompany my photographs.

*Two More Footprints*

A lone cat paw print embedded in
a brick on our back wall
an amusing oddity
to share with friends
A memento to curiosity
or nonchalance
Nevertheless the mark
of a life
lived over a
hundred years ago

Someone's
frozen footprints in
the icy sidewalk.
Boot treads a
personal signature—

individual, distinct
a trail of,
deliberation then
uncertain
disappearing into
the chaos of the day.

## 3 Aesthetics and Design Thinking: Conversations with Nature

Amélie: My encounters with nature are as situational as they are occasional. I often walk with the intention of going somewhere to do something. Likewise, when I carry my Nikon camera with two lenses, one for close-range and one for long-range shots, I do so with an intention of taking snapshots of experience. I started taking courses in digital photography as a young adult about ten years ago, and in most courses, I learned the basics: angle plotting; rule of thirds; colour schemes; layering background; highlighting textures; focal points; bokeh; and so on. This training undoubtedly frames, along with my training in visual arts, an understanding of aesthetics based on both values and design. Our values define who we are. Based on the accumulation of responses to our life experiences and influences, values are non-volitional. They emerge spontaneously as qualitative responses (affect-laden) to any given situation. Awareness of, and response to, social issues are a values exercise. Design concerns are inevitably value laden as well. Our enjoyment of walking in a park, for example, is a value. But the physical features—colour, textures, rhythms, and so forth—to which we decide to pay attention, are deliberate considerations. Taking photographs requires an engagement with both these facets. Underlying these dimensions is the potential of full intentionality as a phenomenological ideal because consciousness consistently oscillates and is always in a state of flux, ever changing and shifting. In this process, new layers of awareness dance with older ones—replacing, blending, clashing with them. The turn to posthumanism may happen if those awarenesses direct their focus to that particular mindset which is what happened in our case. In other words, posthumanism is thought through, apprehended, and embraced as we read and abide by the scholarship we read on the topic, and also the inevitable climatic changes we are currently undergoing as humans. Recognising how our entanglements with nature are, in fact, daily ephemeral transactions with the earth, and that we as humans, artists, educators, are just one piece of the puzzle and a part of that landscape—a culmination of atoms—is worthwhile (Barad, 2007).

## 4 Third Agent as a Trigger for Social Change

We offer considerations on the significance of photographic inquiry in conjunction with walking methodologies. Photography is part of the non-human realm; photography extends dualities between viewer and image, mind and world, to focus on matter and snapshots of movement (Zylinska, 2017). While some images can unsettle and trigger social change, there can be no assurance that our snapshots will fulfill their intended promise. However, we strongly resonated with Zylinska (2017) when she argued that "[i]t is the image itself—the material artifact of the photograph—that touches us and calls us to responsibility" (p. 141). It is our hope that the following picture of Boyd, juxtaposed with Geren's "Art is an Illusion," will strike a chord with our readers and prompt consideration of making art for social change. Remixing a pond reflection of Van Gogh's Starry Night with a picture of a genderless body, Geren's art speaks to the entanglements and intra-actions that we both described earlier in our practices as walkers and photographers. Pondering on these images—fine prints of the third agent—brings us to consider our own responsibility in art for social change. Following the visual artworks in Figures 10.4 and 10.5, I (Amélie) offer an ekphrastic rumination that extends those considerations.

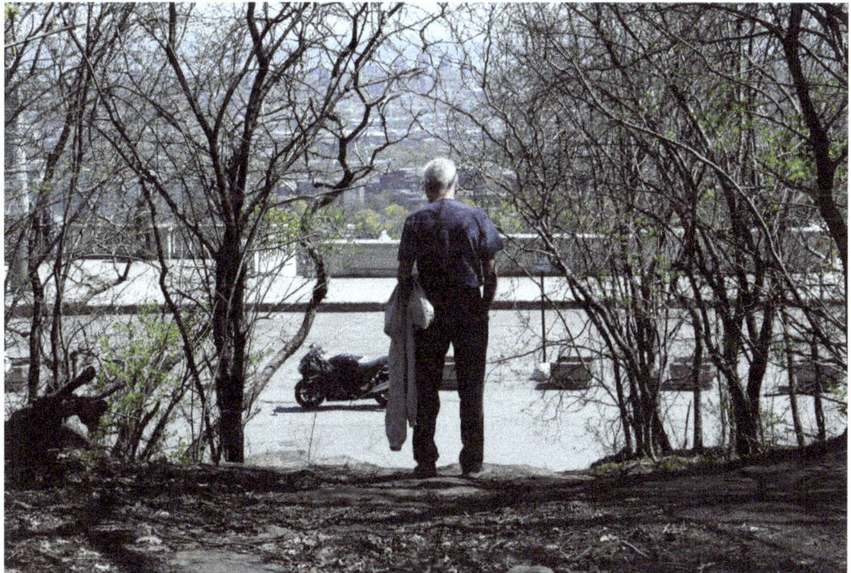

FIGURE 10.4 Camera as third agent and trigger for social change

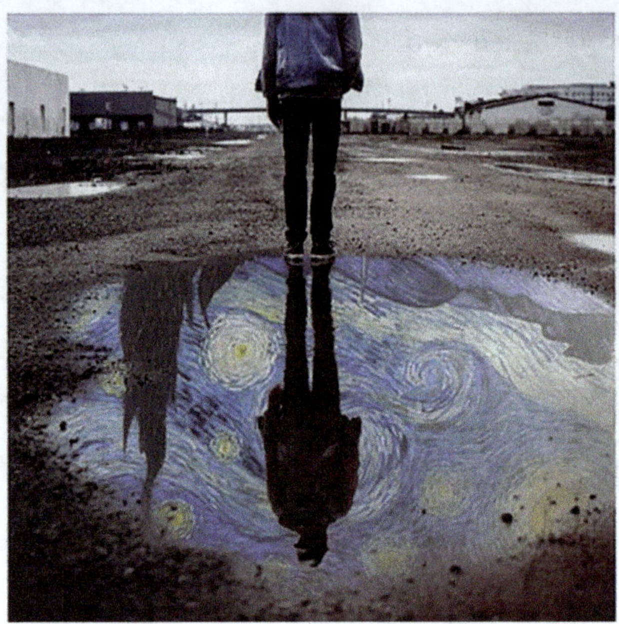

FIGURE 10.5 "Art is an illusion," digital collage. (Artwork by Mehmet Geren)

Solo figure, mind of the world,
Reflections as thoughts in the shallow comfort of
Water
Swirls ahead, city in the horizon
Infinite, fragile horizon,
Textured synthetics collides with an arm as a hanger
Arm as hidden in pockets
Invisible to the world yet feeling it thoroughly
Grasping the moment with growing ideas as grounded branches
Seasoned ponds punctuate the ground waiting for the next change
In chemical composition with
toxic vapors as colours
colliding textures as assemblages
meshing chemicals as neurological synapses flickering
together as one

## 5 Conclusion

As with any manuscript, the final version of this chapter is the result of many steps (metaphorical and literal), readings and re-readings of scholarship on new materialism, walking methodologies, phenomenological hermeneutics, arts-based research, and how all these perspectives converse and coalesce as we engage with what Honeyford (2015) calls "mindful walking" (p. 216), which, in our case, included using the camera as third agent. The results of our exercise are, of necessity, highly subjective. That subjectivity raises a challenge. In Melissa Cahnmann-Taylor's (2018) concluding chapter in her and Richard Siegesmund's co-edited Arts-based research in education (2nd ed.), she states,

> All arts-based researchers must ask: what and whom are the subjects of this work and to what extent does this project further some aspect of public good? By 'public good' … I mean luring oneself and others into seeing self-other connections that expand multiplicity and complexity. (p. 248)

In other words, we are beholden, as artists in whatever branch we find ourselves practicing, to question the value of our personal viewpoints to others. Our intention in this chapter is to explore something as non-confrontational as walking in a forest as an avenue leading to social change. It is unlikely that our images and words will duly unsettle readers, but we hope they will at least question why we did what we did. Such questions are desirable insofar as they may "signal the possibility of an ethical opening" (Zylinska, 2017, p. 144). Acting on these possibilities channels the power and agency of art as an agent of social change.

## Notes

1 The art story: Modern art insight. Richard Long: British sculptor and land artist. Retrieved from https://www.theartstory.org/artist-long-richard.htm

2 Westmount is an autonomous, relatively affluent city within the larger City of Montreal. In the late 19th century, the land was owned by McGill University. The university donated the land to the City of Westmount in the early 20th century, on condition that the land be kept as a bird sanctuary (Westmount Summit. Wikipedia, n.p.).

## References

Barad, K. (2007). *Meeting the universe halfway: Quantum physics and the entanglement of matter and meaning*. Duke University Press.

Cahnmann-Taylor, M., & Siegesmund, R. (2018). *Arts-based research in education: Foundations for practice* (2nd ed.). Routledge.

Elliott, A. (2019). *A mind spread out on the ground.* Doubleday/Penguin.

Fairchild, N. (2019). Do you just want to walk around? *The Sociological Review.* https://www.thesociologicalreview.com/do-you-just-want-to-walk-around/

Grosz, E. (2017). *The incorporeal: Ontology, ethics, and the limits of materialism.* Columbia University Press.

Haas, P. (Director). (1989). *Stones and flies: Richard Long in the Sahara* [Motion picture]. Milestone.

Honeyford, M. (2015). Thresholds of possibility—Mindful walking, traditional oral storytelling, and the birch bark canoe: Theorizing material intra-activity in an afterschool arts space. *Literacy Research: Theory, Method, and Practice, 64*, 210–226. https://doi.org/10.1177/2381336915617615

Jung, Y. (2014). Mindful walking: The serendipitous journey of community-based ethnography. *Qualitative Inquiry, 20*(5), 621–627. https://doi.org/10.1177/1077800413505543

Mills, K. A., Comber, B., & Kelly, P. (2013). Sensing place: Embodiment, sensoriality, kinesis, and children behind the camera. *English Teaching: Practice and Critique, 12*(2), 11–27.

Sontag, S. (1977). *On photography*. Penguin.

Springgay, S., & Truman, S. E. (2017). A transmedial approach to walking methodologies: Embodiment, affect, and a sonic art performance. *Body & Society, 23*(4), 27–58. https://doi.org/10.1177/1357034X17732626

Springgay, S., & Truman, S. E. (2019). Counterfuturisms and speculative temporalities: Walking research-creation in school. *International Journal of Qualitative Studies in Education, 32*(6), 547–559. https://doi.org/10.1080/09518398.2019.1597210

Triggs, V., Irwin, R. L., & Leggo, C. (2014). Walking art: Sustaining ourselves as arts educators. *Visual Inquiry: Learning and Teaching Art, 3*(1), 21–34. https://doi.org/10.1386/vi.3.1.21_1

Van Manen, M. (2014). *Phenomenology of practice: Meaning-giving methods in phenomenological research and writing*. Routledge.

White, B. (2014). Student generated art criticism. *The Canadian Review of Art Education, 41*(1), 32–55.

White, B., & Lemieux, A. (2017). *Mapping holistic learning: An introductory guide to aesthetigrams*. Peter Lang.

Zylinska, J. (2017). *Nonhuman photography*. MIT Press.

CHAPTER 11

# Expression and Action for Change

## *A Contemporary Arts Center and School Collaboration*

*Deborah Randolph and Karen Morris*

### 1 Introduction: Confronting Global Issues through Expression

This chapter begins with the story of high school dance students in Winston-Salem, North Carolina, who confronted the reality of the refugee crisis at an art exhibition, responded with creative movement, began thinking of themselves as catalysts for change, and, with other students, helped move the school culture towards more inclusivity. The dancers' story is just one of many student expressions that were made because of a collaboration between a public arts high school and a contemporary arts center over the course of a school year. After multiple visits to the exhibition, *Dispatches*, and visits with artists, students in several arts and non-arts classes responded to the exhibition with various forms of expression as part of their classes' curriculum.

Students in the dance class were moved by the refugee crisis presented in the exhibition, especially noting that over half of the six million refugees displaced in the early years of the Syrian civil war (2011–2014) were under the age of 18. These students created dance movements expressing the chaos in the Middle East, the loss of home and innocence, and the journeys to unknown and unwelcoming places. The dance movements and performances were inspired by the photo essay, "Syria: The Lost Generation" by award winning photojournalist Ed Kashi. The photo essay was seen by students during visits to the art center. When Kashi visited the school, he explained that the alarming number of refugee children coming out of Syria compelled him to create a film and photo essay about children who were refugees in camps in Northern Iraq and Jordan. The dance teacher said, "Being able to see the exhibits and see the human side of what we hear about in the media gave the students something to hold onto. It made them create meaningful movement and dances." She continued, "They gained a voice that they didn't know they had. They began to think more in terms of being citizens of the world." (Quotes from teachers and students were extracted from video interviews conducted by student Sam Stopyra at RJ Reynolds High School in May 2017.) The presence of English as Second Language (ESL) students at one of the rehearsals of this dance added a certain poignant layer. A newly arrived Syrian girl and one from Yemen, who acted as

 DOI: 10.1163/9789004442870_011

her interpreter, shared stories of their home countries with the dancers, young men and women who were their same age, but who had had very different life experiences. Kashi also attended this rehearsal and spoke to students about his time in Syria prior to the civil war and his experiences with refugee families. The verbal exchange among the dancers, Syrian and Yemeni students, and this artist made the dances stronger and more authentic. One dance student said, "We showed our expression of how we saw the issues through dance ... Expression in the form of art can give a clearer idea of the message."

Dónal O'Donoghue (2015) has written that "one is made different by participating in such works that seek to activate an experience of one kind or another" (p. 105). Through the stories of students and faculty, such as the one above, in this chapter we illustrate the transformative quality of this collaboration. Not only were students and faculty changed, but because of the impact of this school/arts center partnership, the school culture became more inclusive.

## 2 Collaboration

RJ Reynolds High School (RJR) and the Southeastern Center for Contemporary Art (SECCA) have had a long-standing relationship. We, the authors, a museum educator and the arts coordinator for the school, have collaborated on several occasions. Without this history, the trust, time, and commitment needed from both partners to implement this project would not have been forthcoming. The collaboration, centered around the *Dispatches* exhibition, gained particular traction in the school and at SECCA. In this chapter, we strive to capture that momentum and the resulting changes in students and the school culture, while providing an example for others who might be considering similar partnerships.

The literature suggests that field trips to art museums have the capacity to increase critical thinking skills (Bowen, Greene, & Kisida, 2014) and integrating the arts with non-art content has been shown to increase empathy (Bradshaw, 2016) and other relational capacities. In keeping with the literature, this project's three-part process of field trips, artists' visits, and student expression certainly produced critical thinkers and built relational capacities including social imagination and social action. Students took action through artmaking supported by research into current issues. Writing about social imagination sparked through art, Maxine Greene (2009) has suggested that

> if we release our imaginations, if we allow ourselves to move out to such works, we may well find them becoming part of our lived experience ...

> [and] we may also ask, 'What next?' or 'What can be done?' or 'How does it affect what I make of my life?' (p. 1)

Students and teachers alike took inspiration from the artists and the arts center, internalised the lessons learned, and courageously questioned the culture and processes of the school to make them more inclusive and relevant.

### 2.1 *RJ Reynolds High School*

RJ Reynolds High School (RJR), a public school located in Winston-Salem, North Carolina, is a focus of this chapter. In 2007, RJR became an arts magnet school and launched the "arts for academics" program that comprehensively weaves arts exposure, arts integration, and arts education into the high school experience for all students. In 2014, RJR joined the A+ Schools network, an international network of schools using the arts for whole school reform. RJR is one of the most diverse high schools in the district and closely reflects the racial and economic demographics of the county. Students come from all over the county and from eighteen different countries speaking nine different languages. Families from both the most affluent and most impoverished neighborhoods in Forsyth County choose RJR for their children's high school. This fact alone is a point of pride among the student body and is a defining part of the Reynolds experience.

### 2.2 *Dispatches at the Southeastern Center for Contemporary Art*

On November 1, 2016 at a time of anticipation that would become a kairotic moment in the history of America, the exhibition *Dispatches*, curated by Cora Fisher, opened at SECCA in Winston-Salem, North Carolina. The exhibition featured artists whose work responded to current social, political, and ecological issues. According to Fisher (2016), "The artists in *Dispatches* reshape our understanding of our world and the fullness of what's at stake in the news reports we receive" (n.p.).

The exhibition had five sections: borders and migration; ecological justice; grass-roots activism; post 9/11 realities; and the 2016 US Presidential election. (The exhibition opened one week before the election took place.) The Curator's intent was to create a platform from which visitors would be moved to action by addressing the issues presented either individually or as a community. The art and education curators worked closely to ensure that visitor experience went beyond passively viewing objects. Their work reflects the concepts proposed by McGhie (2019) who reminded us that "[i]t is not enough to aim to connect people with the museum. The museum should aim to connect people with the world" (p. 24).

## 3 Process

The process began in June, 2016 when SECCA's curators of art and education met with 26 RJR educators to discuss the exhibit and brainstorm potential connections. That summer, teachers met to plan lessons and design learning experiences that would intersect with the issues presented in *Dispatches*. SECCA invited teachers to preview the exhibition during an educator night before the field trips began. Student experiences unfolded in three parts over four months and two semesters: field trips; artists visits; and expressive responses. Field trips occurred throughout the exhibition from November 2016 through February 2017 and were personalised for each class, learning objective, or curricular intersection. Students and teachers often viewed the exhibition more than once with different classes, making over 4,000 combined visits. Ten artists, musicians, and photojournalists presented at the school and visited both non-arts and arts classrooms. Students prepared and performed group and individual expressive responses to the issues presented. Teachers met weekly in Professional Learning Teams (PLTs) to reflect, plan, and coordinate the ways in which each particular class would experience and respond to *Dispatches* and to plan standards-aligned lessons for each group. Students from the entire school created art based on the school-wide arts integrated collaboration, made real by the artists' visits, and activated through student expressions and conversations.

## 4 Field Trips

SECCA's art and education curators and the RJR staff worked hand in hand to design curriculum and experiential learning opportunities for students. During the run of *Dispatches*, 89% of the Reynolds student body attended the exhibition with their classes. Guides tailored each field trip to meet the curricular needs of that class. One teacher remarked, "It totally opened a new world of how to go to an exhibit and view the work and come home and make it your own." Incidents that happened during field trips are worth describing here. Suspended from the ceiling was a rubber boat similar to those that carried refugees across the Mediterranean; this sparked the imagination of visitors. One student said, "[The boat] made me feel what others may have felt ... [SECCA] could have just shown a picture, but instead, they had the actual boat." Around the boat were images of items left behind photographed by renowned photojournalist Ron Haviv. These photographs provided a glimpse into the lives of refugees who landed in Greece after dangerous water crossings and from there began journeys to sanctuary. The items included floaties, baby shoes, official documents, and food. A student who spoke Arabic translated a prayer depicted in one of the images. His teacher explained that as he was reading and translating the prayer, students "were silent and frozen. They were consumed by the idea that this prayer was something someone would grab as they were leaving their home and that it was lost in transit."

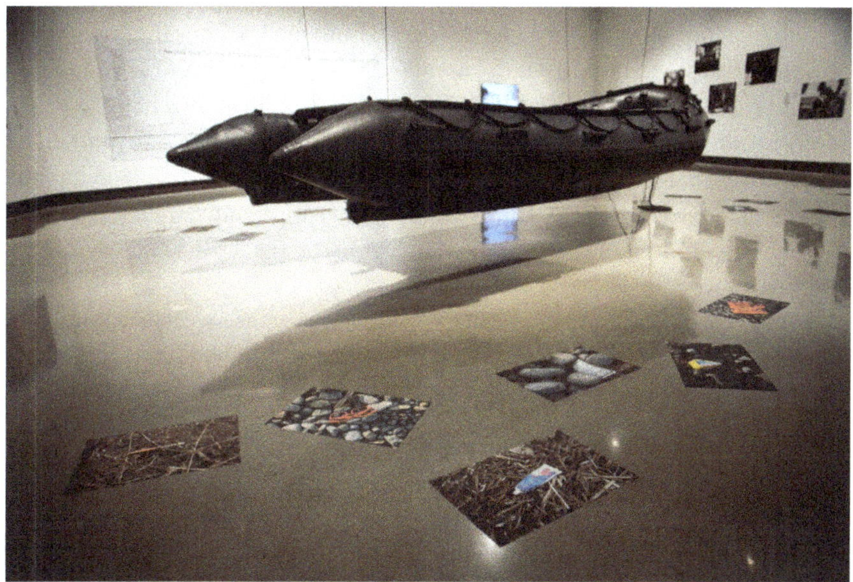

FIGURE 11.1 "Installation Photograph of *Dispatches*, Potter Gallery, SECCA" (Cliff Dossel, 2016). (Source: Southeastern Center for Contemporary Art)

## 5 Visiting Artists

The collaboration included school visits by six artists featured in *Dispatches* and four musicians. Curator Cora Fisher (2016) said,

> The artists and visual storytellers in this exhibition hail from all over the world. In their studio work and fieldwork ... they create dispatches, producing responsive new works on the defining issues of our day with perspectives that go far beyond the 24-hour news cycle. (n.p.)

Artists met with students in their classrooms and gave presentations to large groups in the auditorium. They had conversations about current affairs linked to their work in *Dispatches*. The questions raised by the artists were directly connected to class curricula. For example, a World Lit class was studying the book *A Thousand Splendid Suns* (2007) by Khaled Hosseini and one of the photojournalists who had covered an election in Afghanistan discussed his experiences. His work gave students context and set the stage for further research. Other topics included surveillance, racism, refugees, sexual orientation, child labor, and pollution. Students learned about drone strikes by launching a drone over campus with artist Tomas van Houtryve, whose work "Blue Sky Days" mimics habitual foreign strike targets with images from the US. They discussed racial tensions with Ron Haviv, who documented the Ferguson protests in his project "A Winter's Day of Discontent." They argued about climate change with Ed Morris of the Canary Project, one of the creators of *The Arctic Is*, a film noting the extreme changes in climate experienced by the Inuit in Greenland and the world's connectedness to it. They played music with Lonnie Holley, who gave them the impromptu advice, "Show love for each other. Love is an energy and you have to work it."

Among the visiting artists was iO Tillett Wright whose work at SECCA was "Self Evident Truths", a photographic portrait essay of individuals who identify as other than 100% heterosexual. One teacher remembered, "When iO came to our classroom the black box was just humming with this really cool energy." Students talked with Wright about sexuality, discrimination, and gender bias. "All of the students in the room felt really comfortable talking to iO and talking to each other." Another teacher said, "[Students] were so grateful for iO's presence as an artist and doing something transformative through the lens of art." These conversations with Wright and other artists were inspirational and led directly to meaningful connections with the art and each other, thus allowing students to genuinely express these experiences.

## 6 Expression and Action

Expression and action took many forms through arts integration in the classrooms. Earth/Environmental Science students researched personal carbon footprints after seeing Ed Kashi's film, *Curse of the Black Gold*, about the environmental impact of oil exploration in the Niger Delta. Theater students created performances to showcase contemporary issues highlighted by the exhibition and artists' visits. One student, inspired by Sim Chi Yin's photographs of Chinese miners, put his back to the audience and embodied a miner who was examining an x-ray of his lungs, destroyed by toxins. Students connected with the miner whose plight was being met with silence from the government.

Because of exposure to artist Sheryl Oring's "I Wish to Say" project, students became more involved in national, state, and local governmental issues through letter writing campaigns. Oring's longstanding performance art project gives individuals the opportunity to write notes to the President, and in the case of *Dispatches*, the future president. One teacher said, "By the time we were seeing the exhibit things had changed … Some of the notecards had become historical. Looking back at them even though they were just a few months old was really powerful … Our words could freeze a moment in time."

Experiences that started at the arts center became whole school events. For example, students engaged in the For Freedoms lawn signs project at SECCA. This experience became a catalyst for whole school installations. For Freedoms is an organisation led by artists who "believe citizenship is defined by participation, not by ideology."[1] Students made lawn signs prompted by the words "Freedom Of" and "Freedom From," citing "freedom from fear" and "freedom of choice" as examples. They linked their responses to the Civic and American History curriculum.

As a follow-up to the lawn signs project, 27 visual and performing arts, history, foreign language, and English classes read the United Nations Declaration of Human Rights. They identified the provisions that were most fundamental, timely, or sorely missing, and linked them to current issues. As an artistic Declaration, students created a campus-wide display of flags modeled from prayer flags from around the world. These fabric strips were adorned with written wishes for access for the world. Materials were available so that anyone in the school could add flags to the display that hung prominently at the school for three months.

One 3-D Design class took the project even further by creating an interactive installation entitled "Framing Access." Students each researched an amendment from the UN Declaration of Human Rights as it applied to current issues. Students created works from frames that hung from a centrally located tree. Students took personally relevant framed selfies and posted them on social media. Each student artist wrote an accompanying statement. One student wrote,

> The subject of my frame was saving the environment. I used metallic or technological materials to represent the pollution and manmade objects that are destroying the environment. The metallic paint is advancing in toward the organic material to show how it is taking over … The red lettering also represents the earth's pain as the environment is becoming more and more disrupted. My frame is saying that we need to help save the environment from ourselves.

## 7 Reverberation

The RJR student body and faculty are diverse, so finding commonalities in order to facilitate growth for all can be challenging. The school uses arts and experiences to do just that. Alberto Ibargüen, CEO of the Knight Foundation, speaking at the 2018 Power of Giving Symposium said, "Art binds. Culture generates social capital and strengthens a community's character. Art brings people together physically … and culturally, through its capacity to tell a community's shared story … and form connections that transcend difference." An RJR teacher said simply, "[The experience] gave a feeling of community and empathy across groups of students."

The increased social capital generated by the magnitude of this project continues to reverberate in the school culture. Teachers are seeking out field trips and speaker opportunities and using arts integration more consistently. One teacher stated, "Anyone can teach English, social studies, math, or science, but who has the courage to teach empathy?" Although hesitant at first to take students to an art museum, she now embeds field trips into each semester's plans.

Another example of reverberation is the ESL storytelling project. Faculty realised the power of telling stories through images and words after the *Dispatches* experience. They worked with filmmakers from the University of North Carolina School of the Arts to make storyboards with photos from their home countries and their current lives. Students wrote poetry in two voices that showcased the commonalities and differences in their two worlds, mounted the photo montages, and developed artist statements that were displayed at SECCA. This project has become a cherished part of ESL classes and has expanded to include conversations with non-ESL students as a way of sharing their perspectives.

## 8 Conclusion

During the school year, from this one school alone, more than 1600 individual students and 120 teachers were touched by this exhibition. In post-project surveys, 44% of teachers stated that the most impactful part was combining all three aspects (field trips, artists' visits, student expressive responses) of the project. This combination increased student engagement with both school curricula and current global issues.

Most importantly, individual students became more aware of current issues and decided to take action. Students and teachers noted that this collaboration increased empathy, created visible compassion, and fostered a commitment to critical issues. One student said, "We can't vote, but we can share what we know. It is about education and spreading [the message], and then vote." Another student was deeply inspired by one of the photojournalists and said, "That is something I would like to do in the future, be an active part of what is going on in the world." She continued, "We really have to be taught to go and make a difference as young people. We have to be exposed to issues in the world. I think art is such a good way to do that." Four theatre students summed up their experience in a scene calling for action. The students, surrounded by cardboard boxes inscribed with labels, stated:

> We need to step up together and break these boxes. How? With unity, acceptance, love, inclusion, hope, awareness, understanding. Don't put people down. Don't 'other' them. Notice the spectrum of similarities and differences. Accept it. Don't hate people for their identity. Love people for their personality. Give people the freedom to be themselves, love themselves, and encourage others to break out of their own boxes. Always remember the words of iO Tillett Wright, 'Familiarity is the gateway drug to empathy.'

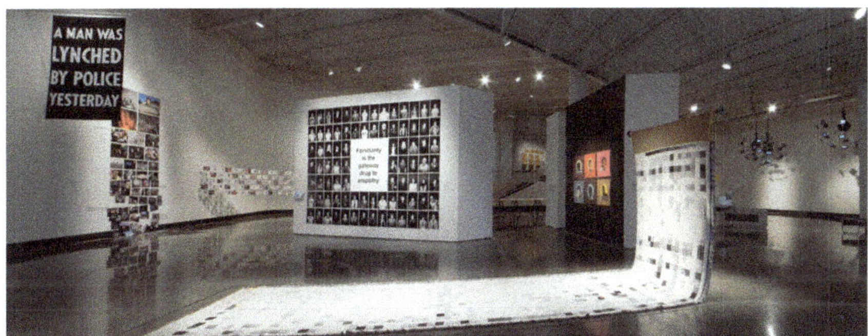


FIGURE 11.2 "Installation Photograph of *Dispatches*, Main Gallery, SECCA" (Cliff Dossel, 2016). (Source: Southeastern Center for Contemporary Art)

## Note

1 For Freedoms, see https://forfreedoms.org

## References

Bowen, D., Greene, J., & Kisida, B. (2014). Learning to think critically: A visual art experiment. *Educational Researcher, 43*(1), 37–44. https://doi.org/10.3102/0013189X13512675

Bradshaw, R. D. (2016). Art integration fosters empathy in the middle school classroom. *The Clearing House: A Journal of Educational Strategies, Issues and Ideas, 89*(4–5), 109–117. https://doi.org/10.1080/00098655.2016.1170441

Fisher, C. (2016). *Dispatches* [Exhibition title wall text]. Southeastern Center for Contemporary Art, Winston-Salem, North Carolina.

Greene, M. (2009). *The arts and the search for social justice*. https://maxinegreene.org/about/social-imagination

Ibargüen, A. (2018, March 22). *Art binds people to place and each other*. Presentation to The Third Annual Symposium of The Power of Giving: Philanthropy's Impact on American Life, National Museum of American History, Washington, DC. https://americanhistory.si.edu/topics/philanthropy/pages/power-giving-2018

McGhie, H. (2019). Climate change engagement: A different narrative. In W. Filho, B. Lackner, & H. McGhie (Eds.), *Addressing the challenges in climate change across various audiences* (pp. 13–29). Springer.

O'Donoghue, D. (2015). The turn to experience in contemporary art: A potentiality for thinking art education differently. *Studies in Art Education, 56*(2), 103–113. https://doi.org/10.1080/00393541.2015.11518954

CHAPTER 12

# Moving beyond Celebration toward Action

## *Affordances and Tensions in Screening and Audiencing Cellphilms and Participatory Verbatim Films*

*Casey Burkholder and Matt Rogers*

## 1 Introduction

As facilitators of participatory visual research projects in New Brunswick, Canada, we consider the complicated ways in which participatory verbatim films, which are dramatic cinematic representations of qualitative research data, (Abdullah & Khalaf, 2016; Rogers, 2017a, 2017b) and cellphilms, which are cellphone + film productions (see Dockney, Tomaselli, & Hart, 2010; MacEntee, Burkholder, & Schwab-Cartas, 2016, 2019) are screened and audienced.[1] Casey works with queer, trans, and non-binary youth to produce cellphilms that respond to queer and safe spaces in curricula and schools (Nackawic Needs a Gender Sexuality Alliance (GSA) Now!! (2018) archived on our YouTube channel, #QueerCellphilmsNB[2]). Matt worked with female-identifying and non-binary youth to produce a participatory verbatim film (Social Proof, 2018) on intersections of violence in the online lives of girls and young women (see Bell, Copage, Rogers, & Whitty, 2019). We reflect on our experiences facilitating the screenings of the films that emerged from our two projects, and ask four questions:

- What complexities arise when participatory verbatim films and cellphilms are screened in community contexts and in film festivals?
- How might facilitators and project participants navigate some of these complexities?
- How do audiences respond to participatory verbatim films and cellphilms when they are screened in different venues?
- What might facilitators consider when screening participant-produced films and cellphilms in different contexts?

By describing the ways in which we have facilitated screenings of our two projects in community contexts for participants and their families, teachers, policy makers, and also at local film festivals, our chapter considers the opportunities and challenges to screening youth-produced participatory verbatim films and cellphilms. We begin by describing the context of the two projects, Nackawic Needs a GSA Now!! and Social Proof before describing how they

 | DOI: 10.1163/9789004442870_012

have been screened. We then discuss the politics of screening youth-produced participatory verbatim films and cellphilms in (1) community settings, and (2) at film festivals. We explore the ways in which different audiences (for example, teachers, community members, youth, and government workers) have responded to the works. Finally, we offer a series of questions for facilitators to consider when they are seeking to screen youth produced participatory verbatim films and cellphilms in different spaces.

## 2 Context

### 2.1 *Nackawic Needs a GSA Now!!*

Since December 2018, Casey has been collaborating with a group of 13 to 17-year-old queer, trans, and non-binary young people from New Brunswick, Canada, in monthly art-making workshops. In the summer of 2018, she and PhD student Amelia Thorpe (see Burkholder & Thorpe, 2019), explored the Social Studies curricula and adjacent materials for representations and erasures of queer, trans, and non-binary people as well as women. They found only one mention of homosexuality in curricular-adjacent materials to support a unit on Ancient Greece. As a result, they sought participants for a media-making project to explore the ways in which queer, trans, and non-binary histories have been included in and/or erased in Social Studies classes and schools. The project, called Where are Our Histories, focuses on fostering opportunities for youth to speak back to these erasures and to disrupt silences (see Burkholder & Mitchell, forthcoming). In the first media-making workshop, the participants created stencils and short cellphilms about queer and safe spaces in schools. One participant, Alia, noted that her school did not have a GSA (gender sexuality alliance), and, more generally, was rife with homophobic and transphobic violence. The group brainstormed, storyboarded, and shot a multi-shot cellphilm, Nackawic Needs a GSA Now!! that imagined the life of a non-binary young person navigating a family and school structure that did not affirm their identity. Together, the group created the YouTube channel #QueerCellphilmsNB and produced and uploaded Nackawic Needs a GSA Now!![3] The cellphilm calls urgently for Nackawic to create a GSA to support queer, trans, and non-binary students. To date, the group has screened the cellphilm at a community screening for participants and families, for members of the school district, and at the Pink Lobster LGBTQ+ Film Festival in Fredericton, New Brunswick.

### 2.2 *Social Proof*

Matt Rogers's participatory verbatim cinema collaborations are an extension of an earlier research project called Preventing and Eliminating Cyberviolence against Young Women and Girls that focused on addressing issues like stalking, harassment, exploitation, and extortion in the lives of young women and girls in New Brunswick.[4] In 2016, Matt was invited to be involved in the dissemination phase of the research. The project involved province-wide qualitative interviews that focused on young women's lived experiences of cyberviolence and how communities and social and legal institutions address the issue. The research revealed that sexism, blaming, and paternalistic discourses framed discussions about cyberviolence when this topic was addressed in schools, in the media, or by law enforcement. This information encouraged the researchers involved in the Preventing and Eliminating Cyberviolence against Young Women and Girls project to pursue participatory approaches in disseminating the findings. In helping to rethink the project, and address youth knowledge and agency, Matt proposed working with a group of young women through a combination of what Brickell (2015) thinks of as participatory video drama and the verbatim cinema methods set out by Abdullah and Khalaf (2016). Reflecting on, interpreting, and responding to the insights gathered in the Preventing and Eliminating Cyberviolence against Young Women and Girls project, the new group collaborated to write, direct, and produce the narrative film, Social Proof. Produced through a participatory approach, the film involves dramatised recreations of elements of the earlier research texts. For example, the film explores issues of paternalism and victim-blaming and uses quotes from the Preventing and Eliminating Cyberviolence against Young Women and Girls project in some of the characters' dialogue. Social Proof has been shown in teacher professional development symposia, professional meetings, academic conferences, and through Atlantic Canada's Silver Wave Film Festival.

## 3 Screening in Community-Based Settings

Community venues can offer spaces for the filmmakers to speak back to peers, to community stakeholders, and to authority figures. These screenings can create meaningful opportunities for dialogue that might not have taken place otherwise. However, facilitating screenings in community settings also has some challenges. We have noticed that community-based audiences have been celebratory of the participants' media-making practices, but often do not take seriously the messages that the media productions seek to center. While these responses have been positive, we have noted audience members sometimes being patronising and dismissive of the issues presented.

Casey has screened Nackawic Needs a GSA Now!! for participants and their parents. She has also screened the cellphilm for teachers who work at Nackawic school, officials from the Anglophone West school district, and the NB Department of Education and Early Childhood Development (EECD) (without the participants' involvement). Each audience has responded differently. For example, the participant and parent screening led to emotional responses. Parents were proud and some were brought to tears by their children's activism and production capabilities. Parents knew how the school had othered and oppressed their children, and one parent spoke of being "so proud of the way that [name of child] could express [themselves] and talk about gender and sexuality in such deep ways—so much deeper than in [their] own adolescence." In screening with EECD and Anglophone District West officials—without the participants' presence—Casey noted mild celebration of, as well as discomfort with, the cellphilm. An EECD official said it was exciting that the project illustrated how young people can engage in activism about their school lives. The district officials, however, were concerned about the naming of the school in the cellphilm itself, "I mean we don't want to offend anyone. And, it's just a conservative space. We wouldn't want to make the teachers or the admin feel bad." Casey was disappointed, but not surprised by these reactions from community stakeholders. The cellphilm sought to disrupt the ways in which stakeholder adults (teachers and administrators) minimise the experiences of queer, trans, and non-binary youth. Unfortunately, the stakeholders' reactions reified the participants' concerns about the ways in which queerness was acceptable in schools—a queerness that does not stand out from others, demand anything of administration, or disrupt hegemonic heteronormativity as practiced in school

Discussions about audiencing Social Proof began early in the dissemination phase of the research into cyberviolence. The young filmmakers were excited to share their work with co-researchers, government officials, educators, and wider audiences at festivals. Whereas discussions about audiences occurred early and often, the team encountered complexities along the way. After some post screening audience interactions, the filmmakers talked to Matt about how adults in community settings responded to the film with paternalistic and dismissive attitudes (see Bell et al., 2018). He also encountered paternalistic responses to the film when he screened it (with no filmmakers present) to a group of high-level NB Education and EECD officials at a local conference. These screening experiences were disheartening since they showed how difficult it is to encourage some adults to appreciate work that affirms youth knowledge and agency. However, when the team was invited to screen Social Proof at a conference for provincial policymakers, Matt had an encouraging exchange with one government worker. During the invitation, this person suggested that

> [it would be] good to get [Social Proof] on the agenda sooner rather than later. I think it would be important to have it shown and then a bit of a Q&A after. When I was reading the report [that Rogers prepared] and news articles [on Social Proof], what stood out for me was the filmmakers' take on how adults interpret their work. I think it's important for them to have the air to address that and how their inclusion on projects is necessary when so often we don't bring them to the table… [I] just [want] to ensure [the film] would be an appropriate fit … as it may not be the right audience.

It is clear that this person was interested in screening the young people's film, but they wanted to be thoughtful about who the audience members might be, how they might respond, and how seriously they might take the work. They also brought up the importance of participatory screening, bringing the young people in to speak about a potential screening, and for them to be a part of the decision to screen or not screen depending on whether the audience was the right fit.

## 4 Film Festival Screenings

Screening participatory visual works at film festivals might mean reaching wider, and perhaps unanticipated, audiences in productive ways. As Carol Roy (2016) has explained, regional film festivals occupy an interesting liminal space in society that can provide contexts for communities to engage with political issues. Furthermore, many film festivals give a platform to niche genres (e.g. queer cinema) and audiences that are under-served in mainstream media, and these festival screenings have the potential to mobilise young people.

One of the complexities associated with screening participatory visual works at film festivals relates to issues of aesthetics and expectations based on cinematic conventions. The film festival submission process may include a critical screening by conference programmers and an adjudication for awards. Audiences attending festivals often tacitly compare the quality and production value of films screened. Furthermore, film festival audiences are often populated by filmmakers who may view films in more critical ways than would general audiences. This level of scrutiny of participatory visual works is not always appropriate.

Casey and her collaborators screened Nackawic Needs a GSA Now!! at the Pink Lobster LGBTQ+ Film Festival in February 2019. As one of the filmmakers, Raven, explained, "I was disappointed in the screening. The other films looked so good. Ours looked so cheap in comparison. The others were professional looking. Ours didn't look like that." In other words, Raven highlighted a concern that if the audience's attention plateaus at the value of production, there is the possibility that the political themes in the film might be missed or unrecognised. The root of our discussions on the aesthetics of participatory works draws on Cole and Knowles's (2008) view that aesthetics are a valid concern in arts-based research; as they pointed out, "Art is a medium ... Attention to the aesthetics of a particular genre are, therefore, important; aesthetics of form are integrally tied to communication" (p. 66).

Casey did not experience the cellphilm screening in the same way as Raven did. She felt that the screening provided a local context for queer filmmaking, which emerges from DIY traditions and responds to queer activism and DIY aesthetics more broadly. Casey noted that audience members were congratulatory in their responses to the cellphilm, even noting, "I can't believe that was shot on a cellphone." Perhaps the audience has different expectations regarding production and time. Reflecting back on these interactions now, Casey wonders what it means when people say, "I can't believe that was shot on a cellphone." What are the audience members' aesthetic assumptions and their ways of reading these film texts?

Much like Casey's experience with young people being apprehensive about the aesthetics of their work following the screening at a festival, when Social Proof was accepted for screening at the Silver Wave Film Festival the filmmakers were nervous about how the production quality of their film would compare to other films in the festival. There was some concern that the audience, or their peers, might belittle the work or them as filmmakers, based on aesthetic issues. Although participants in both projects expressed concerns relating to audience expectations and whether their film would measure up to the quality of other films shared in festival screenings, both the Social Proof filmmakers and the Nackawic Needs a GSA Now!! group have continued to submit their participatory visual media productions to other festivals since.

## 5 Opportunities for Pre-Screenings

What else might we do to prepare participant-filmmakers as well as audiences to engage deeply with screening practices? As a filmmaker, Matt finds pre-screenings with test audiences helpful in terms of getting a clearer understanding of how people might interpret his work. He suggests that offering a pre-community or pre-festival screening for a close group of critical friends might be useful in understanding how people outside the projects might interpret or take up the work. Pre-screenings also allow filmmakers and facilitators to see where audiences may get distracted or lose the message, thus creating an opportunity to re-edit based on audience feedback. Casey notes that she has engaged in similar pre-screenings and re-editing processes, but with participants themselves in cellphilm production workshops. However, she has not yet sought outside feedback in order to re-edit the cellphilms but sees useful opportunities in this practice.

We also see the need to engage in audience work, particularly with film festival audiences. We wonder if there is something about youth produced media (or DIY aesthetics) that prevents the audience from engaging deeply (beyond celebration) with the ideas presented in the media? For example, the audience might have difficulty reading the text in the way that they are used to doing with Hollywood films. While we do not wish to set up a deficit model of the films, Casey notes that she often uses coded words like DIY before she screens the youth-produced media. We wonder if such practices set up the film in a deficit fashion, even as we try to prepare the audience and disrupt simplistic readings based on the audience's notion of aesthetic worth. Even when we think we are presenting the work in ways that are agentic, what do we do that might reinforce surface level readings of the film texts? Should facilitators present the meanings behind the cellphilms and films in a prescriptive way for audiences?

## 6 Concluding Thoughts and Lingering Questions

Insight from our experiences screening cellphilms and participatory verbatim films in community and festival contexts have some implications for participatory visual methods practitioners who audience participant work. We offer Table 12.1 for participatory visual researchers to consider when they are facilitating screenings of participant-produced media with audiences.

TABLE 12.1 Reflexive strategies for facilitating participatory media screenings

| Consideration | Questions |
|---|---|
| Power and participation | How is the power relationship between researcher and participants negotiated in the screening processes?<br>Who decides where and when to screen the films?<br>How might the audience be prepared for participatory film screenings?<br>How might oppressive structures, discourses, institutions, or audiences have an impact on the screenings?<br>What is the role of the facilitator/researcher when audiences react to films in ways that minimise, infantilise, and/or misrepresent the participants' messages? What should be done if audiences other or oppress the filmmakers? |
| Authorship and ownership | Who is named as the author of the film?<br>Who introduces the film?<br>How are participants invited to speak about, set up, or contextualise the film? Does this happen before or after the screening?<br>Who answers questions from the audience?<br>What might participatory approaches to authorship look like? |
| Ethics | What ethical issues might emerge from screening the participatory media for diverse audiences (e.g. young people, teachers, policy makers, and/or the general public)?<br>How might the group/participants/facilitator respond to paternalistic or oppressive comments from audience members?<br>How might potential harm be addressed by the facilitator?<br>What are the facilitator's responsibilities in screening the participatory media when participants are not present at the screening? |

Through our reflections on the different ways that our youth-produced cellphilms and participatory verbatim films have been audienced and screened, we suggest that as facilitators it is necessary for us to work with the audience to see the works beyond empty celebration (e.g. "they did good work," "good for them for making a film," "they're so brave," etc.) (Low, Brushwood Rose, Salvio, & Palacios, 2012; Rogers, 2016, 2017). We argue in this chapter that it is our ethical responsibility as facilitators to make the audiences take seriously the issues that the young people have raised. Nackawic Needs a GSA Now!! highlights the ways in which the perpetuation of the gender binary in schools through sex-segregated spaces is an act of violence against trans and non-binary youth. Social Proof describes the ways in which online violence against girls and young women online has serious and embodied offline repercussions. There are consequences to minimising the activism and work of young people as celebration (Mitchell, Lamb, & Raissadat, 2018; Treffry-Goatley, Wiebesiek, de Lange, & Moletsane, 2017; Walsh, 2012). As facilitators and allies, it is our responsibility to work with audiences toward action—to agitate for systemic change—based on what we have seen.

## Notes

1 In this chapter, we do not discuss explicitly the screening of participatory media in academic contexts, but point to the scholarship of Arcidiacono, Grimaldi, Di Martino, and Procentese (2016); Koningstein and Azadegan (2018); Mandrona and MacEntee (2015); MacEntee (2016); Mitchell and de Lange (2013); and Mitchell, de Lange, and Moletsane (2017) who describe the complexities of this work in great depth.

2 #QueerCellphilmsNB, Home, see https://www.youtube.com/channel/UCXORsJs6oOVKJ7TS-DnEl6xg

3 This chapter does not describe the opportunities and challenges to the QueerCellphilmsNB cellphilm archive. For more analysis, see Burkholder and Thorpe (2019).

4 Other project coordinators include the Murial McQueen Furgussen Centre, New Brunswick Social Workers Association, and the New Brunswick Office of the Child and Youth Advocate. The project has been funded by Status of Women Canada (Project to Prevent and Eliminate Cyberviolence against Young Women and Girls in New Brunswick).

## References

Abdullah, A., & Khalaf, A. (2016). Truths ethics and politics and their relations to verbatim theatre. *Journal of Humanities, 17*(4), 258–267. http://repository.sustech.edu/handle/123456789/17134

Bell, R., Copage, K., Rogers, M., & Whitty, P. (2019). Fleeting encounters & brick walls: Animating embodied literacies in our everyday relations. *Language and Literacy, 20*(4), 5–22. https://doi.org/10.20360/langandlit29434

Brickell, K. (2015). Participatory video drama research in transitional Vietnam: Post-production narratives on marriage, parenting and social evils. *Gender, Place & Culture, 22*(4), 510–525. https://doi.org/10.1080/0966369X.2014.885889

Burkholder, C., & Mitchell, C. (forthcoming). Storing, sharing and circulating images. In C. Mitchell (Ed.), *Doing visual research* (2nd ed.). Sage.

Burkholder, C., & Thorpe, A. (2019). Cellphilm production as posthumanist research method to explore injustice with queer youth in New Brunswick, Canada. *Reconceptualizing Educational Research Methodology, 10*(2–3), 292–309. https://doi.org/10.7577/rerm.3680

Caterina, A., Daria, G., Salvatore, D., & Fortuna, P. (2016). Participatory visual methods in the 'psychology loves porta capuana' project. *Action Research, 14*(4), 376–392. https://doi.org/10.1177/1476750315626502

Cole, A. L., & Knowles, J. G. (2008). Arts-informed research. In J. G. Knowles & A. L. Cole (Eds.), *Handbook of the arts in qualitative research: Perspectives, methodologies, examples, and issues* (pp. 55–70). Sage.

Dockney, J., Tomaselli, K., & Hart, T. B. (2010). Cellphilms, mobile platforms and prodsumers: Hyper-individuality and film. In N. Hyde-Clarke (Ed.), *The citizen in communication: Revisiting traditional, new and community media practices in South Africa* (pp. 75–96). Juta Press.

Koningstein, M., & Azadegan, S. (2018). Participatory video for two-way communication in research for development. *Action Research, 1*(1). https://doi.org/10.1177/1476750318762032

Low, B., Brushwood Rose, C., Salvio, P., & Palacios, L. (2012). (Re)framing the scholarship on participatory video: From celebration to critical engagement. In E.-J. Milne, C. Mitchell, & N. de Lange (Eds.), *Handbook of participatory video* (pp. 49–64). Altamira Press.

Macentee, K. (2016). Facing responses to cellphilm screenings of African girlhood in academic presentations. In K. MacEntee, C. Burkholder, & J. Schwab-Cartas (Eds.), *What's a cellphilm? Integrating mobile phone technology into participatory visual research and activism* (pp. 137–152). Sense Publishers.

MacEntee, K., Burkholder, C., & Schwab-Cartas, J. (2016). What's a cellphilm? An introduction. In K. MacEntee, C. Burkholder, & J. Schwab-Cartas (Eds.), *What's a cellphilm? Integrating mobile phone technology into participatory visual research and activism* (pp. 1–25). Sense Publishers.

MacEntee, K., Burkholder, C., & Schwab-Cartas, J. (2019). Cellphilms. In P. Leavy (Ed.) *The Oxford handbook of methods for public scholarship* (pp. 419–442). Oxford University Press.

Mandrona, A., & MacEntee, K. (2015). From discomfort to collaboration: Teachers screening cellphilms in a rural South African school. *Perspectives in Education, 33*(4), 42–56. http://hdl.handle.net/11660/3820

Mitchell, C., Lamb, P., & Raissadat, H. (2018). Exploring the impact of youth-produced images on family, community, and policy. *International Journal of Qualitative Methods, 17*(1), 1–10. https://doi.org/10.1177/1609406918807609

Moorehouse, A., Milchenko, L., Sharpe, T., Pinney, A., & Rogers, M. (Producers), & Moorehouse, A. (Director). (2018, November). *Social proof* [Motion Picture, festival release]. Fredericton, New Brunswick: Muriel McQueen Fergusson Centre for Family Violence Research.

Rogers, M. (2016). Problematising participatory video with youth in Canada: The intersection of therapeutic, deficit and individualising discourses. *Area, 48*(4), 427–434. https://doi.org/10.1111/area.12141

Rogers, M. (2017a). Conceptualizing and implementing critical filmmaking pedagogies: Reflections for educators. In J. Cummings & M. Blatherwick (Eds.), *Creative dimensions of teaching and learning in the 21st century* (pp. 229–238). Sense Publishers.

Rogers, M. (2017b). Participatory filmmaking pedagogies in schools: Tensions between critical representation and perpetuating gendered and heterosexist discourses. *Studies in Social Justice, 11*(2), 195–220. https://doi.org.10.26522/ssj.v11i2.1522

Roy, C. (2016). *Documentary film festivals: Transformative learning, community building & solidarity*. Sense Publishers.

Squires, A., Scott, R., Hartley, N., Thorpe, A., & Burkholder, C. (Producers), & Scott, R., & Squires A. (Directors). (2018). *Nackawic needs a GSA NOW!!* [Cellphilm]. QueerCellphilmsNB. https://www.youtube.com/watch?v=T8hg8QzfiU4

Treffry-Goatley, A., Wiebesiek, L., de Lange, N., & Moletsane, R. (2017). Technologies of nonviolence: Ethical participatory visual research with girls. *Girlhood Studies: An Interdisciplinary Journal, 10*(2), 45–61. https://doi.org/10.3167/ghs.2017.100205

Walsh, S. (2012). Challenging knowledge production with participatory video. In E.-J. Milne, C. Mitchell, & N. de Lange (Eds.), *Handbook of participatory video* (pp. 225–241). AltaMira Press.

CHAPTER 13

# Cameraless Film-Making in the Education Classroom

## *A Professor-Student Artistic Collaboration*

*Lisa A. Mitchell and Kerri Kennedy*

In this chapter, we share our experiences of collaborating as professor and undergraduate student on designing and delivering a cameraless film-making workshop in the Bachelor of Education program at Trent University, where we are currently Assistant Professor and Teacher Candidate respectively. The cameraless film-making workshop was delivered in a cross-section of Education classes to approximately 150 teacher candidates over an 18-month period. Our research uses a conceptual framework of Appreciative Inquiry (AI) to explore

- the nature of the collaborative working relationship between us as an Arts professor and student artist respectively
- the Arts-based film-making experience itself and how teacher candidates responded to engaging in this collaborative process.
- In this pilot project, our research explored the following questions:
- How did we (the professor and student) experience the collaborative teaching process?
- What elements of the collaborative teaching process can be identified that had a significant, positive impact on the project participants?
- What positive lessons can be learned from this collaboration that, potentially, could inform future collaborative teaching approaches between professors and students in Arts, Education, and other university teaching and learning contexts?

## 1 Our Voices

### 1.1 *Student*

Before I began the Bachelor of Education program at Trent University, I was in the university's Cultural Studies program, where I discovered and developed my passion for film, and, more specifically, cameraless film-making. Through taking courses in film studies, I learned about the intricacies and technicalities of working with 16mm filmstrip as an art form. When I began my Bachelor of

 | DOI: 10.1163/9789004442870_013

Education degree, I wanted to bring my experience and the passion I had as an artist and independent film-maker into my classroom, if possible. Fortunately, my very first practicum placement as a teacher candidate included a grade 10 Media Arts class in which I could share my skills and passion for cameraless film-making with my own students.

My Trent University faculty advisor and professor at the time in the Education program, Lisa Mitchell, attended this Media Arts class during this practicum placement and observed me teaching a class on cameraless film-making to a group of students who had little to no prior experience of film-making. During the class, my students created their own cameraless films from scratch, using 16mm clear leader filmstrip and a variety of mediums—markers, paint, nail polish and the like—to design their animated filmstrips frame by frame. Lisa then approached me to ask if I would be interested in collaborating with her to create, develop, and deliver a cameraless film-making workshop to her students (my own teacher candidate peers) in the Bachelor of Education program at Trent. I was thrilled and excited to do so because I am passionate about film and see the value in teaching teachers themselves about this art medium with which many people are unfamiliar. I believed that exposing my peer group to a new kind of knowledge to which they may not already have access would be a valuable learning opportunity for them, and for me as a new teacher myself.

The experience of working collaboratively to create, develop, and deliver this film-making workshop with Lisa, who is an experienced teacher and professor, was invaluable in that I learned so much about teaching itself and how I could improve my own pedagogy in the classroom. In addition, knowing that Lisa was looking to me as an expert in the area of film-making helped to create a positive learning opportunity and demonstrated to me that a professor could be truly excited about learning about something new.

### 1.2 *Professor*

In the weeks before I observed Kerri Kennedy teach in a secondary classroom during her first Bachelor of Education practicum placement, I had been reviewing a collection of academic articles for possible inclusion in a Master of Education curriculum theory course that I was tasked with designing. During my preliminary course construction, I came across Gilbert's (2006) article entitled, Let us say yes to who or what turns up: Education as hospitality, that prompted me to consider how the concept of hospitality might be otherwise operationalised in a teacher education program. Gilbert's definition of hospitality in which unconditional welcome in K–12 schools and classrooms is emphasised, draws on Derrida's (2000) notion of the reciprocally linked relationship between foreigner and other. Derrida made the argument that hospitality is a kind of ethos whereby we "give place to [the foreigner], that [we] let them come, that [we] let them arrive, and take place in the place [we] offer them" (as cited in Gilbert, 2006, p. 25). Similarly, Gilbert (2006) makes the argument that hospitality "demands that we accept what is not yet intelligible; knowledge or understanding cannot be a precondition of welcome. We are to welcome the stranger before we know who or what he or she is" (p. 27). Gilbert's argument that the very nature of inclusive education practices should be hospitable for all learners in classrooms is particularly compelling for me as both a former classroom teacher and as a current education professor.

As I sat in the back corner of Kerri's grade 10 Media Arts class and watched her motivate and inspire her own secondary school education students through the sharing of her artistic skills and passion for experimental cameraless film-making, I began to consider two key questions.

- What might happen if I invited Kerri into my own university classroom and asked her to collaborate with me as an equal partner in the teaching and learning process?
- Could I let go of my preconceived ideas of who Kerri might be, and, instead, be willing to invite her into a collaborative, emergent professional learning partnership without yet knowing what she may or may not bring to the table as an artist, collaborator, and teacher?

By voluntarily relinquishing my comfortable sense of power as a professor, I wondered if this process of what I thought of as letting go might result in something new and unexpected in the learning environment. As a former secondary school music teacher and a current Integrated Arts professor, the medium of film-making was largely outside my comfort zone. In order to collaborate with Kerri and offer a cameraless film-making workshop to my own university students, I would have to engage in a steep learning curve myself, with Kerri as the mentor and me as the student.

While Gilbert (2006) focuses specifically on the complexities surrounding inclusive education practices for LGBTQ students in the elementary and secondary classroom context and how the notion of hospitality might help to create spaces for critical action, dialogue, and reflection, I was nonetheless eager to consider how hospitality could be considered in the entirely different context of a university classroom in a Bachelor of Education program in which I was currently teaching. Gilbert wrote, "If education is a relation of hospitality, then we will affect and be affected by our encounters with others" (p. 33). Indeed, my initial encounter with Kerri in her own teaching environment has subsequently affected me profoundly, complexly, and in intersecting ways as a teacher, mentor, collaborator, learner, and as an artist. Working closely with a student in a collaborative capacity has prompted me to question my own role as assumed expert in a Bachelor of Education program and has led me to refresh and renew my commitment to lifelong learning as a student and artist myself.

## 2 A Context for Film-Making

The medium of film has been around for well over a century and has been used to document some of the most memorable and iconic historical images, yet many people remain unaware of what the term film refers to. Hollis Frampton (see Jenkins, 2009), an American experimental film artist, describes film in his famous performance piece, A Lecture, as "a narrow transparent ribbon uniformly perforated with small holes along its edges so that it may be handily transported by sprocket wheels … it consists of a long row of small pictures, which do not move at all. The projector accelerates the small still pictures into movement" (as cited in Jenkins, 2009, p. 127). In this context, film describes the physical material of the celluloid filmstrip with respect to its creation and the projection of still images that create the illusion of a motion picture.

During the film-making workshops we created, designed, and delivered, students participated in cameraless film-making. Cameraless film is a genre of experimental or art film that requires the artist to produce footage without the use of a film camera. The content of the film is created by the artist painting, drawing, scratching or collaging directly onto the filmstrip to produce their still images or frames. Unlike what happens in other genres of experimental film-making, here the filmstrip becomes a blank canvas providing the artist with limitless possibilities for creativity.

Although there are unlimited ways of creating cameraless films, there are two basic methods of production that are used most frequently. In the first method, the artist starts with film that has already been developed to manipulate the already developed image. This may be footage created by the same artist or it may be found footage. For example, the artist can hand-tint a black and white film or use tools to create texture on an already developed film. In the second method, which is the method our students followed during the cameraless film workshops, the artist starts with blank undeveloped film and creates their own original images. For this second method, there are two different types of undeveloped filmstrip an artist can use. This first is black leader, which is film with light sensitive emulsion on the surface. With the black leader method, the artist works with the negative image by removing the emulsion to reveal the light. The second is clear leader, which is film without emulsion.

With clear leader, the artist works with the positive image by applying pigment to diffuse and manipulate the light.

Cameraless film-making allows an artist to explore visual representation in a temporal space. The artist must consider their frames (the still images found between the perforations of the filmstrip) and how these frames will appear when seen in quick succession, projected at the rate of 24 frames per second. In *The Emergence of Cinematic Time*, Doane (2002) has stated that "the viewer fills in the gap between two still images and that motion is superadded by the action of the mind" (p. 71). This optical illusion is a crucial element in how the film medium works, how a viewer sees still images in motion, and is especially significant when one is creating cameraless images. Since the footage is entirely produced by hand and not mechanically replicated with a camera, the frames must maintain some consistency to create a lasting impression on the viewer's eye. The film artist must therefore create a series of still images that together create a pattern or visual rhythm that translates into the illusion of movement.

## 3 Rationale

Clover (2007) has proposed that "researchers must be willing to let go of the art as their own product, representation, and way of knowing and be able to see the power in collective production" (pp. 96–97). With this understanding, we (as professor and student) entered into the collaborative film-making project hoping that a collaborative artistic and teaching experience would provide us and our workshop participants with a more complex, nuanced teaching and learning experience that would not have been possible had we been operating as individuals. Faculties or Schools of Education are sites in which teacher candidates are asked to consider themselves as lifelong learners. Professors, whose job it is to train those new teacher candidates, are well-advised to do the same and to take this one step further in modelling the very professionalism they wish to instill in their own students. As previously noted, strongly underpinning this point of view is Gilbert's (2000) notion of education as hospitality, where "if education is a relation of hospitality, then [professors] will affect and be affected by [their] encounters with others" (p. 33) and should therefore embrace, and be willing to learn from, the unique expertise of who and what shows up in their classrooms. We hope that by sharing our positive experiences of professor-student emerging collaboration, we might inspire other professors and students to seek out and create similar learning opportunities in their university classrooms and beyond.

## 4 Conceptual Framework

In the interest of understanding how professors can collaborate effectively with student-experts in their classrooms, our research uses Appreciative Inquiry (AI) as a conceptual framework and as one for the analysis of initial thematic findings. The process of applying AI as a conceptual framework is based on valuing personal, positive, narrative-rich stories whereby learning can be fostered through engagement, and respect can be deepened among participants. The AI process is, therefore, naturally inclusive and collaborative, giving equal voice to all stakeholders (including researchers and participants alike). Essentially, AI "builds on positive experiences to spark positive change by honouring the expertise resident in an organization and its people … by uncovering what works well in a system and devises ways to expand upon those strengths" (Filleul, 2010, p. 38). AI was used to frame our understanding of collaborative and arts-informed learning in a Faculty of Education learning environment, where collaborative approaches to teaching and learning are often espoused as being highly effective tools for both new and experienced teachers. Framing the research through an appreciative model, rather than a deficit one, allowed us to focus on the depth of the positive and affirming stories arising from the variety of participant experiences.

## 5 Methodology

As professor and student, we worked collaboratively to deliver the cameraless film-making workshop to over 150 teacher candidates in a cross-section of Education classes. Initial data for this research is in the form of interviews, photographs, and four resulting short films. Using AI as a conceptual framework has allowed us to focus on a positive, collaborative, and participative approach to conducting research in Education, which is nicely aligned with our initial goal to approach the teaching experience as a collaborative endeavor. Most models for AI as a research methodology focus on four stages: discovering; dreaming; designing; and delivering, with the most crucial aspect of the methodology being the participant interview as Shuayb, Sharp, Judkins, and Hetherington (2009) have reminded us. We used the first stage of the four-stage methodology to guide our individual self-interviews and those of the workshop participants themselves. In this discovering stage, the primary goal is to find out the best and most positive experiences participants had during the phenomenon being studied. To this end, we conducted individual self-interviews (as professor and student) and with a small randomised cross-section of participants (teacher candidates) who took part in the cameraless film-making workshops and had the opportunity to provide written feedback on their experiences. The interviews were then transcribed, open coded, and cross-compared for common themes between and among participants.

## 6 Themes

Preliminary findings from this project demonstrate that collaboration between professors and students in a Faculty of Education offers a rich, dynamic learning opportunity for learners that would not otherwise be possible, demonstrates authentic commitment to lifelong learning on the part of both professor and student, and illuminates and builds upon shared expertise of both professors and students alike. Threads of understanding are woven together intricately across four specific thematic areas, each of which is supported by the written interview narratives and the visual film expressions with accompanying descriptions themselves. The first of these four thematic areas is the notion of flattened hierarchy. For Participant A,

> I feel like a collaborative opportunity is beneficial for both students and professors ... It really benefits students to explore the collaborative nature of teaching in general and values the unique knowledge that students bring into their program rather than professors just treating them as empty vessels.

The second thematic area covers the idea of hybrid teaching. Kerri said, "I've learned so much through learning from and collaborating with Lisa, my professor, that I wouldn't have otherwise thought of attempting in my own teaching." The third can be described as personalised learning, For Participant B, "Many students have different experiences and expertise that can be explored and utilised in the classroom; it just takes the willingness of a professor to explore those possibilities." The fourth addresses the concept of affective expression. For Lisa, "Working closely with Kerri, a student-artist, has renewed my sense of what it means to infuse artistry into my own approach to curricular development and teaching. It has refreshed my love for being artistically creative in the classroom."

An additional, and perhaps the most significant piece of learning that has emerged from this work is the opportunity for professors to proactively highlight, recognise, and give voice to undergraduate student expertise in the university learning environment. This strongly suggests that through experiencing the model of professor-student collaboration as a learning strategy, learners may have access to knowledge or ways of knowing that have been historically marginalised, ignored, or even actively discouraged in the university classroom.

## 7 Future Research

The findings from this initial collaborative artistic project are being used to frame a larger research study that investigates the collaborative teaching and learning possibilities between professors and undergraduate students in Education and other fields. Most research on the nature of collaboration focuses on the professor-professor, or professor-graduate student working relationship. This new resulting research will highlight the need for professors to consider forming collaborative partnerships with undergraduate students and to seek out ways in which the expertise of those undergraduates can be highlighted positively and recognised in university classrooms. Additional research questions to be explored include

- To what extent are professors in Arts, Education, or other university contexts already collaborating with undergraduate students?
- What elements are enabling/constraining professor-student collaborative approaches to teaching and learning?
- How are collaborative partnerships being formed between professors and students?
- Do particular subject areas or fields (e.g., arts or education) lend themselves more easily to professor-student collaborative teaching approaches than other subject areas or fields?

Ultimately, the idea of calling forth undergraduate student expertise arose many times during the initial research (during both data collection and analysis) and this prompts us to consider more complex issues in plans for future research. For example, we intend to examine how educational power dynamics that traditionally disempower students and reinforce broader social power dynamics may be disrupted, and subsequently reformed, renegotiated, and reconceptualised. Celebrating students' expertise empowers the student expert, but also also makes it possible for recipients of that expertise (in this case, both the professor and the student's peer group) to access knowledge that may have been historically marginalised, uninvited, ignored, or even actively discouraged in the university learning context, and thus, not as readily available to them. Collaboration between professors and undergraduatestudents has the potential to bridge this gap and invite social change in university classrooms.

## References

Clover, D. E. (2007). Tapestries through the making: Quilting as a valuable medium of feminist adult education and arts-based inquiry. In D. E. Clover & J. Stalker (Eds.), *The arts and social justice: Re-crafting adult education and community cultural leadership* (pp. 83–101). National Institute of Adult Continuing Education.

Doane, M. A. (2002). *The emergence of cinematic time: Modernity, contingency, the archive*. Harvard University Press.

Filleul, M. (2010). Appreciative inquiry: From positive narrative to systemic change. *Education Canada, 49*(4), 38–40.

Gilbert, J. (2006). Let us say yes to who and what shows up: Education as hospitality. *Journal for the Canadian Association of Curriculum Studies, 4*(10), 25–34.

Jenkins, B. (Ed.). (2009). *On the camera arts and consecutive matters: The writings of Hollis Frampton* (pp. 125–130). The MIT Press.

Shuayb, M., Sharp, C., Judkins, M., & Hetherington, M. (2009). *Using appreciative inquiry in educational research: Possibilities and limitations*. National Foundation for Educational Research. https://www.nfer.ac.uk/publications/AEN01/AEN01.pdf

CHAPTER 14

# Choreography as Poetic, Pedagogical, and Political Action in Contemporary Times

*Tone Pernille Østern*

Led by the following research questions relating to artistic practice, I began to focus on the choreographic processes of which I was part as choreographic leader and researcher in 2016.

- What is choreography in contemporary times?
- What does choreography contribute in contemporary times?
- What are contemporary times?
- If choreography is understood as action in contemporary times, what does it then mean to choreograph?
- What does it mean to choreograph in a way that takes in impulses and values from contemporary times, in process as well as in product?

This article functions as a stop point in the ongoing investigation of these research questions that keep occupying me as a choreographer, teacher, and researcher. I have been a choreographer and a creative leader for nineteen years in a small dance company in the independent art field,[1] and as a teacher-researcher in the academy[2] for the last ten of these years. In what I think of as my artistic-research-with-others, these two positions are fused. I am based in Norway and work here, so my cultural context encompasses the Nordic countries.

First, I will contextualise the study briefly within a larger choreographic research field. I will then discuss the methodology and define central theoretical concepts. Finally, I will analyse the two choreographic processes, *200 Billion and 1* and *Baby Body*, with my research questions in mind.

## 1 The Research Field and Impulse behind This Project

Antje Hildebrandt's (2013) provocation *The End of Choreography*[3] was the direct inspiration for this project. Hildebrandt argued that choreography as an aesthetic phenomenon turns its back on established aesthetics and techniques found within dance, as well as on being associated with handicraft, special skills, and control over the dance and the dancers (Østern, 2018). Solveig Styve

 | DOI: 10.1163/9789004442870_014

Holte (2016) writes about choreographic thinking that leads to the notion of choreography as practice becoming democratised. As I look around me in Norway, the Nordic countries, and globally, I see that choreography is being extended to artistic, pedagogical, and research settings, often in different crossovers between and among these three. With this project, I seek to take part in this extension.

Jenn Joy (2014) has written about how choreographic engagement means relating to another or several others and to providing impulses towards movement, moments of waiting, opportunities to listen, and chances for participation in a state of deep dialogical presence and focus. The choreographic working processes are, in many contexts, changed into open, explorative and collaborative processes. The choreographic processes analysed in this article serve as examples of this.

## 2 Arts-Based Research within a Post-Qualitative, Performative and Agential Realism Paradigm

Arts-based research often has a collaborative approach as Patricia Leavy (2018) has reminded us, and so does this project. Collaborative approaches emphasise transformation, change, participation and voice (Savin-Baden & Howell Major, 2013). Central to collaborative approaches is the idea that knowledge is not located only with privileged experts like academic researchers, but, rather, knowledge must be produced in collaboration with the voices of the knowers. In a collaborative research project, there is a fine line between research participants and co-researchers, and often the same people find themselves in both roles. This is also true of the two projects under discussion here; the researchers in the project were research participants along with the other participants.

The project is positioned within a performative research paradigm with an emphasis on Karen Barad's (2007) notion of agential realism. For Phillip Vannini (2015), performative paradigm in these terms means that the research itself is seen as creative and non-representational. Doing arts-based research is about creating something new, not representing a reality that exists independently of the research project. Further, post-qualitative research moves away from established research methods and is based on the belief that each research project must develop its own methods that best suit that particular project. Post-qualitative research is oriented towards the creative and expressive capacities of the body, including the researcher-body, as well as the agential capacities of non-human materials.

In this study, I speak about diffraction when I am explaining how I understand my analytic approach because I position myself in relation to Barad's (2007) theoretical philosophical approach to agential realism that shifts focus from an interest in individual essences to one in entangled relations; meaning is supposed to be created in discursive-material relations. Inspired by Donna Haraway, Barad's analytical tool is that of diffraction, as opposed to reflection. Reflection turns the gaze back towards the researcher (like looking in a mirror) and makes meaning-making a task for the individual researcher. In qualitative research reflection is important, and the analytical result often one of creating patterns of sameness (like themes or categories). Diffraction is interested, rather, in differences; like reflection, it is also an optical phenomenon, but it is focused on what kinds of differences are produced when something (like a light wave, for example,) encounters (is in a relation with) something else. Barad developed her philosophy from studying quantum entanglement. On a quantum level, diffraction occurs. When, for example, a light wave encounters an obstacle, a new diffractive pattern arises. As Barad emphasises, diffraction is not about any kind of difference, but about differences that make a difference.

To think of my analytical process as diffracting through choreographic processes is an experiment. It is not easy to seek to diffract instead of reflect, and, quite certainly, I do something of both. When I speak of diffracting in this article, I mean that I will try to bend my thinking into new directions, allowing them to change as I encounter obstacles in the choreographic processes. These obstacles I see as positive, creating differences that make a difference, thus giving an impulse for change. The obstacles are performative; they help in creating something new. These diffractions have no clear beginning or end, but they are there, right now, performative for my thinking-acting as choreographer-researcher. In this research project, then, I lean on Barad's philosophical notions, and I am oriented throughout towards differences that make a difference for the choreographic processes in which I take part, to function as and be understood as poetic, pedagogical, and political action in contemporary times.

## 3 Contemporary Times

I am interested in how choreography can be active—how choreography can do something, contribute, and have agency in today's world. I keep coming back to the question of what contemporary times are, what these times do, and perhaps also what they lack or need. In 2014, I made an explorative intervention with twenty-two dance artists in Oslo, Norway (see Østern & Irgens,

2016). We were investigating the three concepts choreographic processes, dance pedagogies, and contemporary times, and the relationships between and among these three. On post-it notes the dance artists came up with 145 different references to what is meant by the notion of contemporary times, but it was not possible to sort or group their references in any particular way. There was no clear pattern to how they understood contemporary times. The pattern may, instead, be the "fragmentation and lack of shared basics, with an emphasis on the now, endless possibilities and a flow of information, combined with a worry for the climate" (Østern & Irgens, 2016, p. 7).

This was in 2014. Now, in 2019 as this chapter is being written, the concern for the climate is even more urgent, and so is the worry about migration, democracy, gender equality, and equal rights. This worry has manifested itself in the UN's sustainability goals,[4] with several of these involving the environment, climate, gender equality (goal 5), reduced inequality (goal 10), and peace, justice and strong institutions (goal 16). Action directed at the same concerns is seen in the revised Norwegian national curriculum for pupils aged 6–19, in which three cross-curricular themes will now be emphasised across all subjects: Health and wellbeing, Democracy and citizenship, and Sustainable development.[5] All of this seems to me to call for attention and action in contemporary times, and, in my opinion, also for choreography as action.

## 4 Choreography as Action

Collaboration is at the heart of the choreographic processes in *200 Billion and 1*[6] and *Baby Body*[7] and collaboration was in many ways the main aim of the choreographic exploration. In *Baby Body* I, a creative leader/choreographer, a dancer/choreographer, a musician/composer, and a dramaturg worked actively with a focus on co- in the process. The aim was to develop choreography through co-working with materials, co-creating with one another, and co-choosing artistic choices (Østern & Hovik, 2017). The result was a performance for toddlers.

*200 Billion and 1* was an artistic project within a larger pedagogical research and development project of the same name, focusing on how science, religion and philosophy, and arts could be combined to develop deep education with 13- and 14-year-old children at secondary school. The theme death, decay, and new (biological) life was investigated from the perspectives of biology, religion and philosophy, and arts. The performance *200 Billion and 1* was created in a collaborative team consisting of seven artists from different arts fields, whereas the whole research and development project consisted of a larger team including about 60 pupils, and several teachers, teacher educators, and artists. The results were, in addition to the performance, different cross-curricular pedagogical designs, research presentations, and a book about deep education through a cross-curricular, relational, and artful approach.

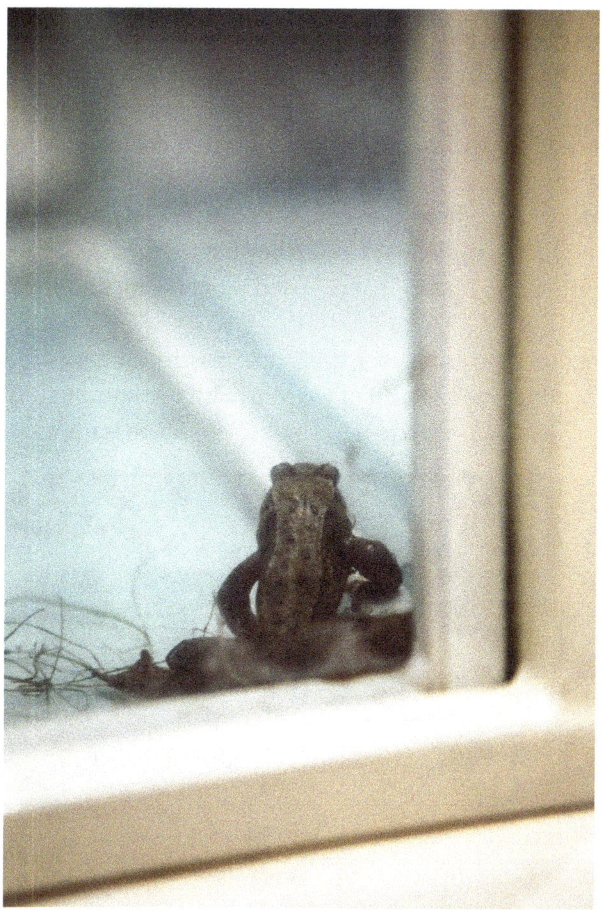

FIGURE 14.1 As part of *200 Billion and 1*, frogs in an aquarium had their own performance. The frogs symbolised the ability to survive the cold and awaken when spring and warmth come. (Photograph by Daniel Almli)

In *Baby Body* and *200 Billion and 1*, I challenged myself to have different choreographic approaches, as creative leader of the projects. This challenge – for me–was to create ruptures in traditional workflows as choreographer, and to distribute ownership, power, and responsibility to the involved (human and non-human) bodies in new ways. Just to take on this challenge, in an outspoken way, I saw a choreography-as-action that demanded an effort from me, and all the others involved. The single most important aspect in this effort is that power is being distributed in different ways in the artistic working structures. The choreographic processes can become empowering in the redistribution of power over artistic working methods and choices.

In *Baby Body* the effort was to try to co-work in all stages of the process, not only with one another but also with the materials, colours, and music (non-human bodies) that we brought into or produced through the process. What does it mean to listen to the colour yellow, for example, in a choreographic process working towards a toddler performance? What does the colour want us to do in terms of movement choices and music composition? This co-working succeeded better in some phases than others, and the dancer and musician said that in those phases where co- worked better, they felt that they contributed as artists more than in other phases that were led more by me (Østern & Hovik, 2017).

*200 Billion and 1* was a different, and larger, project, consisting of creating a performance for a young audience, but also of working with biology and religion around the theme of death, decay, and new (biological) life in school.

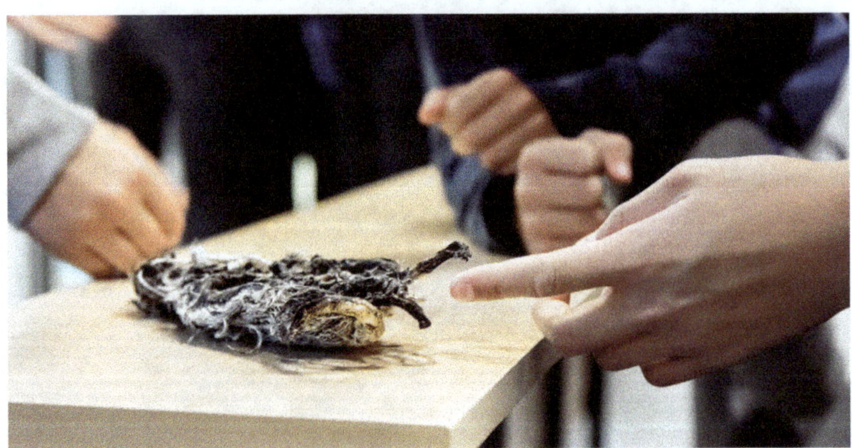

FIGURE 14.2 The school pupils followed a newly dead rat, picked up from the local university hospital labs, through the process of decay. The dead rat's body gave birth to a multiplicity of new life in terms of bacteria, maggots, and flies. (Photograph by Arne Hauge)

Being a (choreographically thinking) leader of the whole project, I understood my task as giving impulses that made new things happen in an entangled context, where things were already happening (Østern, 2019). I, (thinking choreographically), wanted to create movement. The most important thing I did was to give impulses that opened up the other participants' creativity, and to listen to what they gave back to the whole we were creating together.

In a way, choreography as action in *200 Billion and 1* was about creating movement across the whole project and being moved along with the project myself. To me, choreographic thinking in *200 Billion and 1* exceeded the performance production itself. Venke Marie Sortland (2016) has indicated that perhaps there can be choreography where there is no dance since there can be musicality where there is no music. In *200 Billion and 1* I experienced my leadership as project leader for the whole project, including those parts where no dance was happening, as choreographic. This choreographic leadership consisted of creating structures and meeting points for relations, networks, and workflows to become created. In this, movement was made, and power was re-distributed (see Østern, 2019).

## 5 Choreography as Poetic, Pedagogical, and Political Action in Contemporary Times

In *Baby Body* I see how the *poesis* of the performance, the form, is shaped by the artistic, pedagogical, and ethical choice to emphasise *co-* during the whole process. The expression of the performance and the two actors (a dancer and a musician) is performative, not fictional, and this came out of the co-creative process. The actors never enter clear cut roles and do not represent anybody else but themselves on stage, and the play instead takes part *in* and *with* their own bodies. The body becomes *presence* instead of *fiction*. In work with toddlers, a strong fiction and representation can become alienating and even frightening for the very young audience (0–3 years) (Østern & Hovik, 2017). In *Baby Body*, the dancer at certain points in the performance was a chicken, cat and bird, but more as a play with bodily references and sounds, rather than as actual role figures (Østern & Hovik, 2017).

In *200 Billion and 1* the most interesting movement that challenged our ethics happened off-stage. A pupil and her mother got very upset about the fact that a rat was going to be killed[8] and used in a school experiment. The mother wrote e-mails to the whole project group and encouraged upset at the school through the petition LET THE RAT LIVE! This allowed for valuable discussions connected to the subject of religion and philosophy, which in Norwegian schools is mostly about philosophy and ethics as Jesper Aagaard Petersen (2019) has observed. Also living frogs were used in the performance to show how frogs can survive the cold and wake up again when the spring comes. This became an issue of ethical discussion with the teenagers. Given the choice, an overwhelming number of pupils wanted us to put the frogs back into nature when the performance was over. And so, we did; the biologist in the project returned the frogs to a lake in the forest, where they belonged. He documented the return of the frogs through a series of photos and sent the documentation back to the schools for the pupils to see. The pupils' engagement secured a life in their natural environment for the frogs after the performance period.

As a result of (and at the same time starting points for) my diffractions through the choreographic processes described here, I have come to think the following about choreographic processes.[9]

- Choreography in my experience is poetic because is about creating form. *Poesis* in Greek was first a verb, meaning to create. Choreography as poesis is about the forms created, the choices made, and the communicative potential emerging from the work. Choreography as poesis is art.
- Choreography, in my experience, always opens up a pedagogical space. There is a team, and very often a choreographer as leader, or some other kind of choreographic working structure. As soon as a team is trying to create something together, pedagogical aspects like care, ethics, change, upbringing, influence, and power come into play. Choreographers have great influence on others in choreographic processes. Power is active all the time.
- Choreography, in my experience, is political because art communicated in a public sphere is always, on some level, a political statement, even though the theme of investigation is not necessarily a political one. Art is public action, and art, whether intended or not, expresses something about the artists' values and views. Values are being played out in process and product.

## 6 Choreography as Social Action

In asking, "How can choreographic processes be understood as poetic, pedagogical and political action in contemporary times?" I am interested in how choreography can contribute in the world as social action. As a result of the diffractions investigated in this chapter, I propose that for choreography to become social action, it needs to engage actively in what contemporary times are, do, and need. How do contemporary times have agency on choreography as tradition? Contemporary times as a concept may contribute as disturbance and friction in choreographic processes in order to keep choreography alive as action in the world. Contemporary times push choreography out of the studio into exchange with a fragmented, digitalised, migrating, diverse, and innovative world in which it seems important to fight for a sustainable and democratic future. In my experiences with *Baby Body* and *200 Billion and 1*, choreography as action is poetic, pedagogical, and political, all at once, in entangled ways. In this, choreography can contribute not only to artistic, but also to pedagogical and social change. It takes an effort to work with choreography as social action since it is easy to relax into well-known choreographic traditions. Still, in doing so it is equally rewarding to find oneself in a constant state of learning and change.

## Notes

1 https://www.dance-company.no/
2 https://www.ntnu.edu/ilu
3 https://vimeo.com/80257439
4 https://www.un.org/sustainabledevelopment/sustainable-development-goals/
5 https://www.udir.no/laring-og-trivsel/lareplanverket/overordnet-del/prinsipper-for-laring-utvikling-og-danning/tverrfaglige-temaer/
6 See teaser at https://www.dance-company.no/200-milliarder-og-1
7 See teaser at https://www.dance-company.no/baby-body-2017)
8 The rat was killed humanely at the university hospital lab. It had been used for research and was not killed specifically for this school project and would have been killed anyway. The research project followed ethical standards for medical research.
9 See also https://www.dance-company.no/choreography-as-2016-20

## References

Barad, K. (2007). *Meeting the universe halfway: Quantum physics and the entanglement of matter and meaning*. Duke University Press.

Hildebrandt, A. (2013). *The end of choreography*. https://vimeo.com/80257439

Joy, J. (2014). *The choreographic*. The MIT Press.

Leavy, P. (2018). Introduction to arts-based research. In P. Leavy (Ed.), *Handbook of arts-based research* (pp. 3–12). The Guilford Press.

Østern, T. P., & Irgens, E. J. (2016). Interfering with the lived field of dance pedagogy from organizational and leadership studies perspectives: An explorative intervention with performing and teaching dance artists. *Research in Dance Education*, 1–17. https://doi.org/10.1080/14647893.2015.1124079

Østern, T. P., & Hovik, L. (2017). Med-koreografi og med-dramaturgi som diffraksjon—med som metodologisk agent for skapende og forskende prosesser i Baby Body [Co-choreography and co-dramaturgy as diffraction: Co- as methodological agent for creative and researching processes in Baby Body]. *Journal for Research in Arts and Sports Education, Special issue "Å forske med kunsten"* [Doing research with the arts], *1*(5), 43–58. http://dx.doi.org/10.23865/jased.v1.906

Østern, T. P. (2018). Koreografididaktiske sammenfiltringer/Choreographic-pedagogical entanglements. In S. Styve Holte, A.-C. Kongsness, & V. M. Sorland (Eds.), *Koreografi/Choreography 2018* (pp. 24–30). Colophon.

Østern, T. P. (2019). Kunstfag og koreografi distribuert som meningsskapende mulighet i en flerfaglig praksis [Art subjects and choreography distributed as a potential for meaning-making in a cross-curricular practice]. In T. P. Østern, T. Dahl, A. Strømme, J. A. Petersen, A-L. Østern & S. Selander (Eds.), *Dybde//læring—en flerfaglig, relasjonell og skapende tilnærming* [Deep education—a cross-curricular, relational and artful approach] (pp. 135–162). Universitetsforlaget.

Petersen, J. A. (2019). *Religionsfag distribuert som meningsskapende mulighet i en flerfaglig praksis* [Religion and philosophy distributed as a potential for meaning-making in a cross-curricular practice]. In T. P. Østern, T. Dahl, A. Strømme, J. A. Petersen, A.-L. Østern, & S. Selander (Eds.), *Dybde//læring–en flerfaglig, relasjonell og skapende tilnærming* [Deep education: A cross-curricular, relational and artful approach] (pp. 101–134). Universitetsforlaget.

Savin-Baden, M., & Howell Major, C. (2013). *Qualitative research—the essential guide to theory and practice.* Routledge.

Sortland, V. M. (2016). *Arbeidsstrukturer som kritisk praksis* [Working structures as critical practice]. In S. Styve Holte, A.-C, Berg Kongsnes, & R. Borch Skolseg (Eds.), *Koreografi/Choreography* 2016 (pp. 79–86). Redaktørene og forfatterne.

Styve Holte, S. (2016). Koreografens død—spira til ei ny forståing av koreografi [The death of the choreographer: The beginning of a new understanding of choreography]. In S. Øverås Svendal (Ed.), *Bevegelser—Norsk dansekunst i 20 år* [Movements: Norwegian dance arts for 20 years] (pp. 245–267). Skald Forlag.

Vannini, P. (Ed.). *Non-representational methodologies. Re-envisioning research.* Routledge.

CHAPTER 15

# Teaching the Mind-body

## *Integrating Knowledges through Circus Arts*

*Madeline Hoak, Alisan Funk and Dan Berkley*

We, the three authors of this chapter, all come from professional careers in the circus arts. We also have a deep interest in and involvement with our academic domains, including physics, history, and education. We have found that combining circus arts with these traditionally academic subjects in academic institutions has motivated our students to engage with their own learning processes in unique ways. Through our discussions, we have identified three common ways in which students experience agency through the integration of circus practice and academic knowledges. First, students are able to build new knowledge from their domains of comfort into domains of discomfort. Second, combining embodied and academic knowledge expands student access to creative solutions, thereby expanding their knowledge horizons. Third, we notice that the collaboration inherent in the practice of circus arts enables community building, which, in turn, elicits the development of trust in new situations. We see each of these elements as foundational for social change. This chapter situates our findings in relation to theories of creativity that include quotidian, personal discoveries (Beghetto, 2010; Csikszentmihalyi, 1997/2013; Sawyer, 2012) and theories of embodiment that show how the mind and body mutually inform and affect each other (Gallagher, 2006; Steinman, 1995). We further contextualise our findings within the greater conversation of circus arts in education (Cadwell, 2018; Funk, 2018) and the long-term effects of learning arts on the development of other knowledges.

## 1 Defining Circus Arts

Circus arts have undergone many aesthetic, ethical, technical, and cultural transformations in the two hundred years since Philip Astley began producing equestrian spectacles in a thirteen-meter ring (Albrecht, 2006). Although the word circus still conjures up images of clowns, animals, death-defying feats, and sequins, contemporary circus companies, which began forming in the 1960s and 70s, were united by an interest in diversifying the aesthetic, technical, and presentation locations of circus performance as Albrecht (2006) has

 | DOI: 10.1163/9789004442870_015

observed. Continuing to co-exist, traditional and contemporary circus performances are built on the common foundation of what Barlati (n.d.) refers to as the six families of circus activity. Each family describes the type of motor skills a practitioner employs when training in that category: floor acrobatics, aerial acrobatics, balancing, clowning, juggling arts, and equestrian arts. Within these families are individual disciplines, such as trapeze, tight wire, unicycle, and tumbling.

Many contemporary circus artists attend secondary, post-secondary, and university programs for circus performance; they learn circus arts concurrently with general education requirements (Burtt & Lavers, 2017; Funk, 2018, 2019). A number of studies have found that learning circus arts provides a non-competitive context wherein individuality and diversity are valued as each participant develops expertise in a discipline of their choice (Cadwell, 2018). For this reason, circus skills have been used widely to bring together groups of people in at-risk communities through social circus initiatives around the world (Bessone, 2017). We believe that the positive experiences reported by social circus practitioners and educators make circus skills relevant for inclusion in standard academic curricula.

## 2 What We Do

We each have a different approach to integrating circus practice with traditional academic subjects with different age groups and in the context of different learning outcomes. Dan Berkley uses embodied circus experiences to teach introductory physics in secondary schools as a means of engaging students directly with the content. While he values the learning and the acquisition of physics-specific content knowledge, he believes student understanding of the process of science is more important, especially in an era when any fact can be acquired in seconds via the internet. Secondary education in physics is considered a gateway subject because research shows that completing an introductory physics course opens more pathways into science, technology, engineering, and mathematics (STEM) fields and it directly correlates with the likelihood of majoring in a STEM field in college (Feder, 2011). By using embodiment to build more types of knowledge connection to fundamental concepts, Berkley aims to make physics more accessible for students and to provide them with more opportunities to pursue science careers. While the barriers to successful careers faced by underrepresented groups in STEM fields extend beyond access to, and success in, an introductory physics course (Cech & Waidzunas, 2017), the path to those careers often begins in the K–12 classroom (Fries-Britt, Younger, & Hall, 2010). Berkley uses circus in his classroom to try to change the notion that physics is a realm open only to a small, elite population. By using embodiment to build more types of knowledge connection to fundamental concepts, he aims to make physics more accessible for students and to provide them with more opportunities to picture a possible career in science.

Madeline Hoak teaches the physical practice of aerial acrobatics alongside circus history and theory in a single course at undergraduate institutions. In the United States, recreational circus practice is becoming more accessible and widespread, and this has spurred an installation of more formal department-supported classes at the collegiate level. However, recreational circus classes are rarely structured to develop or increase historical knowledge of circus arts or to provoke an interest in its theoretical study. Technical virtuosity does not rely on historical knowledge, so it is extremely important to contextualise the practice in more formal academic settings for the students' benefit and the longevity of the art form (Hoak, 2018). Teaching aerial practice in a university context enables the integration of cultural contexts and circus histories, and this serves to educate students comprehensively.

Alisan Funk is head of the Bachelor program in circus at the Stockholm's University of the Arts. This is a three-year undergraduate course designed to develop and support professional circus artists through intensive discipline training and artistic research (Circus Bachelor, n.d.). The curriculum insists on physical and artistic learning outcomes as the primary expression of accomplishment since this feeds directly into the professional work expected of anyone in a circus arts career (Burtt & Lavers, 2017; Funk, 2019). Unlike most undergraduate programs, traditional academic documentation is given secondary status; writing is required and evaluated, but always in service to the artistic process and professional development of each circus student. Subjects that are traditionally presented in a lecture format, such as anatomy, history, and philosophy, are integrated into practice-based environments in which students can begin quickly to work with the concepts in their own body, circus discipline, and artistic interests to discover where to incorporate the knowledge. Degree programs in circus arts provide an opportunity to explore how knowledge can be transferred in alternative and embodied formats (Funk, 2019).

## 3 Embodied Learning: Building Knowledge across Domains

The nature of the circus as both a popular and commercial art form means that throughout its history practitioners have searched continually for new ideas and inspiration and incorporated these into their acts and presentations. As a living art form, circus is truly interdisciplinary. It draws on the various modes of expertise of athletes, engineers, sociologists, physicists, historians, linguists, designers, and many other professions (Albrecht, 2006). Contemporary circus artists typically have a disciplinary specialty within one or more of the circus arts families, but they also incorporate knowledge from many domains in order to develop performances. These include conceptual, dramaturgical, and scenographic disciplines as Burtt and Lavers (2017) have shown. Professional circus artists are required to engage actively with knowledge across multiple domains, making integrated learning within a circus curriculum essential for the development of professional circus artists. Education in circus universities can center entirely around the practice of circus itself whereas circus concepts taught in traditional university environments must adhere to standardised outcomes required by educational administration. In order to help students conceptualise these standardised objectives through circus arts, Hoak and Berkley use each student's strengths from other more familiar domains.

Hoak believes that a practitioner of any art form must have knowledge of that form's history in order to fully understand their role in the form's present-day context. Therefore, her curriculum blends fundamental aerial techniques and the historical and cultural realities of circus practice. Learning history helps students understand the different physical and environmental risks taken and achievements made by other circus performers throughout different eras. She observes a palpable difference in the classroom after the students have had their first taste of circus history. The students approach the apparatus with more reverence, and they inquire about further historical resources. In addition to situating circus practice within circus history itself, students are required to cross reference circus history events and stories with other academic subjects. Because Hoak's aerial students major in a plethora of subjects, writing assignments and in-class discussions are rich exchanges of ideas and questions with circus studies as an interdisciplinary foundation. Students have connected circus history to gender studies, economics, physics, biology, theater, dance, politics, race relations, marketing, and more. By being exposed to circus history they learn about an exciting field that correlates to many other academic subjects. This engages critical thinking and fosters interdisciplinary research as envisaged by Steinman (1995). The physical practice enlivens the history, and the history imbues the practice with relevance.

At its core, physics is the study of matter and energy. Tying circus techniques to scientific concepts creates a shared embodied experience of the concepts being investigated. In his secondary-level (high school) physics classroom, as advocated by Jackson, Dukerich, and Hestenes (2008), Berkley uses Modeling Instruction, a research-based pedagogy that engages students in the process of science as scientists. Following this pedagogy, instruction begins with observation, thereby reversing the traditional paradigm of lectures followed by laboratory work. For instance, in Berkley's class, students will use the body as a force-sensor while executing introductory acrobatic and juggling skills. This in-class experiment allows students to experience different forces as pushes and pulls on their bodies. They feel and observe the scientific concept of force through the circus activity. This shared experience adds a richness to the definition and discussion of what a force is and what it does, as well as introducing more advanced concepts such as action/reaction force pairs, torque, and angular momentum. Circus serves as the medium that connects the body with the mind providing physics students with a different way to think about how their bodies operate and interact with the world (Gallagher, 2006). By physically experiencing the phenomenon being studied the necessary scientific and mathematical abstractions are grounded in a way that is not strictly intellectual. Through circus, Berkley's students are encouraged to explore the novel and the everyday with their senses while harnessing the mind of a scientist; this shows the students that thought processes from one domain can enhance the knowledge and experience of another. This pedagogy leads to student-led development of both mental and mathematical models of the physical world discovered and internalised through embodied practice.

## 4 Building a Creativity Response

Creativity research looks at how new ideas and concepts are formed. These theories are then used by a society in order to foster creativity with the goal of preparing populations to solve unknown future problems (Sawyer, 2012). Different domains and eras have defined and understood creativity differently. Most contemporary scholars define creativity as an invention that is new to the creator regardless of its novelty to the world. Personal creative achievements are termed small-c creativity, while the term Big-C Creativity is reserved for new ideas that change entire domains, such as psychoanalysis and relativity, or that change societies on a large scale, such as cell phones changing communication methods (Beghetto, 2010; Sawyer, 2012). Big-C creative ideas are the result of many small-c discoveries over time. Creativity exists within every domain; it is just as present and important in engineering and medical science as it is in the arts and humanities. To be considered creative, an idea, small or large, must be original, appropriate, and understandable to others within a domain, because otherwise it cannot be applied. While significant creative inventions are usually conceived of by people with expertise in a domain, inspiration is often drawn from other fields or models of reality

(Csikszentmihalyi, 1997/2013; Sawyer, 2012). Because creativity requires both deep domain knowledge and an understanding of the spectrum of patterns within different disciplines, traditional academic knowledge domains contribute significantly to the development of Big-C Creativity (Beghetto, 2010; Sawyer, 2012). However, the curriculum in many traditional academic settings does not facilitate diverse approaches to a particular topic within the subject itself. While creativity is prized in professional sectors, the tools necessary to develop creatively minded professionals are not typically provided in traditional education structures.

Integrating the exploration of circus techniques into traditional academic domains has the potential to enrich student understanding of the content of those domains because circus is an approachable medium for all bodies and minds. Circus arts encompass a diversity of skills that can be learned by people of nearly any age and any physical ability (Bessone, 2017; Cadwell, 2018). Similarly, circus studies connects with nearly every academic subject, making it an excellent foundation for interdisciplinary studies. Circus naturally fosters diverse approaches to multiple domains. When Berkley's students are embodying physics concepts through the actions of partner acrobatics, weight-sharing, object manipulation, and juggling, they begin from a place of familiarity (their own bodies) to discover and extrapolate from the laws of physics. Their personal experiences become a reference point and a problem-solving strategy that gives them access to developing new ideas from an embodied initiation (Gallagher, 2006). In Hoak's course, students root the development of aerial skills within the diverse cultures and histories of circus arts, and this allows them to practice bringing cultural context to their physical experience. Hoak encourages them to seek the context and histories of other cultural phenomena, and this prompts them to discover connections between those domains and circus, thus activating the habit of quotidian little-c creativity.

Integrating circus arts into a traditional curriculum provides an opportunity to embody concepts through collective creative practices which make space for the development of a student's understanding of different subject areas. This deeper, broader knowledge of academic domains may increase the number of connections students form and the number of patterns they can identify, thereby laying the foundation for both small-c and Big-C discoveries. In Berkley's and Hoak's educational practices, they strive to spark students' curiosity to seek out the greater context and interconnections of any subject matter in order to acquire deeper knowledge in their chosen field. By integrating embodied and conceptual knowledge, they aim to develop students' ability to unearth connections between and among domains that are traditionally separated between body and mind. In this way, they guide their students toward cultivating personal and professional creative intuition.

## 5 Circus Builds Community

Many circus educators have found that the practice of circus arts builds community between and among the participants (Bessone, 2017; Cadwell, 2018). Cadwell describes how learning difficult and often risky collaborative and non-competitive skills in a group builds each student's trust in their own abilities, increases their trust in others, and facilitates the experience of being trusted by others, peers and educators alike. In our own teaching, we have seen how practicing circus arts builds communities through these three areas of trust in frequently surprising and enriching ways.

Framed by these three types of trust, we first see students experience being trusted by others—specifically the educator—to learn difficult skills. Learning acrobatic and aerial technique is physically challenging and sometimes scary. When teachers are able to show that they trust their students to learn difficult skills and to collaborate safely, the students begin to embody being trustworthy (Cadwell, 2018). Being trusted to manage risk leads to increased self-esteem as students accomplish difficult tasks; they develop trust in themselves and their peers.

As they experience being trustworthy, students reciprocate by trusting each other, especially when asked to collaborate on physical skills or creative experiments. For instance, Hoak's students learn to assist their peers in the air, which develops physical trust and activates participation in each other's struggles and successes. Berkley's students work through individual and partner-balance skills that require clear communication between students so they may safely achieve a new skill. In both cases, common language must be agreed upon in order to communicate effectively. Because students are working toward similar physical goals, each has embodied knowledge of how difficult acquiring a skill can be. When a success occurs for an individual student it results in a communal experience of accomplishment, celebration, and pride. Therefore, through common, embodied experiences, participants share a sense of achievement that fosters a positive connection that is unique from other artistic practices or classroom structures. For both Hoak and Berkley, the classroom becomes a microcosm of the social circus movement which has exemplified how circus, as a non-competitive athletic activity, builds community.

Being trusted and learning to trust others enables students to have confidence in their own practice and process. The process of practicing circus arts honors individual contributions toward a group goal. Each person's role is vital, naturally creating respect and connectivity between and among participants. For instance, Berkley's students who identify as scientifically inclined mix with students who may identify as athletes, artists, and/or historians, for example. Together, they use the body as a force-sensor to investigate physics. This becomes a common experience that the entire class can discuss and through which they can bond. Similarly, when circus history is used as a foundation for interdisciplinary studies in Hoak's class, students are able to share individual academic interests and expertise while relating to a common source. Each student is able to make meaningful contributions from within their unique identity, which can lead to the realisation that their strengths are equally vital to the learning process. Students watching each other embody and investigate circus also demonstrates that the different paradigms defining beauty, strength, intelligence, and success can be redefined. When students feel they can contribute their individual perspective towards a collective answer, they become more willing to take intellectual and creative risks. Although their students may not be pushing the boundaries of physics or history, Berkley and Hoak witness their students embracing and valuing their individual strengths within a new domain; this is a realisation that can lead to better engagement, achievement, creativity, and community.

## 6 Conclusion

Since circus has become a contemporary art form, the practice of circus arts has been used effectively with at-risk populations to build self-esteem and community (Bessone, 2017; Cadwell, 2018). Academic work has been integrated into circus schools in order to encourage aesthetic and intellectual engagement for burgeoning circus professionals (Funk 2018, 2019). We have shown that integrating physical circus practices into traditional academic environments has the potential to increase student engagement with subjects by drawing on artistic, physical, collaborative, and creative strategies. Additionally, students can develop the complexity and nuance of individual domains by building on knowledge from a zone of comfort into unfamiliar subject matter and practices. By fostering community building and collaboration based on trust, this integrated approach may enable some students to envision themselves following paths that were previously invisible or inaccessible to them. It may also increase their opportunity to gain the necessary tools for little-c creativity and Big-C Creativity which are foundational skills for individuals and communities to leverage their knowledge and strengths from different domains to solve existing problems with new, constructive solutions. In these ways, circus arts can significantly contribute to envisioning and generating social change.

## References

Albrecht, E. (2006). *The contemporary circus: Art of the spectacular*. Scarecrow Press, Inc.

Barlati, A.-K. (n.d.). *Circus disciplines*. http://ecolenationaledecirque.ca/en/school/circus-disciplines

Beghetto, R. A. (2010). Creativity in the classroom. In J. C. Kaufman & R. Sternberg (Eds.), *The Cambridge handbook of creativity* (pp. 447–463). Cambridge University Press.

Bessone, I. (2017) Social circus as an organised cultural encounter embodied knowledge, trust and creativity at play. *Journal of Intercultural Studies, 38*(6), 651–664. https://doi.org/10.1080/07256868.2017.1379962

Burtt, J., & Lavers, K. (2017). Re-imagining the development of circus artists for the twenty-first century. *Theatre, Dance and Performance Training, 8*(2), 143–155. https://doi.org/10.1080/19443927.2017.1316305

Cadwell, S. J. (2018). Falling together: An examination of trust-building in youth and social circus training. *Theatre, Dance and Performance Training, 9*(1), 19–35. https://doi.org/10.1080/19443927.2017.1384755

Cech, E., & Waidzunas, T. (2017). *STEM inclusion study organization report: American Association of Physics Teachers* (AAPT). University of Michigan.

Circus Bachelor. (n.d.). Circus-bachelor. https://www.uniarts.se/ english/courses/bachelor-programmes/circus-bachelor

Csikszentmihalyi, M. (1997/2013). *Creativity. The psychology of discovery and invention.* Harper Perennial.

Feder, T. (2011). Convincing US states to require physics. *Physics Today, 64*(7), 29–30. https://doi.org/10.1063/pt.3.1163

Fries-Britt, S. L., Younger, T. K., & Hall, W. D. (2010). Lessons from high-achieving students of color in physics. *New Directions for Institutional Research, 2010*(148), 75–83. https://doi.org/10.1002/ir.363

Funk, A. (2018). Gender asymmetry and circus education. *Performance Matters, 4*(1). http://performancematters-thejournal.com/index.php/pm/article/view/149

Funk, A. (2019). Le cirque en équilibre: Les écoles supérieures de cirque au Québec. In *Arts du cirque et spectacle vivant: Les formations en arts du cirque et en activités physiques artistiques* (Vol. 1). ÉPURE—Éditions et Presses universitaires de Reims et CNAC, Centre national des arts du cirque.

Gallagher, S. (2006). *How the body shapes the mind.* Clarendon Press.

Hoak, M. (2018). The risk of circus studies: Mapping the current landscape in US higher education. *CircusTalk*. https://circustalk.com/news/the-risk-of-circus-studies-mapping-the-current-landscape-in-us-higher-education

Jackson, J., Dukerich, L., & Hestenes, D. (2008). Modeling Instruction: An effective model for science education. *Science Educator, 17*(1), 10–17.

Sawyer, R. K. (2012). *Explaining creativity: The science of human innovation* (2nd ed.). Oxford University Press.

Steinman, L. (1995). *The knowing body: The artist as storyteller in contemporary performance*. North Atlantic Books.

CHAPTER 16

# Contemplative Arts-Based Practices in Education

## *Weaving Our Way towards Social and Ecological Justice through Transcultural Storymaking*

*Giang Hoang Le Nguyen, Trinh Ngoc Phuong Bui and Jodi Latremouille*

## 1 Becoming Storymakers

"We are storymakers, not just storytellers. All stories are connected, the new one is woven from the threads of the old" (Wall Kimmerer, 2013, p. 341).

We live in "ecologically sorrowful times" (Jardine, 2015, p. xv) of devastating social and ecological injustice. Characterised by worn–out stories of immense social inequality, rampant destructive corporate capitalism, and ecological destruction, these times also hold the potential to open up possibilities for greater solidarity and powerful change. As storymakers, educators must weave new stories, new ways of being in the world, and new pedagogical practices to allow for these possibilities. Human beings, as intellectual, physical, emotional, and spiritual individuals, may take up the contemplative creative arts to help both teachers and students to understand, live with, and address social and environmental inequities (Wapner, 2016, p. 68).

In this chapter of three woven threads, we bring our diverse ancestries and experiences to a poetic transcultural weaving of the contemplative art genres of Photo–Story, life writing, holistic teaching practices, and creative mindfulness art (Finley, 2008). Given that we understand the importance of reflexive writing, here we discuss the impact of reflexive inquiry in our work oriented towards social and environmental justice.

## 2 Thread One: Being Courageously Holistic: Security, Love, and Discipline

### 2.1 *Jodi*

As a non-Indigenous educator working towards decolonising and more holistic ways of learning and being, I reflect on a contemplative arts-inspired ecological journey from head to heart. Drawing on eco-hermeneutic life writing (Derby, 2015; Hasebe-Ludt, Chambers, & Leggo, 2009), I consider which


DOI: 10.1163/9789004442870_016

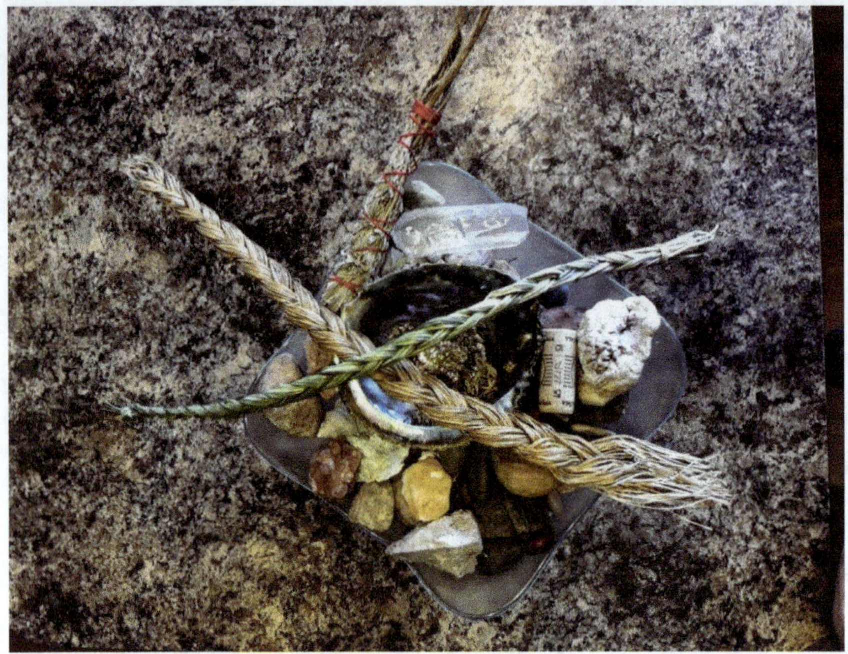

FIGURE 16.1 "Security, Love, and Discipline: Braided Ways of Knowing." (Photograph by Jodi Latremouille)

courageously holistic teaching practices might be called for in these times of ecological and social upheaval.

In Indigenous philosophies and holistic ways of knowing, the divides between the mind and the body, culture and nature, and humans and the earth are false and disruptive to what Leroy Little Bear (2000) has described as cyclical, multiple, and interdependent earthly relationships. In a holistic education course hosted by the University of Alberta, Elder Bob Cardinal shared his principles of Security, Discipline, and Love.[1] Following Little Bear (2000) he encouraged me to embrace a deep cultural shift towards an honest participation in relational Being, as I journey, in Cree terms, *kistikwânihk êsko kitêhk* (from the head to the heart). On this head to heart journey, I interpret Security through the listening circle, Love through the practice of smudging, and Discipline through the braided ways of knowing of the Four Directions. These three principles are incorporated into the image in Figure 16.1. I wonder, "How do I maintain the courage to teach and live in the ways that I know are proper to the earth and all my relations?" These teachings help me as I try to be courageously holistic in my work as a teacher.

Elder Bob Cardinal's teaching about Security came through in the listening circle. We understood, that, like the listening circle, our earth is a nurturing and abundant place (Jensen, 2002). I have taken up the practice of the listening circle in my own M.Ed. classes at Thompson Rivers University. Elder Bob encouraged us to pray in our own way, so I learned to open and close the circle with poetry readings that create a base of trust. In the listening circle, we are asked to participate honestly and slowly, and to listen with open heart-minds.

I experienced Elder Bob's teachings about Love when he shared the smudge. He reminded us to listen in a good way, to see in a good way, to speak in a good way, and to act in a good way. I always finished my smudging by focusing on my heart, because I wanted to love in a good way. David Jardine, following Wendell Berry (2013), says, "[T]he secret goal of education is to fall in love with the world. You can't fall in love with something if you don't know it. And you can't know it if you don't stay put" (D. Jardine, personal communication, October 15, 2015).

Dwayne Donald's reminder that "decolonization is a process of getting to know one another again" (D. Donald, personal communication, February 28, 2014), reminds me of our classes at Thompson Rivers University. My students and I hail from Merritt, Kamloops, Nigeria, Vancouver, China, the Upper Nicola Indian Band, Turkey, India, the Dene Nation, and Vietnam. Together, we read Confucius, Leroy Little Bear, bell hooks, Jeannette Armstrong, Chimamanda Adichie, Paulo Freire, and Al Ghazzali. We read the land, the water, the mountains, and we read each other's histories and philosophies. We try to do this gently and with compassion, even when our stories clash and challenge one another. Elder Bob's smudge reminds me that we can, with love and careful judgment, try to "get to know one another again," as we take care of our places and each other so we can "become who we are" (Chambers, 2008, p. 117).

Elder Bob's teaching of Discipline lives in the braid of the spiritual, intellectual, physical, and emotional ways of knowing of the Four Directions. There is indeed a deep discipline to holistic learning and teaching that cannot be contained within the language of efficiency, measurement, and comparison. Like strands of a braid of sweetgrass, this work has its own sense of rigour that needs to be in proper measure to the earth and our relations.

I have noticed that in education, this holistic work is often seen as a deviation from what is known as the real work, as a luxurious frill, as slightly wild and unmanageable, and neither serious enough nor academic enough. I try to heed the call to a disciplined and honest participation by standing up for this work with strong and careful words and concepts: spirit; love; ancestors; the great smallness of human beings and our earthly responsibilities; humility; heartbreak; wonder; the wisdom of poetry; and the consciousness of nature.

## 3 Thread Two: Heart-to-Heart Connection through Photo-Story

### 3.1 *Giang Le*

Telling stories through photos builds heart-to-heart connections. Photo-Story, derived from Photovoice methodology, for Wang and Burris (1997), uses a series of connected photos through which people describe their lived or witnessed experiences and perspectives on inequity. As a teacher from the Far East who was a victim and survivor of oppression, I discovered the power of Photo-Story for social change: it can connect people through uniting their memories of injustice.

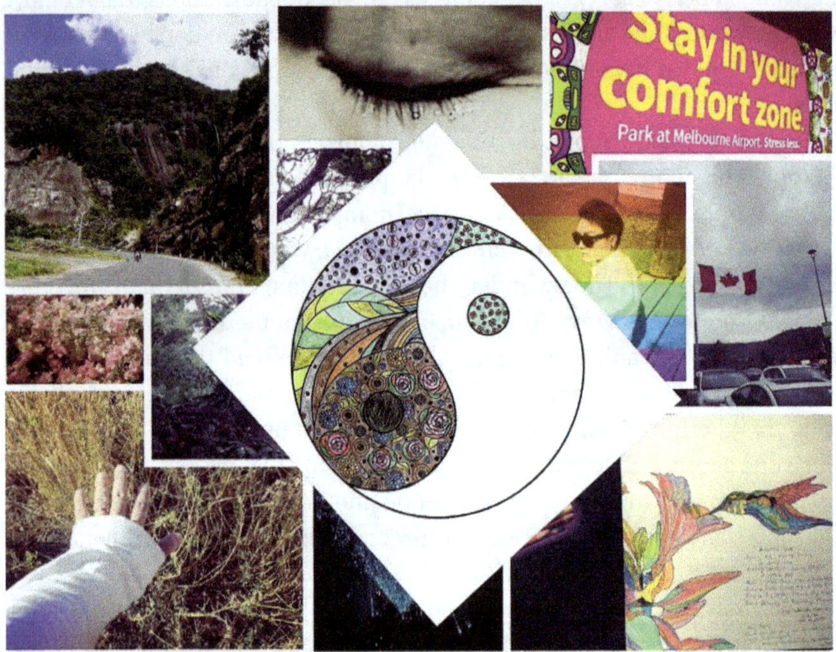


FIGURE 16.2 "A Collage of My Story." (Photographs by Giang Le)

In using Photo-Story, researchers are artists seeking empathic interconnections between themselves and their audience members. Expanding on Photovoice as a visual participatory research method for empowerment, Photo–Story incorporates a balanced inter-weaving of photographs and story-sharing. In a social justice-oriented classroom, Photo-Story visualises a sequence of lived stories woven within the photographs that interpret and give meaning to images. Oppressed people may speak of their experiences of social issues to express crucial community concerns and to amplify their message (Wang & Burris, 1997).

I believe in the power of visual arts as effecting spiritual connection that helps people explore their deepest psychological corners. Visual arts can open these spaces and relieve some of the pain we all suffer through social injustice. Photo-Story as a pedagogy opens up an arts-creating space for teachers and students to co-explore; the boundaries between knowledge holders and receivers are blurred. This approach may enliven student interest and curiosity, help navigate the spontaneous ebb and flow of teaching and learning, and ignite an imaginary for social change.

I share an example of Photo-Story to tell my lived experiences as a child with divergent gender identity born in a traditional Vietnamese family, an oppressed student, and a marginalised teacher in the academic workplace. Through the collage of photos gathered from painful memories, I can see and read the stories in each picture: they are full of hatred, bliss, laughter, freedom, and fetters. I re-experience and learn to live with all these feelings; I come to understand and accept them to be vulnerable parts of my life. The wounds are healed, and my soul settles into peacefulness.

A collage of my photos tells my own story from childhood to adulthood (see Figure 16.2). I was born in a small area of central Vietnam where people did not have a good understanding of difference regarding gender, race, and religion, such as LGBTQ+. I always had to hide my divergent gender identity and was afraid of standing outside my comfort zone. Growing up, I started to explore the world outside bravely, travelling to different countries and especially studying abroad. I came to Canada, where my epistemology and ontology have changed.

I have come to know that I am not so different or alone in this world, and there are no reasons for continuing to hide what I think of as my true self. I am proud of being born different since the difference is the root of my power for social change. I borrow the Tai Chi symbol from Taoism, indicating yin yang, two contrary forces, but also complementary, interconnected, and interdependent in the natural world as Taylor and Choy (2005) have shown. They are not two but a unity of balanced power. I incorporate the Tai Chi symbol with my personal imagination of a harmonious cohabitation of yin yang coloured by what I have experienced, acquired, and believed.

## 4 Thread Three: Learning through Meditative Art

### 4.1 *Trinh Bui*

The art-making process evokes creativity, reflective, empathetic, and emotional responses (Dewey, 1919; Eisner, 2002) that can lead to meaningful learning experiences (Dewey, 1934; Vygotsky, 1971). Recognising the universal aspect of attentive, compassionate, and joyful art-making and mindfulness practice, I use meditative drawing as a way to observe the world, and to recognise patterns that lead to social and ecological injustice and, thus, following Hanh (1991) and Smith (2014), to cultivate knowledge for change.

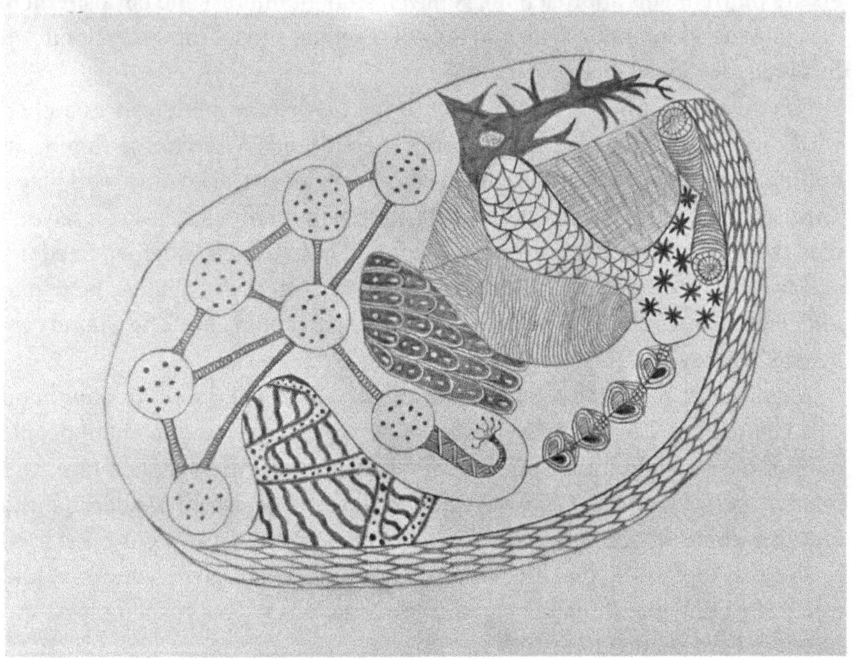

FIGURE 16.3 "The World Cell." (Drawing by Trinh Bui)

The story emerges from my own experience as a student and a young professional in the educational field. In the Vietnamese education system, art is extracurricular and accessible only to the talented students. I was considered an average student and did not get the chance to learn about it. Fortunately, in a course entitled Psychology of Art, art captured my interest as a young undergraduate student. My instructor, who is very passionate about observing and admiring different types of art, told us about its application in therapy, entertainment, and philosophy. Nevertheless, throughout the course, never once were we asked to create our artwork or showcase any performance art forms. Art still felt like a private club reserved only for the ones with talent and something that we, as regular students, should learn about only by respectfully gazing from afar.

When I moved to Canada, I had a chance to use creativity and aesthetic expression to represent my knowledge and, therefore, to include art in my critical and reflective thinking and learning process. In the Master of Education program at Thompson Rivers University, we were encouraged to explore multiple approaches to conceptualising and interpreting knowledge including drawing, life writing, poetry making, rapping, blogging, photography, crafting, and so on. I experienced the "the natural form of education" (Read, 1943, p. 207) that contains the activities for self-expression, observation, and appreciation. Art and craft making is a full-body experience that connects our body, mind, and soul holistically.

I remembered returning to the streets of Ho Chi Minh City as an adult, unable to spot the blue sky from my childhood because it had been taken over by a thick greyish smoke. I saw a group of high school students hold a beautiful picture of the earth with the sign saying "Save the Earth, Do Not Litter." I listened to the children as they talked passionately about how we can each do our part in saving the planet and explained how Vietnam is being polluted by industrialisation. Artistic expression can be a powerful instrument for learning because it requires profound observation, allows self-expression, but also inspires a sense of appreciation and responsibility for the world, thus inspiring people to protect and preserve what they love.

I remember attending a troubling lecture on social justice issues during the second year of the master's degree program that shook my mind, body, and soul. I felt an urge to do something with the new knowledge, so I picked up a pencil and started drawing. I experienced a period and space of being absolutely present during which my mind took the noise of anger and shifted it into silence, stimulating a profound easing of tension and a feeling of love and compassion. This resulted in my drawing shown in Figure 16.3. The spark of joy permeated every sense of my being. This state was similar to my experiences of meditating on a cushion, surrounded by the aroma of Agarwood incense. I did some research and found that I was engaging in meditative drawing, unknowingly yet mindfully at the same time. I have continued to use meditative drawing to translate my social and ecological thoughts and perspective in a mindful manner ever since that incident.

At Thompson Rivers University, we teach every new international student about social and environmental etiquette during orientation sessions about intercultural learning and sustainability. There is a need to educate students about the diverse Canadian culture, and the sustainability officer speaks a sustainable mantra of reducing, reusing, and recycling plastic. The message is clear: it is essential for everyone to get along and know how to recycle. They always start with a standard lecture and end with a series of quick quizzes using a fun digital program. While most students pay attention to this critical information, I cannot help but wonder about a creative way to cultivate such knowledge. What if we asked the students to create something with this information? Perhaps, giving students a creative task could make them feel a sense of appreciation and responsibility for the place and community they are coming into. Rather than using a reward system to help students memorise facts, we could engage in a collaborative and mindful art-making activity aimed at gaining a much more meaningful understanding of diversity and sustainability.

## 5 Keeping the Ends Out: Weaving Our Way towards Social and Ecological Justice

### 5.1 *Jodi*

The teachings that Elder Bob shared with us have given me the language to see the security, the love, and the discipline in this work, proper to the land, the places, the stories, the elders, the more-than-human beings with whom we live together. How do I maintain the courage to teach and live holistically in the ways that I know are proper to the earth and to all my relations?

### 5.2 *Giang Le*

I am transformed from the oppressed to the courageous. From aesthetics to self-consciousness, I construct an art-creating space for myself; I give freedom and authority to my artistic character as I more fully embody who I am, and what I feel. I learn to draw power from the photos that capture every meaningful moment of my life and other lives. There are always stories to tell in those photos, and I believe in them. With them, I can connect my thoughts, my feelings, and my stories with others. At that moment of aesthetic connection, I am the artist of my photos but also a reader of my audience's stories. We are connected through art and story-sharing.

### 5.3 *Trinh Bui*

Maybe with a little hope, we can use mindfulness art as an agent to engage meaningfully in ecological and social justice education. To build a socially and environmentally conscious generation, institutions must encourage students to participate in actively creating their knowledge through an art–based approach instead of passively receiving information from lecturers and speakers. Learning and creativity complement each other, and the addition of the mindfulness practice gives way to a critical and embodied understanding of the world.

Following Kahlo's (2000) words, "I never paint dreams or nightmares. I paint my own reality" (p. 91), we as educators with our students may inquire into our lived realities, our assumptions, our challenges, fears, and questions. We can keep the ends of our braid out, open to new understandings, open to dialogue and active responses. Through these arts-based contemplative inquiries, we become transcultural *storymakers* in our work towards deeper, more meaningful, and more possible stories of social and ecological justice.

## Note

1 I gratefully acknowledge Elder Bob Cardinal of the Enoch Cree Nation, and thank him for permission to print excerpts from the oral teachings that he shared, and his ongoing and generous support of all the work stemming from the 2014 course that he co-taught with Dr. Dwayne Donald, entitled "Holistic Understandings of Learning."

## References


Chambers, C. M. (2008). Where are we? Finding common ground in a curriculum of place. *Journal of the Canadian Association for Curriculum Studies, 6*(2), 113–129.

Derby, M. (2015). *Place, being, resonance: A critical eco-hermeneutic approach to education.* Peter Lang. https://doi.org/10.3726/978-1-4539-1656-8

Dewey, J. (1919). Imagination and expression. *Teachers College Bulletin, 10*(10), 7–15. https://doi.org/10.1177/002205741909001602

Dewey, J. (1934). *Art as experience.* Perigee Books. https://doi.org/10.2307/2016688

Eisner, E. (2002). *The arts and the creation of mind.* Yale University Press.

Finley, S. (2008). Arts-based research. In G. Knowles & A. L. Coles (Eds.), *Handbook of the arts in qualitative research: Perspectives, methodologies, examples, and issues* (pp. 71–81). Sage Publications. https://doi.org/10.4135/9781452226545.n6

Hanh, T. N. (1991). *The miracle of mindfulness: A manual on meditation.* Random House.

Hasebe-Ludt, E., Chambers, C. M., & Leggo, C. (2009). *Life writing and literary métissage as an ethos for our times.* Peter Lang.

Jardine, D. W. (2015). Introduction: How to love black snow. In M. Derby (Ed.), *Place, being, resonance: A critical eco-hermeneutic approach to education* (pp. xv–xviii). Peter Lang.

Jensen, D. (2002). *Listening to the land: Conversations about nature, culture, eros.* Chelsea Green.

Kahlo, F. (2000). Frida Kahlo 1907–1954: Life and work. In A. Kettenmann, & F. Kahlo (Eds). *Frida Kahlo, 1907–1954: Pain and passion* (pp. 92–94). Taschen. https://doi.org/10.1016/b978-0-12-375038-9.00255-7

Little Bear, L. (2000). Jagged worldviews colliding. In M. Battiste (Ed.), *Reclaiming indigenous voice and vision* (pp. 77–85). University of British Columbia Press.

Read, H. (1943). *Education through art*. Faber and Faber.

Smith, D. (2014). *Teaching as the practice of wisdom* (Vol. 5). Bloomsbury Publishing USA.

Taylor, R. L., & Choy, H. Y. F. (2005). *The illustrated encyclopedia of Confucianism* (Vol. 1.). The Rosen Publishing Group.

Vygotsky, L. (1971). *Psikhologiia Iskusstva* (The psychology of art) (I. Scripta Technica Trans.). The MIT Press.

Wall Kimmerer, R. (2013). *Braiding sweetgrass: Indigenous wisdom, scientific knowledge, and the teachings of plants*. Milkweed Editions. https://doi.org/10.5840/envirophil201613137

Wang, C. C., & Burris, M. (1997). Photovoice: Concept, methodology, and use for participatory needs assessment. *Health Education and Behavior*, 24(3), 369–387. https://doi.org/10.1177/109019819702400309

Wapner, P. (2016). Contemplative environmental studies: Pedagogy for self and planet. *The Journal of Contemplative Inquiry*, 3(1), 67–83.

CHAPTER 17

# The Generative Act of Critical Pedagogy

## *Animating Children's Books and Games as Research Practice*

*Sue Uhlig, Amy Migliore and Jacqueline Reid-Walsh*

## 1 Animation as Participatory Education

In this chapter we link the act of critical pedagogy with the creative generation of ideas by sharing projects that derived from a graduate course on children's books and toys that Jacqueline Reid-Walsh taught in the College of Education. The projects were constructed in response to a playful challenge, to a discussion of which we will return presently, that Reid-Walsh issues to all her graduate classes. The term that she uses to refer to her critical, engaged, and creative pedagogy is "animation."

In English, the term animation has been used variously over the centuries to refer to the state of being alive, being lively, and being enthusiastic, but its current context is connected to a specific type of art and film that uses cartoons and movement to convey often humorous events. For example, the online *Oxford English Dictionary* defines the term as "the technique of photographing successive drawings or positions of puppets or models to create an illusion of movement when the film is shown as a sequence" hence we refer to an "animated" cartoon or film ("Annimation", n.d.). Reid-Walsh returns to earlier meanings of the term to emphasise the notion of animation as connected to creative thinking and practice, and to French usage where these activities often occur in groups.

Reid-Walsh has adapted these definitions to refer to the class activity of using techniques to enable active participation by members of a group to enhance our collective knowledge. This is her challenge.

She links this strategy to a pedagogy based on Paulo Freire's notion of emancipatory critical, participatory education which is the opposite of a stifling banking education. Described initially in his *Pedagogy of the oppressed* (2000), a participatory, engaged pedagogy was adopted later by feminist educators such as bell hooks in her *Teaching to transgress: Education as the practice of freedom* (1994) and remains important to liberatory pedagogies. The aim of an animation is to encourage critical interrogation of new, or, perhaps, all too familiar topics. Reid-Walsh also links the term to a set of possible practices in class. For her, an animation is the opposite of a lecture or formal presentation. It may take any form of interactive and/or creative activity, such as making a


DOI: 10.1163/9789004442870_017

piece of art, playing a game, staging a performance, and so on. The aim is to provoke our thinking individually and collectively. Since an animation should challenge and stimulate our thinking on the topic or issue under investigation in some way, an animator may use any creative or scholarly strategy they see fit. Amy Migliore and Sue Uhlig discuss how they seized on the challenge and created memorable and provocative arts-based engagements that have had an afterlife in their dissertation work.

## 2 Animation on the Un-Snap Chat: A Generative Approach to Transformative Dialogue

### 2.1 *Amy Migliore*

The Un-Snap Chat animation is designed to provoke authentic conversation and build empathy with others through a creative encounter. As a participatory activity, it is designed to encourage partners to engage in reflective sharing and active listening. While these practices are common to many diversity awareness activities, Un-Snap Chat seeks to enhance the dimensionality of the encounter by adding a generative visual activity. People are asked to engage with other participants who are unfamiliar to them. The partners are then encouraged to re-examine stereotypes and generate strength-based portraits of each other as a reflective/reflexive act. The concept of the Un-Snap Chat resulted from a number of ideas based on the generative theories of art practice as an informing and transformative method of research (Sullivan, 2010) and strengths-based practices rooted in the field of positive psychology (Seligman & Csikszentmihalyi, 2000).

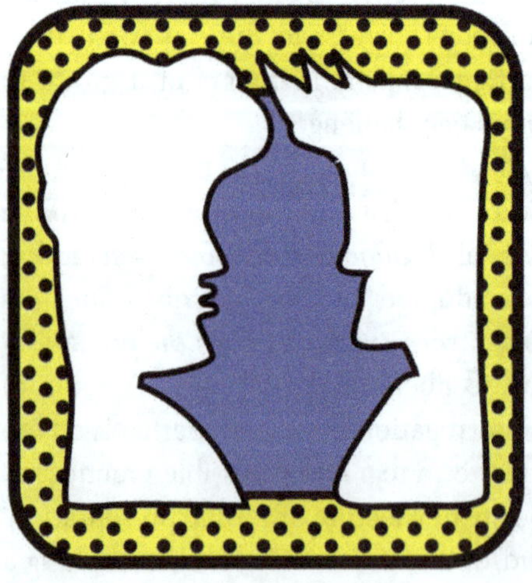

FIGURE 17.1
Un-Snap Chat (Amy Migliore, 2018)

My approach in creating this animation was to combine the generative actions of art practice with the positive psychological views of focusing on strengths and re-mixing those with the diversity awareness activity "Circles of my multicultural self" by Paul C. Gorski (n.d.).

I sought to cultivate a generative and interactive space in which individuals could listen, reflect, and visually see another's strengths. In the Un-Snap Chat animation, partners share the perception that is typically imposed on them by others based on how their gender, clothes, lifestyle, skin color, family of origin, and other identifying factors are perceived. Participants are encouraged to share, listen, see the other, and then share back to their partner through a visual. In this way, the reflective/reflexive loop is extended to include a multidimensional component of making and looking again through imagery. By following the guide and question prompts, partners will ultimately re-imagine the other person through a visual portrait. The newly generated image should focus on the strengths and authenticity of the partner's voice and her reality.

TABLE 17.1 Un-Snap question prompts and activity guide

| | **Question prompts & guides for Un-Snap Chat** |
|---|---|
| 1. | On the back of the chat card, individually list five identifiers that you feel are important parts of your life story (such as mother, professor, artist, friend …). |
| 2. | Reflect on a time when you were proud to claim one of these identifiers and a time when it was painful or embarrassing to be associated with the perceptions of others of that identifier. |
| 3. | Describe a stereotype about that identifier that seems to be overused by others. Think of ways to re-frame that perception of your identity to make it more accurately fit your reality. |
| 4. | RE-FRAME yourself by starting with the phrase: "I am a/an __(personally chosen identifier)__, but I am NOT a/an __(imposed stereotype)____" |
| 5. | Interact with a partner that you do not know well and take turns sharing several of your re-framed identities with each other. |
| 6. | After listening actively to each other, imagine a new snapshot of the other person whom you have just encountered, and doodle a visual to represent their re-framed identity. (Be imaginative with your representation. The portrait does not need to be recognisable. You might choose to add arrows, notes, and symbols to represent your encounter with this person or make an abstract design of colours and patterns to represent what you heard and remember of them.) |
| 7. | Share your image with your partner and then listen to/watch their response. What did you capture, hear, or see that was important to the other person? |

Why might an animation like this be necessary or worth the time and energy it takes to engage with another who is different? In her book *The Strength Switch*, Lea Waters (2017) has argued that our brains are predisposed to a negativity bias towards differences, but this can be ameliorated through the intentional focus of switching the way we perceive, talk to, and think about others.

Today's emergent globalisation and interaction of cultures holds promise of incredible collaboration with world and local neighbors, but how then does our habit of being alarmed at differences impact those emerging diverse relationships? If left unaddressed, the lingering negativity bias in our brain could become dangerous to newly forming 21st-century communities because the perceptions of an old evolutionary brain may interpret the unfamiliar, such as another's religious beliefs, cultural or ethnic background, and other defining qualities, as an invisible predator. Waters (2017) has argued that

> [f]or the situations we encounter today—which usually demand complex reasoning and problem solving, sophisticated cooperation and communication, reserves of persistence, or expert facility in a specific skill—the negativity bias can put us at a disadvantage because it blinds us to opportunities, keeps us from seeing the larger picture, and bars access to the expansive thinking that unlocks innovation, collaboration, adaptability, growth, success, and fulfillment. (p. 8)

For all the benefits Waters has listed that help us meet our changing global community, it seems critical to provoke change intentionally through creative and critical acts of engagement with our neighbors. Intentional practices are needed to re-frame our image of the other and examine critically the lenses we use to see the world. As Waters (2017) has suggested, "Attention on the negative helped us survive. Attention on the positive helps us thrive" (p. 9).

In our graduate classes with Reid-Walsh, we investigated creative ways of re-framing through story, image, and play. The Un-Snap Chat animation is intended to be an encounter of participatory play with others and to be an active listener and engage long enough with another and through visuals to see that person not only as different, but differently. While this activity interprets ideas from commonly played ice-breaker games and other team-building activities, there is an added generative component. In their review of art practices used in research, Marshall and D'Adamo (2011) advocate for the powerful contributions made by generating responses and conducting research in visual ways. According to them,

> Visual imagery sets the stage for vicarious, empathetic experiences that generate deep empathetic understandings (Eisner, 2008; Leavy, 2009)

> and raise consciousness (Leavy, 2009; Weber, 2008). Visual Imagery is particularly suited for this because it is captivating and evocative; it grabs attention in powerful aesthetic ways (Leavy, 2009; Weber, 2008). (p. 13)

The Un-Snap Chat requires participants to portray their partner through symbolic references visually. Partners generate imagery to represent each other. Often, artists notice the nuances present in another's speech, words, and body language, so the visually generated meanings are both reflexive and projective. "These meanings are determined not only by the artist, but also by the viewer (Leavy, 2009; Sullivan, 2010; Weber, 2008)" (Marshall and D'Adamo, 2011, p. 13). By adding the important visual component to this type of engaging activity, the reflective/reflexive loop is activated in the in-between space of participants. This in-between and multidimensional space holds great promise for transformative dialogs and insight.

## 3 Animation on a Sense of Place: Critical Placemaking through Making

### 3.1 *Sue Uhlig*

A Sense of Place is an activity kit based on geography and place in which learners engage with place-based ephemera through creative play and exploration. Accompanying the activity box is an in-class animation that focuses on individual narratives of place and memory. In the activity box and the animation, critical placemaking is examined through ephemera, handmade books, and related creative activities inspired by children's books, toys, and activity sets from the 18th and 19th centuries which we examined in the special collections library during the course.

In her book *The lure of the local: Senses of place in a multicentered society* (1997), cultural critic and artist Lucy Lippard stresses the importance of place through a carefully curated collection of pieces of contemporary art and historical narratives, as well as through geographical and cultural context. Lippard has contended that artists can make the issues and concerns of place visible to others through art. Artwork, places, and sites of learning can also be considered pedagogical and relational (Ellsworth, 2005). In this project and animation, I consider ways in which a collection of place-based ephemera set in a bookmaking activity kit can foster pedagogical sites of critical placemaking by the learner in the making.

I interrogated my own understanding of place by traveling to three large cities in the United States over one semester. To document my own sense of placemaking, I walked as research methodology, took numerous photographs of objects of and in place, and collected objects and ephemera in each location. Ephemera, such as print materials, tourist brochures, postcards, and pamphlets are important to the activity kit since these items present what Darts (2004) would consider a culture jamming of traditional consumerist culture because of their creative employment of everyday materials used as resistance and disruption. The activities move beyond passive consumption of consumerist culture to being actively engaged with the place-based ephemera, altering the images so that they take the place of the places depicted.

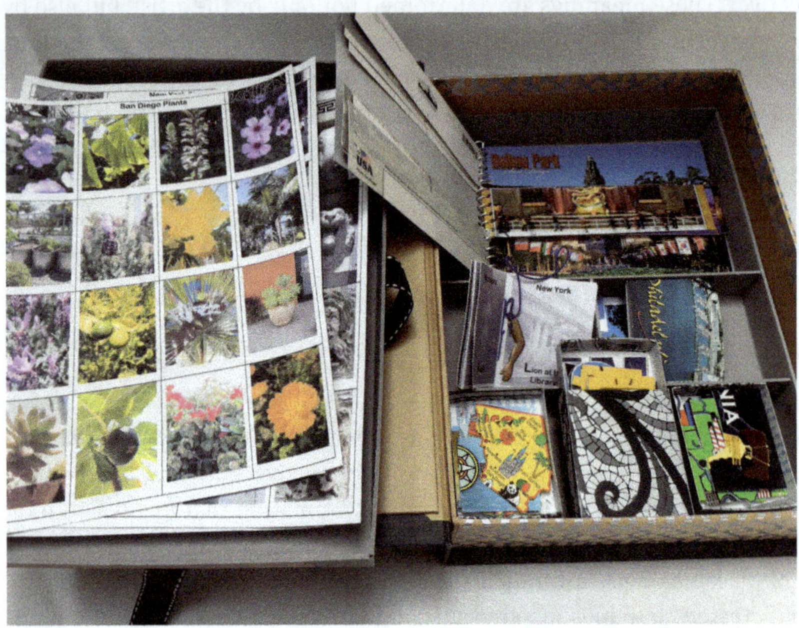


FIGURE 17.2 A Sense of Place Activity Kit (Sue Uhlig)

In the "A Sense of Place" activity kit, activities are housed in a book-like box, with a gray cover and spine and a decorative pattern on the recessed side of it. Inside are two layers of trays that contain art materials and five different activities that are based on the historical children's books, toys, and games seen in the archives and read about in class. The top tray contains two sets of sixteen images from each from three US cities. The images are themed according to what I noticed was in abundance in each city. There are examples of New York visual culture and signs, grotesque sculptural figures found in the historical architecture of Philadelphia, and the abundant plants and flowers that are found throughout San Diego. The format of these sheets is based on lottery sheets, which are, historically, "a type of print for children" that contain "small engravings covered with little pictures laid out in rows" (Immel, 2005, p. 66) and were first available for purchase in the late 17th century. Lottery sheets are also known as "catchpenny prints" (see The Memory of the Netherlands, n.d.; LaPlantz, 2001) since these were inexpensive printed graphics readily available for the consumer market that children used to make a scrapbook of images as Immel (2005) has reminded us. The lottery sheets in this activity box also act as ephemera and are intended to be used creatively; they may be cut, pasted, drawn on, used to create a story, and as material for a collage.

The bottom tray of the activity box contains four different activities: an abecedary, a horizontal myriorama, three blank books, and three place puzzles. The abecedary is a 24-page alphabet book that explores characteristics of urban environments through photographs representing each letter of the alphabet. It is in a chapbook format, which means that the book was printed front and back on one single sheet of paper, cut, and then bound. Traditionally, chapbooks were made using inexpensive materials and processes so the books could be sold cheaply to the masses (Department of Rare Books and Special Collections, 2002). A myriorama is a "moveable picture" that consists of a set of cards depicting landscape vistas, which may be then be combined in various ways to form an infinite number of different views (Jerden, 1824, p. 14). Typically, myriorama are vertical segments, but, in my activity kit, they are aligned horizontally to accommodate nine postcards which are cut into three segments each and are spiral bound. This allows the participant to move the segments to create new landscapes with characteristics from the three cities. On the back, the postcard format encourages writing, which can also change depending upon how the cards are turned. Miniature blank books made in a matchbook format have covers made with postcards. Instructions on how to create these easy-to-make books (based on McCafferty, 2012) are included in the activity kit so more books can be made and enjoyed for future exploration and creative use. Three boxes shaped like matchboxes each hold a postcard puzzle of one of the three cities. The historical reference to these place puzzles is from the dissected maps of John Spilsbury and others beginning in the mid- to late-18th century intended to be entertaining yet also educational to teach geography (Norgate, 2007).

The accompanying animation conducted in class focused on critical placemaking and memory through bookmaking. Learners made matchboxes and matchbooks to house visual and material objects to show their understanding, experience, narratives, and cultural context of place(s) important to them. To further the connection of critical placemaking and storytelling, the children's book, The Matchbox Diary (Fleischman & Ibatoulline, 2013) accompanies the animation. In *The Matchbox Diary*, a grandfather's immigration story of coming to the United States from Italy is told through a collection of objects set in a series of matchbooks. In this way, objects, images, and books open up possibilities to help tell layered narratives of human geography.

## 4 Conclusion

As can be seen, each animation is a generative act of critical pedagogy that opens up possibilities for serious reflection in a playful, hands-on context. In both the Un-Snap Chat activity and the Sense of Place activity, different visual and tangible art methods from the past and present are used to engage all the class members in critical making projects. These require the participants to reflect on the issues involved, make a project using the specified guidelines, and use the handmade product as a means to examine the topic under investigation. By doing animations such as these, not just discussing a topic, all the class-members engage in participatory learning within a safe, creative, and critical space.

## References

Animation. (n.d.). *OED Online*. Oxford University Press. https://www.oed.com/view/Entry/7785?redirectedFrom=animation&

Darts, D. (2004). Visual culture jam: Art, pedagogy, and creative resistance. *Studies in Art Education, 45*(4), 313–327.

Department of Rare Books and Special Collections. (2002). *What is a chapbook?* University of South Carolina. http://library.sc.edu/spcoll/britlit/cbooks/cbook1.html

Ellsworth, E. (2005). *Places of learning: Media, architecture, pedagogy*. Routledge.

Fleischman, P., & Ibatoulline, B. (Illustrator). (2013). *The matchbox diary*. Candlewick Press.

Freire, P. (2000). *Pedagogy of the oppressed* (30th anniversary edition.) Continuum International Publishing Group.

Gorski, P. (n.d.). *Circles of my multicultural self.* http://www.edchange.org/multicultural/activities/circlesofself_handout.html

hooks, b. (1994). *Teaching to transgress: Education as the practice of freedom*. Routledge.

Immel, A. (2005). Frederick Lock's scrapbook: Patterns in the pictures and writing in the margins. *The Lion and the Unicorn, 29*, 65–86.

Jerdan, W. (Ed.). (1824). The myriorama, or many thousand views. *The Literary Gazette: A Weekly Journal of Literature, Science, and the Fine Arts*. https://babel.hathitrust.org/cgi/pt?id=mdp.39015033904775&view=1up&seq=22

LaPlantz, S. (2001). *The art and craft of handmade books*. Lark Books.

Lippard, L. (1997). *The lure of the local: Senses of place in a multicentered society*. New Press.

Marshall, J., & D'Adamo, K. (2011). Art practice as research in the classroom: A new paradigm in art education. *Art Education, 64*, 5, 12–18.

McCafferty, K. (2012). *Making mini books: Big ideas for 30+ little projects*. Lark Crafts.

Norgate, M. (2007). Dissected maps and the origins of the jigsaw puzzle. *The Cartographic Journal, 44*(4), 342–350.

Seligman, M., & Csikszentmihalyi, M., (2000). Positive psychology: An introduction. *American Psychologist, 55*, 5–14.

Sullivan, G. (2010). *Art practice as research: Inquiry in visual arts*. Sage Publications.

The Memory of the Netherlands. (n.d.) *Catchpenny prints from the Koninklijke Bibliotheek: What are catchpenny prints?* https://geheugen.delpher.nl/en/geheugen/pages/collectie/Centsprenten+van+de+Koninklijke+Bibliotheek/Wat+zijn+centsprenten

Waters, L. (2017). *The strength switch*. Penguin Random House Australia.

# PART 3

## *Teaching & Pedagogy*

∵

CHAPTER 18

# Our Words Flowing into Wide Futures

## *Making a Difference through Poetic Professional Learning*

*Kathleen Pithouse-Morgan*

## 1 Starting with My Self

I am a white South African who was born and grew up during apartheid. I qualified as a teacher in 1995, the year after South Africa's first democratic elections and I have now been teaching for 25 years, first as a schoolteacher and then as a university-based teacher educator. Currently, I teach graduate modules and supervise graduate students' research in the specialisation of teacher development studies at a South African university. My students are teachers with varied educational backgrounds, teaching different subjects in schools and higher education institutions. During the apartheid era (1948–1994), most of them would have been racially classified as African, Indian, or coloured.

My academic work is located in professional learning, with a focus on teachers' self-directed learning, undertaken in dialogue with others. In line with the views of Webster-Wright (2009), I am drawn to understandings of professional learning that emphasise how teachers and other professionals can develop vital insights into their own personal and professional selves and practise to bring about change for the better. My scholarship is grounded in professional learning for teachers and teacher educators and has extended into research on polyvocal professional learning across disciplines in higher education (Pithouse-Morgan & Samaras, 2015).

In conceptualising polyvocal professional learning, Samaras and I have built on Mikhail Bakhtin's (1984) in-depth analysis of polyvocality (which he called polyphony) as a narrative approach in the fiction of Fyodor Dostoevsky, who interplayed distinct voices and viewpoints in his writing. Our multifaceted conceptualisation of polyvocal professional learning, epitomised by plurality, interaction and interdependence, and creative activity, is inspired by heterogeneous bodies of knowledge and is characterised by a pluralism of ways of knowing, doing, and communicating (Pithouse-Morgan & Samaras, 2018, 2019).

For the past two decades, I have been studying my own professional learning through self-study and narrative research (see Pithouse, 2005; Pithouse-Morgan, 2019). Through this self-reflexive research, my professional learning

 | DOI: 10.1163/9789004442870_018

has been troubled, deepened, and expanded in critical ways. As a work-in-progress, my teacher self and my teaching practice continue to develop in relationship with students and colleagues.

Through scholarship and teaching, I strive to acknowledge the agency of teachers in lived experiences of professional learning. This emphasis on "teachers as transformative intellectuals" (Giroux, 1988, p. 125) developed in response to my understanding of how authoritarian and technicist apartheid-era teacher training and management continues to constrain South African teachers' professional learning experiences long after the dismantling of apartheid policies (Msibi & McHunu, 2013; Pithouse-Morgan, 2016).

During the apartheid era, the state enforced racial classifications to stratify South African society. A fundamental part of this stratification was a racially segregated education system deliberately aimed at advantaging the white minority and disadvantaging the majority of South Africans (Christie, 1991). Apartheid-era schooling was typified by a "strong behaviourist and non-inquiry ethos" (Henning & van Rensburg, 2002, p. 85). For instance, the teaching of creative writing frequently focused on the reproduction of model essays. Similarly, the teaching of literature and poetry was often confined to the memorisation of model answers and prescribed poems. To illustrate, when Bridget Campbell (2016), a teacher educator of English education in a South African university, asked a class of 54 student teachers about their school-based encounters with poetry, most responded with words such as "horrible," "confusing," and even "torture" (p. 10). They explained that at school they "were not given the opportunity to explore the poems themselves and to form their own opinions as the teachers' ideas and interpretations were imposed on them" (p. 10).

Notwithstanding substantial post-apartheid curriculum policy change, a behaviourist and non-inquiry ethos can still be observed in many South African schools and higher education institutions (Andrews & Osman, 2015; Bharuthram, 2012). With this in mind, I do my utmost to enliven my teaching and research with modes of active inquiry that are informed by "the languages, processes, and forms of literary, visual, and performing arts" (Cole & Knowles, 2008, p. 59). This commitment to the arts is rooted in a love of reading fiction and poetry that was nurtured in my early childhood by my mother (see Pithouse-Morgan, 2019). Also, unlike many South Africans, I am fortunate to have had some very encouraging encounters with the arts at school. For instance, several teachers recognised and nurtured my early interest in creative writing. And, at secondary school, I received merit awards for short story and poetry writing in a prestigious regional creative writing competition. Looking back, I can see how these affirming experiences laid a strong foundation for arts-inspired teaching and research.

## 2 Finding Poetry in Professional Learning

My explorations in self-reflexive and arts-informed research have given rise to a distinctive formulation of poetic professional learning as a literary arts-inspired means of researching and enhancing professional learning (Pithouse-Morgan, 2016; Pithouse-Morgan & Samaras, 2019). I have worked with many others, in South Africa and internationally, to cultivate a portfolio of work that engages the power of poetic inquiry for researching and performing professional learning (Pithouse-Morgan et al., 2015; Pithouse-Morgan, Chisanga, Meyiwa, & Timm, 2018).

Poetic inquiry develops through infusing qualitative research with the imaginative possibilities of poetry (Leggo, 2008). Poetry can be seen to exist on a continuum as Young (1982) has pointed out. Near one end is poetry that can be acknowledged as fulfilling identifiable literary and artistic criteria. Near the other end, playing with poetic language and forms of expression can foster imaginative engagement without necessarily generating poems that demonstrate literary expertise or that have innate artistic merit. My emphasis is on the lived experience of poetry making and poetic communication for the educative purposes of studying and enhancing professional learning.

In this chapter, I show how I looked back over this portfolio of work to inquire about its impetus and impact. I asked, "What difference can poetry make to professional learning?" To respond to the question, I created a "poetic bricolage" (Pithouse-Morgan & Samaras, 2019, p. 5) using words and phrases from nine professional learning poems, composed over a span of five years. Some of these were composed individually and some with others. However, the poems I composed on my own were inspired by the voices and stories of students and colleagues, so, for me, they are all polyvocal.

In the arts, bricolage signifies "construction or creation from a diverse range of available things" (Bricolage, n.d.). Constructing a poetic bricolage offered a "container ... for a gradual distillation of [my] multifaceted and complex learning, experienced over time" (Pithouse-Morgan & Samaras, 2019, p. 7). I chose to arrange this poetic bricolage using the traditional Japanese renga form, which is a type of linked-verse poetry usually generated by two or more poets as a kind of conversation (see Poets.org, 2004a). The title I chose for the renga was, "*Our* Words Changing *My* Story."

*Our* Words Changing *My Story*

Always a learner
Struggling to move, uncertain

Still feeling my way

I find a chest of treasures,
Care at the centre of it

Look back with purpose
Stepping into the unknown
Stand in the midst, *breathe*

*Our words*, blending, flowing out
Like vines, changing *my story*

Listening, connect!
Letting go and opening
To *our wide futures*

As I arranged the renga, I saw how each stanza could serve as an entry point for further conversation. In many of the poetic professional learning pieces I have written with others, we have used dialogue as a literary arts-inspired mode for exploring and representing our co-learning. Building on this, in response to the renga, I created a dialogic bricolage by combining excerpts from eight of these published dialogues, lightly edited for flow and coherence. In what follows, each stanza is followed by an exchange between distinctive voices from different contexts.

*Always a learner*
*Struggling to move, uncertain*
*Still feeling my way*

Edwina Grossi: When I was starting my dissertation, memories and pictures, thoughts and feelings were rekindled and were given a voice as they translated into words that fell into verse. I was free to write from the heart, not the head! However, at the start I feared my work was too simplistic, too non-academic, and too below par for a doctoral dissertation. Was I brave and strong and true enough to weave my simple poetry around the pieces of my dissertation?

Thenjiwe Meyiwa: Doing this work was very humbling as it exposed my poetic vulnerabilities. I had genuine fearful moments.

Delysia Timm: I have learned the importance of providing opportunities to explore areas where we are not necessarily comfortable to go because it is there where our true creativity is unleashed.

Linda Fitzgerald: But many people are coming with a lot of struggles, being told that this is not legitimate, it's not really research. How do you support people through that to keep going?

Lorraine Singh: It seems to be light and effortless. Yet we know otherwise.

Anastasia P. Samaras: It does take somebody who is willing to say, 'Let's go and do this! Let's try this!' Engaging in the arts is the portal, but it needs to be done in a way that does scaffold one into understanding things otherwise.

Kathleen Pithouse-Morgan: What is also important is to keep finding opportunities to show others, especially leaders in our institutions, how and why this work matters.

*I find a chest of treasures,*
*Care at the centre of it*

Nithi Muthukrishna: Most of our students come from a background of exposure to very traditional, linear kinds of research. But what I have found is that they embrace the experience of a dynamic learning community that explores creative ways of doing research, and soon they are eager to take risks and engage in social inquiry using innovative, reflexive methods and artistic modes.

S'phiwe Madondo: I did not know that I could express and make meaning of my own experiences through composing poems. The style of language teaching during my own primary school days in the 1980s promoted rote learning. For example, we were expected to read and memorise poems. I do not remember any poetry lessons that demanded our creative thinking or writing. Many years later, by bringing poetry into my research process, I was able to learn first-hand about developing a flair for poetic communication.

Delysia Timm: I, as many of our students do, come from an educational background where the arts and poetry have not been given much educational value compared to chemistry, mathematics, science, and technology. I was not provided with learning opportunities to express my creativity through performance and fun activities in the classroom. However, through co-learning and engaging in the poetic process, I am now moving towards flourishing in my practice as a university educator and researcher.

Theresa Chisanga: It has been wonderful to see the endless possibilities for doing research right there in the space that had previously felt tight and uncomfortable, and which seemed to be throttling the research capacity in me. There was support and genuine cooperation with a community that encouraged and reminded me constantly that my role was critical.

Kathleen Pithouse-Morgan: We are drawn together through our mutual interest and then, through exploring that interest, trust, understanding, and care can grow.

Daisy Pillay: Because of that prolonged, interactive, caring engagement, it becomes another way to look at the world.

*Look back with purpose*
*Stepping into the unknown*
*Stand in the midst, breathe*

S'phiwe Madondo: Through writing interpretive poetry, I was able to identify significant educational and emotional episodes in my past.

Chris de Beer: The whole process was very emergent and messy; a lot of the decisions were made on the fly, but slightly guided. There was a very slender thread that held it all together. And, I think at times it was almost like we wanted more order but then abandoned ourselves to the process and, lo and behold, something manifested!

Lee Scott: I also think we must never underestimate the teaching that we're doing. We are teaching each other. That's really important. And it's quite a natural way to learn as opposed to reading.

Lorraine Singh: There's a lot of healing that happens that way. You must be there with someone else. Because the breathing and energy that you release helps the next person.

*Our words, blending, flowing out*
*Like vines, changing my story*

Anastasia P. Samaras: I've been continually enriched by my experiences in moving out of my lens. That's been where I've been able to really grow and be inspired.

Relebohile Moletsane: Our multiple perspectives, debated and sometimes agreed upon and at other times diverging, have the potential to enable us to arrive at more 'trustworthy' claims.

Linda Van Laren: So, we're crossing borders?

Inbanathan Naicker: And we've become entangled in the process.

Daisy Pillay: That's what makes us living beings, that ongoing dialogue. It frees us to imagine new possibilities.

*Listening, connect!*
*Letting go and opening*
*To our wide futures*

Thenjiwe Meyiwa: Each person enriches and contributes to the collective journey. Co-learning requires us to listen and accommodate various points of view.

Daisy Pillay: Feeling safe and hopeful and human comes not by using our uniqueness to stay separate and lonely, but to connect with the unique in the other.

Jean Stuart: I think it's related to the openness of our collaboration. There's no resistance against an idea coming in.

Delysia Timm: It is during and through the sharing process that we undergo a transformation. Doors are opened and we venture into new areas.

Kathleen Pithouse-Morgan: I'm reminded of the final line of Grace Nichols' (1984) beautiful metaphor poem, "A Praise Song for My Mother." The poem ends with the words, "Go to your wide futures." Because of our dynamic, creative collaboration, there is that sense of spaciousness and possibility, of wide futures.

## 3 What Difference Can Poetry Make to Professional Learning?

The medley of voices presented in this chapter communicates how students, teachers, and academics who might not call themselves experienced or well-qualified poets can come together and play with the artistic potential of poetic forms and language to generate research data, representations, and interpretations. Even when the poems themselves might not be regarded as literary or artistic texts, the experience of poetry making, especially when it is collective, can permeate professional learning research and practice with imagination, feeling, and sensory impressions in ways that intensify and interconnect self-insight, care for others, and social awareness.

Through assembling words as poems, we can articulate and become engrossed in lived experiences and perspectives that might be tricky to convey or grasp in conventional academic language. Composing poetry with others in a mutually supportive environment can facilitate creative, multi-perspective meaning-making to reimagine ourselves and our educational practice in ways that respond to pressing social concerns. Overall, poetic inquiry can enrich professional learning research and practice in arts-inspired ways that can contribute to personal and social change.

What is more, fostering affirming and generative poetic experiences is particularly critical in the context of South Africa, where the teaching of poetry has often been confined to the memorisation of prescribed poems and where disheartening teaching approaches continue to make many people believe that they are not competent to create or understand poetry.

When teachers in schools and universities enact poetic professional learning, this can inspire them to work differently with poetry in the classroom by opening up supportive and gratifying possibilities for students to delve into reading, writing, and performing poetry in ways that allow them to experience "imagination [as] a source of exploratory delight" (Eisner, 2002, p. 5). Changing the atmosphere of the classroom can motivate students and demonstrate how poetry can become a dynamic part of their lives (Ferguson, 2017).

In closing, to encapsulate my response to my guiding question, "What difference can poetry make to professional learning?" I used words and phrases from the renga poem to create a second poem in the more concise tanka format. The tanka is a Japanese poetic form that moves from depicting an image in the first two lines to responding to that image in the final two lines, with the third line denoting the change of viewpoint (see Poets.org, 2004b). I titled the tanka, "Our Words Flowing into Wide Futures."

*Our Words Flowing into Wide Futures*

Stand in the midst, *breathe*
*Our words*, blending, flowing out
Changing *my story*
Care at the centre, *connect!*
Step into our wide futures

## Acknowledgements

This work is based on the research supported in part by the National Research Foundation of South Africa (Incentive Funding for Rated Researchers, Grant Number 127096).

I am grateful to all the colleagues and students who have enabled my continuing learning through our shared poetic explorations. In particular, I thank Theresa Chisanga, Chris de Beer, Linda Fitzgerald, Edwina Grossi, S'phiwe Madondo, Thenjiwe Meyiwa, Relebohile Moletsane, Nithi Muthukrishna, Inbanathan Naicker, Daisy Pillay, Anastasia P. Samaras, Lee Scott, Lorraine Singh, Jean Stuart, Delysia Timm, and Linda Van Laren for kind permission to include their words and names in this chapter.

The dialogic bricolage presented in this chapter is composed of lightly edited extracts from Pillay and Pithouse-Morgan (2016), Pithouse-Morgan et al. (2018), Pithouse-Morgan et al. (2019), Pithouse-Morgan et al. (2017), Pithouse-Morgan et al. (2015), Pithouse-Morgan and Samaras (2017, 2018, 2019).

## References

Andrews, D., & Osman, R. (2015). Redress for academic success: Possible "lessons"for university support programmes from a high school literacy and learning intervention: Part 2. *South African Journal of Higher Education, 29*(1), 354–372. https://doi.org/10.20853/29-1-459

Bakhtin, M. (1984). *Problems of Dostoevsky's poetics* (C. Emerson, Ed.). University of Minnesota Press. https://doi.org/10.5749/j.ctt22727z1

Bharuthram, S. (2012). Making a case for the teaching of reading across the curriculum in higher education. *South African Journal of Education, 32*(2), 205–214. https://doi.org/10.15700/saje.v32n2a557

Bricolage. (n.d.). In *Lexico*. https://en.oxforddictionaries.com/definition/bricolage

Campbell, B. (2016). Rethinking my poetry pedagogy: An autoethnographic self-study. *South African Journal of Higher Education, 30*(1), 42–56. https://doi.org/10.20853/30-1-556

Christie, P. (1991). *The right to learn: The struggle for education in South Africa* (2nd ed.). Ravan Press and Sached Trust.

Cole, A. L., & Knowles, J. G. (2008). Arts-informed research. In J. G. Knowles & A. L. Cole (Eds.), *Handbook of the arts in qualitative research* (pp. 55–70). Sage. https://doi.org/10.4135/9781452226545.n5

Eisner, E. W. (2002). *The arts and the creation of mind.* Yale University Press.

Ferguson, K. (2017). A poetry coffee house: Creating a cool community of writers. *The Reading Teacher, 71*(2), 209–213. https://doi.org/10.1002/trtr.1610

Giroux, H. A. (1988). *Teachers as intellectuals: Toward a critical pedagogy of learning.* Bergin & Garvey.

Henning, E., & van Rensburg, W. (2002). Academic development in writing composition: Beyond the limitations of a functionalist and pragmatic curriculum. *Journal for Language Teaching, 36*(1–2), 82–90. https://doi.org/10.4314/jlt.v36i1-2.6004

Leggo, C. (2008). Astonishing silence: Knowing in poetry. In J. G. Knowles & A. L. Cole (Eds.), *Handbook of the arts in qualitative research* (pp. 165–174). Sage.

Msibi, T., & McHunu, S. (2013). The knot of curriculum and teacher professionalism in post-apartheid South Africa. *Education as Change, 17*(1), 19–35. https://doi.org/10.1080/16823206.2013.773924

Nichols, G. (1984). *The fat black woman's poems.* Virago.

Pillay, D., & Pithouse-Morgan, K. (2016). A self-study of connecting through aesthetic memory-work. In J. Kitchen, D. Tidwell, & L. Fitzgerald (Eds.), *Self-study and diversity II: Inclusive teacher education for a diverse world* (Vol. 2, pp. 121–136). Sense Publishers. https://doi.org/10.1007/978-94-6300-534-0_8

Pithouse, K. (2005). Self-study through narrative interpretation: Probing lived experiences of educational privilege. In C. Mitchell, S. Weber, & K. O'Reilly-Scanlon (Eds.), *Just who do we think we are? Methodologies for autobiography and self-study in teaching* (pp. 206–217). RoutledgeFalmer.

Pithouse-Morgan, K. (2016). Finding my self in a new place: Exploring professional learning through found poetry. *Teacher Learning and Professional Development, 1*(1), 1–18.

Pithouse-Morgan, K. (2019). My students' stories became a gift: A tale of poetic professional learning. In E. R. Lyle (Ed.), *Fostering a relational pedagogy: Self-study as transformative praxis* (pp. 20–33). Brill | Sense. https://doi.org/10.1163/9789004388864_003

Pithouse-Morgan, K., Chisanga, T., Meyiwa, T., & Timm, D. N. (2018). Flourishing together: Co-learning as leaders of a multicultural South African educational research community. *International Journal of Multicultural Education, 20*(3), 102–125. https://doi.org/10.18251/ijme.v20i3.1607

Pithouse-Morgan, K., Madondo, S., & Grossi, E. (2019). The promise of poetry belongs to us all: Poetic professional learning in teacher-researchers' memory-work. In K. Pithouse-Morgan, D. Pillay, & C. Mitchell (Eds.), *Memory mosaics: Researching teacher professional learning through artful memory-work* (pp. 133–153). Springer. https://doi.org/10.1007/978-3-319-97106-3_8

Pithouse-Morgan, K., Muthukrishna, N., Pillay, D., Van Laren, L., Chisanga, T., Meyiwa, T., … Stuart, J. (2015). Learning about co-flexivity in a transdisciplinary self-study research supervision community. In K. Pithouse-Morgan & A. P. Samaras (Eds.), *Polyvocal professional learning through self-study research* (pp. 145–171). Sense Publishers. https://doi.org/10.1007/978-94-6300-220-2_9

Pithouse-Morgan, K., Pillay, D., & Naicker, I. (2017). "Knowing what it is like": Dialoguing with multiculturalism and equity through collective poetic autoethnographic inquiry. *International Journal of Multicultural Education, 19*(1), 125–143. https://doi.org/10.18251/ijme.v19i1.1255

Pithouse-Morgan, K., & Samaras, A. P. (2015). The power of "we" for professional learning. In K. Pithouse-Morgan & A. P. Samaras (Eds.), *Polyvocal professional learning through self-study research* (pp. 1–20). Sense Publishers. https://doi.org/10.1007/978-94-6300-220-2_1

Pithouse-Morgan, K., & Samaras, A. P. (2017). Thinking in space: Virtual bricolage self-study for future-oriented teacher professional learning. In D. Garbett & A. Ovens (Eds.), *Being self-study researchers in a digital world: Future-oriented research and pedagogy in teacher education* (pp. 133–150). Springer. https://doi.org/10.1007/978-3-319-39478-7_10

Pithouse-Morgan, K., & Samaras, A. P. (2018). "Many stories matter": Taking a polyvocal stance in learning about teaching of self-study. In J. K. Ritter, M. Lunenberg, K. Pithouse-Morgan, A. P. Samaras, & E. Vanassche (Eds.), *Teaching, learning, and enacting of self-study methodology: Unraveling a complex interplay* (pp. 313–328). Springer. https://doi.org/10.1007/978-981-10-8105-7_27

Pithouse-Morgan, K., & Samaras, A. P. (2019). Polyvocal play: A poetic bricolage of the *why* of our transdisciplinary self-study research. *Studying Teacher Education, 15*(1), 4–18. https://doi.org/10.1080/17425964.2018.1541285

Poets.org. (2004a). *Poetic form: Renga*. https://www.poets.org/poetsorg/text/poetic-form-renga

Poets.org. (2004b). *Poetic form: Tanka*. https://www.poets.org/poetsorg/text/tanka-poetic-form

Webster-Wright, A. (2009). Reframing professional development through understanding authentic professional learning. *Review of Educational Research, 79*(2), 702–739. https://doi.org/10.3102/0034654308330970

Young, A. (1982). Considering values: The poetic function of language. In T. Fulwiler & A. Young (Eds.), *Language connections: Writing and reading across the curriculum* (pp. 77–97). National Council of Teachers of English.

CHAPTER 19

# Eight Weeks, Eight Verses

## *Using Arts-Based Inquiry to Explore Educator Subjectivity and Reflexivity during a Time of Social Change*

*Marguerite Müller and Frans Kruger*

## 1 Introduction

In our chapter, we employ collective poetic autoethnographic inquiry as described by Pithouse-Morgan, Naicker, and Pillay (2017), to explore how art can act as an agent of social change in the context of reflexive pedagogy and practice. This piece was inspired by St Pierre's (2019) question, "Why do we think we should know what to do before we begin to inquire?" (p. 4). Using this question as a starting point, our methodological exploration finds expression in poetry, fiction, and drawing as we explore affective experiences of teaching a social justice module at the University of the Free State, South Africa. The chapter includes a poem composed of eight verses. Each verse is a reflexive engagement with our experiences inside and outside the classroom during an academic semester. These verses are, furthermore, collaborative creations that are drawn from what we think of as the data of our day-to-day lives. This evidence includes, for example, notes we made on our cell phones while waiting in a queue at the grocer, or quick drawings done on post-it paper while taking a break from marking in the office. We used this form of art-on-the-go to connect our lives with the academic texts with which we engaged then. In a sense, we used art as a means to respond to our world of academic work as it becomes/is entangled with everyday experiences that unfold in a certain time and place. The eight verses we offer are thus aimed at highlighting the micro-social moments of everyday experience that play out alongside our search for a form of inquiry that is responsive to the world (Kruger, 2019; Müller, Kruger, Lekoala, & Mokoena, 2020), and in particular how this relates to the entanglement of educator subjectivity, memory, and experience with social justice pedagogy, curriculum, and theory.

In recent years, student protests at South African institutions of higher education have highlighted an intensified call for the transformation and decolonisation of curricula and pedagogy. The changing context requires South African educators to respond through transformation of the self, pedagogy, curriculum, and research inquiry. We take up this challenge by grappling with the question

 | DOI: 10.1163/9789004442870_019

of how a creative and artistic engagement with our personal experiences in this context might create possibilities for such transformation and enable new ways of becoming different. In this regard, we understand subjectivity as being composed of an assembled multiplicity that affects and is affected by the educational space in which it unfolds. Although this piece is inspired by our personal experiences, it is, following Eliastam, Müller, Müller, and Trahar (2019), a fictionalised and artistic response, and the characters are reflective of imaginative possibilities rather than representative of individuals. Our inquiry is informed by post qualitative inquiry that does not seek to emulate representational logic but rather make new ways of knowing possible (St Pierre, 2019). We thus find arts-based inquiry useful since it allows for alternative forms of data representation that foreground issues of complexity, affect, and new ways of being and becoming (Cahnmann-Taylor & Siegesmund, 2018). In making use of poetry, drawing, and fiction, we aim to communicate that which would otherwise be impossible to convey (Leavy, 2009) as we explore the intersections, complexity, messiness, and intertwined nature of personal and professional experiences during a time of social change in the South African higher education landscape.

## 2 Eight Weeks: Eight Verses

In this section, we offer an aesthetic exploration of our experiences inside and outside the classroom during eight weeks of teaching on a social justice module. We juxtapose the personal/professional continuum of experiences with literature and theory that resonate with each verse. In Section 3, we offer a description of what informed the construction of each verse.

*A Conversation*

Mom, what are you doing?
  I am writing a story
Is it a story for kids?
  No, not really
Why not?
  It is a story about my work
What do you do?
  I teach teachers

What do you teach them?
    I teach them how to teach
I don't like *my* teacher,
she keeps us in for break
    Why?
Because we talk in class …
Do your students talk in class?
    Yes
Do you know all their names?
Do you know all their birthdays?
    No
    Why?
I have many students,
more than a thousand
    Do they write tests?
    Do they get stickers?
    Do they go on a field trip?
    Do they get a lot of homework?
    Do you love them?

Are we, as a society, embarrassed by love? Does social justice elude us because we cannot have justice without love (hooks, 2018)? Social justice, as love, is not about rewarding and punishing (hooks, 2018) but rather about understanding; it "is an experience of sharing, of communion, which permits the full unfolding of one's inner activity" (Fromm, 1955, p. 31). In this sense then, social justice as love is "an active striving and inner relatedness" (Fromm, 1941, p. 114); it is a praxis of community.

*The Right Story*

Why is education theory and research so often about "the one with the 'Right' Story" (Ellsworth, 1997, as cited in Lather, 1998, p. 488)? About "abstraction and universalization" (Lather, 1998, p. 488)? Research, like the experiences of life we try to capture and express, involves constant movement, uncertainty, joy, faltering. In a sense, we are "actors in a story-telling process" (Gough, 2010, p. 45) and our research inquiry measured and weighted storying.

*Round and Round and Round We Go*

I read Angelina Ballerina to my
three-year-old daughter
Mei, thinks that she *is* Angelina
  "I am a *dancerina*!"
I take her to a ballet class
She goes inside
and I peek through the window
to see the little three-year-old humans
run around in circles of pink
and look at themselves in the mirror

  twinkle twinkle little star
  how I wonder where you are?

I remember being three
I think
and I remember wanting to do
ballet lessons
as my older sister did

Manning (2009) maintains that thought and movement are co-constitutive of one another and that the movement of thought is the "reciprocal action of reaching-toward and in-gathering of environment and body" (Hunt & Kant, 2009, p. 171).

I remember those beautiful
costumes she used to wear for
concerts!
One with sparkly material and
sequins
a butterfly with chiffon wings
but my mom said the teacher
was too mean
rightly so
but now I look at the little ballet
dancers
with a sort of envy
and a sense that I had missed
out
I read Jasmine Ulmer's
*Pivots and Pirouettes*
while I wait
and think of
Patricia Leavy (2009)
who wrote part of a book
while her daughter attended art
lessons
I am writing this chapter on the
go
making little notes on my cell
phone
reading
while I wait
keeping up
with the pirouettes and pivots
of research
emails
teaching
supervision
home
kids
round and round
and round we go

We take up the notion of reciprocal action in terms of *pirouettes* that involves "lifting oneself up and maintaining internal momentum" (Ulmer, 2019, p. 1). Doing this allows us to conceptualise research inquiry as a thoughtfully choreographed performance and as a generative movement of criticality and affirmation.

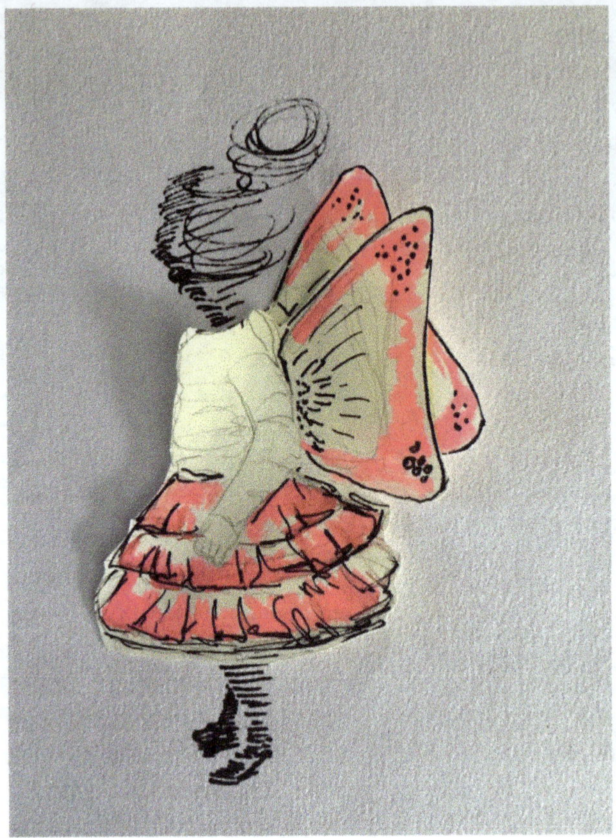

FIGURE 19.1 "Dancerina," 2019, mixed media drawing, 10 cm × 7 cm (Marguerite Müller)

*But You Wouldn't Understand*

Because it is April but students are still waiting
for their funding to become available
A student asks me for R20 to buy some lunch
because he hasn't had food
all day
he is hungry
waiting for his bursary to be paid out
somewhere on campus
a small protest breaks out
a fire extinguisher is emptied in the lecture hall
students are getting impatient
the campus is shut down for a day
The next day we resume lectures

with venues overflowing
and the air conditioner out of order
Bloemfontein is hot
the sun beating down on us
too hard

After class
under the shade of a lonely tree
a group of students talk about graduation
They show me pictures
of designer dresses and stiletto shoes
they talk
of family expectations
the money spent
Getting a degree is everything,
bigger than marriage
but you wouldn't understand
They laugh at my expression of surprise
Why?
    you are white
    but for us …
    getting a degree is everything
    but you wouldn't understand

*A Sticky Mess*

Summer rains have come and
gone
Yellow sunflowers smile at me
Soaking in the autumn sun
A Black-eyed Susan vine creeps
over the wall
spilling into the parking lot
of the shopping mall
where I take my son to lunch at
Wimpy
He eats the kiddies meal too
quickly
He is growing so fast

In his homework book it says he
must learn the spelling of
frequently misspelled words
*Because*, I read
    Easy
he says as he writes
    B E C A U S E
    my teacher taught me:
    Betty eats carrots and uncle sells eggs
Because
He is still a child
His face brightens up when he
receives
the little plastic toy that comes
with the meal
a tub of purple slimy 'goo'
which he plays with on the way
home
and then leaves behind on the
car seat
where his little sister would
later discover it and
get the sticky mess into her hair
eventually I would have to cut
out the slimy bits

*Because*

Because I am in a hurry
on my way to class

Because he is now all grown up
I don't recognize his face
At first
Sitting in the front row
The last time I saw him he was a
boy of fourteen
In a school classroom one
thousand kilometres away
    Do you remember me?

I was the naughty one
I remember you
How is it here at university?
It is ok, but I miss home

Because we are discussing
racism in Unit Two
I show the students a
newspaper article
about a primary school teacher
who separated students into
two groups (Seleka, 2019)
One black and one white
A heated conversation erupts in
class
racial polarization
plays out
in the ruins of Apartheid
as we make our way through
the
anger
and the guilt
and the anger
and the guilt
and the tension in the class
could be cut with a knife
"How do I bear responsibility
for the oppressions and
injustices in my community and
the world?" (Zembylas, 2019, p.
414).
The answer is a resounding
thousand silent stares
Do they hate me?

My truth is not my identity

A well-known African proverb
says:
If you want to go fast

Drawing on the notion of interbeing as developed by Thich Nhat Hahn, Asher (2003) argues that one is able to see the other only by "looking deep into oneself" and giving recognition to "how one's own past, present, and future are linked to those of different others and vice versa" (p. 238). This understanding of interbeing strongly resonates with shared responsibility, a concept that involves "a shared, relational and political practice" (Zembylas, 2019, p. 405). Shared responsibility begs us to consider how each of us bears responsibility for the injustices in our communities and our response-activeness towards any such responsibility we may hold.

go alone,
If you want to go far
go together

*Conviviality and other things*

A foot is tapping impatiently
A folder on the table
Tell us about your student pass
rate
Tell us about your student
evaluations
Have you made your academic
portfolio?
What is your workload?
How many students are you
supervising?
Have you published anything
this year?
and remember to RSVP for the
decolonisation workshop.

The meeting room is cold but I
sit next to a colleague who
brought her traditional baSotho
blanket
and shares it with me
a micro-moment of joy
on a rocky shore (Gannon et al.,
2019).

What is my culture? I ask the
students
Western they say
I show them the picture of a
Christmas Holly
It is a picture from a childhood
book that I have kept
I remember looking at this
picture and thinking

somehow our Christmas *here* is
wrong
We don't have snow
We don't have holly
It is hot
and we eat watermelon

What does it mean to be
African?

Sometimes I listen to music I
don't know
And I love it
Is it possible to love something
you don't know?
Is knowing loving?
Is love familiar and
comfortable?
Or is it really awkward?
Sometimes I hate loving what I
cannot be

A student knocks on my office
door ...
    Look
    A branch of holly
    I picked it for you
    It grows on campus
    near the library

Strange that I have never seen it before

    *It is getting cold outside*

Outside my window there is construction site
They are building a new lecture hall
Right now they are just digging away to make way for a foundation
The beep beep beep of the construction vehicles getting louder
My desk trembles
under the weight of a hundred and twenty essays

Conviviality, for Nyamnjoh (2017), is an affirmation and celebration of incompleteness, of being "open-minded and open-ended" and reaching out to the incompleteness of others (human and non-human) as a means "to make us more efficacious in our relationships and sociality" (p. 263). To what extent does this understanding of conviviality inform our learning spaces and our research inquiry? How might this understanding of conviviality enable us to move towards celebrating plurality and an epistemology of pluriversality (Mbembe, 2016)?

The topic is oppression,
social justice,
and decolonisation
I see an email appear on my screen
When are we getting our marks?
The hole outside my window seems to be getting bigger

What makes a good teacher?
  A teacher must challenge
  A teacher must be inclusive
  A teacher must be reflexive
A teacher must ...

  I get home and it is bedtime for Josh
    Come lie with me 'till I fall asleep
  No I am sorry, but I need to enter some marks
    It can wait 'till tomorrow
  His little hand pulls me away from the screen
  Away from the rows of little numbers
  I wonder what happened to my little baby boy
    I wish you could come to school with me
    so that we would never be separated
  I wait 'till he falls asleep
  Before I let go of his hand

## 3 Creating Eight Verses

Given our approach in this chapter, we deem it important to provide the reader with a glimpse into our thinking during the process of creating our narrative. In what follows, we provide a brief description of what informed the construction and shaping of each verse. These can be thought of as the pre-sketches, or field notes, that were eventually transformed into the eight verses.

In the first verse, *A Conversation*, we interrogate the interplay between social justice pedagogy and love. Drawing on the work of hooks and Fromm, we reflect on how love manifests in our practice and the (potential) role it plays in social justice pedagogy. This reflection is, furthermore, informed by the tension that exists between a desire for a humanising pedagogy that responds to the call for decolonisation in our context (Zembylas, 2018), on the one hand, and the reality of systemic challenges such as teaching courses with large student enrolments and neo-liberal knowledge economies on the other. Thereafter, we respond to the theoretical and methodological expectations and conventions that seek to shape, and sometimes stifle, our artistic engagement with educational research inquiry in *The Right Story*. We continue our response in *Round and Round and Round We Go*, highlighting how our performative practice and embodied experiences of our day-to-day lives interact and become entangled with theory. These two verses also play on the continuous interaction of our personal and professional identities as these collide and merge into one another. In *But You Wouldn't Understand*, we turn our attention to the South African context where issues of funding, access, culture, socio-economic and racial markers continue to permeate and frame the experiences of staff and students at academic institutions. *A Sticky Mess* follows this and here we refocus on the more-than-humanness of our context and how this shapes our experiences and understanding. In keeping with this concern, in verse *Because*, we deliberate on rationality and how pedagogies produce affective encounters that move beyond the classroom walls (Müller et al., 2020). *Conviviality and other things* is a portrait of subjectivity, belonging, and estrangement as we struggle to move beyond the confines of our identity markers towards an affirmative politics of subjectivity that does not rely on a logic of negation (Kruger & Le Roux, 2019). In our final verse, *It is getting cold outside*, we posit personal and professional transformation as a difficult process that involves change towards the unknown.

## 4 Conclusion

In this chapter, we employed post qualitative inquiry to explore the question of how a creative and artistic engagement with our personal experiences might create possibilities for transformation and enable new ways of becoming different. In taking up post qualitative inquiry, we want to "bring into existence that which does not yet exist" (Deleuze, 1994, p. 147) as an alternative to describing and interpreting that which already does exist. As such, we ask ourselves what our experimentation with collective poetic autoethnographic inquiry makes possible as it relates to using art as an agent of social change to explore educator subjectivity and reflexivity in the context of South African higher education. We briefly turn our attention to this to consider the contribution we make in this chapter. Throughout the process of our inquiry, we became aware of the way the texts and theories we explore in/through our teaching practice and research inquiry are abstracted from experience. For Whitehead (as cited in Manning, 2015), experience is always in-act since it concerns "the limits of the not-yet and the will-have-been" (p. 46). To narrow the distance between theory as abstraction and experience in-act, we propose that research inquiry in general, but specifically arts-based approaches to inquiry that seek to work toward social change, should be conceptualised as a practice of artfulness. Such a conceptualisation of inquiry allows one to focus on being "attuned to a skill or craft of learning" (Manning, 2015, p. 45) rather than the product thereof. This would allow one to experiment with "the middling of experience ... where futurity and presentness coincide" (p. 46) and to interrogate how theory and experience relate to one another and manifest in our personal and professional lives and as we work toward social change.

## References

Asher, N. (2003). Engaging difference: Towards a pedagogy of interbeing. *Teacher Education, 14*(3), 235–247.

Cahnmann-Taylor, M., & Siegesmund, R. (2018). Introduction. In M. Cahnmann-Taylor & R. Siegesmund (Eds.), *Arts-based research in education: Foundations for practice* (pp. 1–11). Routledge.

Deleuze, G. (1994). *Difference and repetition* (P. Patton, Trans.). Columbia University Press. (Original work published 1968)

Eliastam, J., Müller, J., Müller, M., & Trahar, S. (2019). Fictionalisation and research. In J. Muller, J. Eliastam, & S. Trahar (Eds.), *Unfolding narratives of Ubuntu in Southern Africa* (pp. 12–28). Routledge.

Fromm, E. (1941). *Escape from freedom.* Farrar and Rinehart.

Fromm, E. (1955). *The sane society.* Rinehart and Winston, Inc.

Gannon, S., Taylor, B., Adams, G., Donaghue, H., Hannam-Swain, S., Harris-Evans, J., & Moore, P. (2019). 'Working on a rocky shore': Mirco-moments of positive affect in academic work. *Emotion, Space and Society, 31*, 48–55.

Gough, N. (2010). Performing imaginative inquiry: Narrative experiments and rhizosemiotic play. In T. W. Nielsen, R. Fitzgerald, & M. Fettes (Eds.), *Imagination in educational theory and practice: A many-sided vision* (pp. 42–60). Cambridge Scholars Publishing.

hooks, b. (2018). *All about love: New visions.* Perennial.

Hunt, J., & Kant, M. (2009). Reviews. *International Journal of Performance Arts and Digital Media, 5*(2–3), 171–178.

Kruger, F. (2019). Crafting new worlds: Critical qualitative inquiry and/as an aesthetics of the wound. *Cultural Studies ↔ Critical Methodologies.* https://doi.org/10.1177/1532708619886333

Kruger, F., & Le Roux, A. (2019). A schizoanalytic exploration of the potential of fabulation for the creation of new social collectivities in pre-service teacher education. *Pedagogy, Culture & Society*. https://doi.org/10.1080/14681366.2019.1629994

Lather, P. (1998). Critical pedagogy and its complicities: A praxis of stuck places. *Educational Theory, 48*(4), 487–497.

Leavy, P. (2009). *Method meets art. Arts-Based research practice*. The Guilford Press.

Manning, E. (2009). *Relationscapes: Movement, art, philosophy*. MIT Press.

Manning, E. (2015). Artfulness. In R. Grusin (Ed.), *The nonhuman turn* (pp. 45–79). University of Minnesota Press.

Mbembe, A. (2016). Decolonizing the university: New directions. *Arts & Humanities in Higher Education, 15*(1), 29–45.

Müller, M., Kruger, F., Lekoala, N., & Mokoena, N. (2020). Pedagogy is a messy affair: A performative narrative of being new. *Qualitative Inquiry, 26*(1), 89–98. https://doi.org/10.1177/1077800419874830

Nyamnjoh, F. (2017). Incompleteness: Frontier Africa and the currency of conviviality. *Journal of Asian and African Studies, 52*(3), 253–270.

Pithouse-Morgan, K., Naicker, I., & Pillay, D. (2017). "Knowing what it is like": Dialoguing with multiculturalism and equity through collective poetic autoethnographic inquiry. *International Journal of Multicultural Education, 19*(1), 125–143.

Seleka, N. (2019, January 19). Timeline: A whirlwind of racism and emotions for Learskool Schweitzer-Reneke. *News24*.

St. Pierre, E. A. (2019). Post qualitative inquiry, the refusal of method, and the risk of the new. *Qualitative Inquiry*. https://doi.org/10.1177/1077800419863005

Ulmer, J. (2019). Pivots and pirouettes: Carefully turning traditions. *Qualitative Inquiry*. https://doi.org/10.1177/1077800419829778

Zembylas, M. (2018). Decolonial possibilities in South African higher education: Reconfiguring humanising pedagogies as/with decolonising pedagogies. *South African Journal of Education, 38*(4), 1–9.

Zembylas, M. (2019). Encouraging shared responsibility without invoking collective guilt: Exploring pedagogical responses to portrayals of suffering and injustice in the classroom. *Pedagogy, Culture & Society, 23*(7), 403–417.

CHAPTER 20

# Dear Artemisia

## *Art as Transformation in Sexual Violence Prevention*

*Victoria L. Dickman-Burnett*

## 1 A Letter to Baroque-Era Painter Artemisia Gentileschi

Dear Artemisia,

Your story is all the metaphors we use today for rape culture made literal. In your trial in 1612 (because it was you who was on trial, not your rapist), you endured thumbscrews, a literal pelvic examination in open court, and men lying about your sexual history to make the trial a matter of your past. While today we count ourselves lucky because these exact tactics have not endured, the spirit of doubting survivors unfortunately has. And that is why I am writing this letter to you because, even though we think of historical figures as adults, you were an eighteen-year-old girl when you were assaulted as Gunnell (1993) has reminded us.

In the rest of this letter, I will tell you about my research and what I learned. I will tell you about the power of art to educate youth about sexual violence. I will tell you about how we conducted research and show you some student artwork as well as some artwork of my own. I am a sexual violence prevention researcher who works in the context of a high school program. I have been carrying out this program with my research partner for two years. While our planning for the project began before the #MeToo movement arose, the program started in the midst of #MeToo (see Dickman-Burnett, 2019). As I write about my experiences with the program, I blend news events with reflections on the program to synthesise what I have learned from it in my specific context.

## 2 Some Information about Sexual Violence to Contextualise Our Project

In the United States, sexual violence is unfortunately very common. In fact, experts estimate that one in every four to six women experiences rape in her lifetime (Rape Abuse Incest National Network [RAINN], 2019). On college campuses, women experience sexual violence at an alarming rate (Fisher, Diagle, &

 | DOI: 10.1163/9789004442870_020

Cullen, 2009). As a result, many universities and even some high schools have created programs to educate students about sexual violence (DeGue, Valle, Holt, Massetti, Matjasko, & Tharp, 2014). Given federal legislation (DeGue et al., 2014), universities in the United States receiving federal funding are required to have prevention programs that all new students must attend. High school programs, in contrast, are typically the result of community organisations, initiatives in a school (DeGue et al., 2014), or the work of researchers like me.

When I talk about sexual violence, I frequently use the term rape culture (see Buchwald, Fletcher, & Roth, 1993). When I use this term, I mean that society has allowed sexual violence to become common through excusing the behavior of people who commit it or through blaming the survivors of sexual violence for what has happened. Furthermore, sexual violence needs to be considered in terms of our making changes to society, not just preventing bad actors or teaching potential victims how to stay safe. For an example of rape culture, consider the way in which the media responded when a Stanford swimmer was caught in the act of sexually assaulting an unconscious woman behind a dumpster on campus. The media conversation surrounding the case included details about the assailant's promising swimming career rather than about his sexual assault of his victim (Miller, 2019). Instances like this one make it easier for perpetrators of sexual violence to get away with these acts of violence. Also, survivors often decide not to press charges against their assailants.

## 3 Methodology

In February 2018, we began our sexual violence prevention unit in a high school in the Midwestern United States. For six weeks, students read *The Mockingbirds* (2010), a novel by Daisy Whitney about sexual violence. They also learned about this through direct lessons in class that involved PowerPoint presentations about it along with information from government websites and other resources like rainn.org. They also completed journals as they read and participated in classroom discussions and in three larger projects—photography, art, and action planning.

The photography project involved having students take pictures with their phones to represent a myth and a fact about sexual violence. The art project asked them to represent artistically for a community showcase what they had learned in the unit. The action plan project involved working in groups to create a plan to address sexual violence in the community. The information we collected took on multiple forms, but the information shaping my letter to you is from student artwork, the rationales they provided with their artwork, two interviews with each of the thirteen students, and my notes from classes in the unit.

In getting ready to write these letters to you, I first coded student artwork, rationales, interview transcripts, and my notes to identify emerging themes. Writing letters allows the complexity of the data to be represented in its full richness without incurring the risk of flattening data in the interest of neat categories (see Carroll, 2015, for a discussion of the epistolary form). I consider these letters to you to be a post-script to the work of my dissertation, somewhere I can make and convey meaning through art.

## 4 What I Learned from My Students

*My students are afraid.* They tell me sexual violence is discussed only in the context of being a potential consequence of drinking alcohol, using drugs, or becoming sexually active. They tell me no one teaches them about consent, but I notice that someone taught them how to preserve evidence for a rape kit. My students, especially the young women, are aware that they live in a world with sexual violence. They are aware that sexual violence is treated as inevitable. Some of them feel that no one has taught them to do anything about this. They most commonly cite the internet as the source of their education on the subject. No one has taught them that a different world is possible.

In the image below, the student artist, Violet, conveys fear through the eyes of the woman and the damage done to her in the tearing up of the photo. While the student writes about the perception of sexual violence as damaging, the fear underlying this artwork is palpable. Another student, Eliza, tells me in her interview that she has only ever been taught about sexual violence as a consequence of using drugs or alcohol, and this scares her.

*My students are hopeful.* As we make art, there is an energy in the room. Even as we discuss the seriousness of the subject, there is a sense of hopefulness. Throughout the program I witness students learn, grow, and change. A young man who, early in the program, denied the role of sexism in sexual violence brings in advertisements as evidence of rape culture. A young woman who was resistant to the program tells my research partner that she hopes that one day all the students in the school can experience it. While the program discusses difficult subjects, the art process allows students an opportunity to visualise the change they hope to make. As they make art, they are prompted to think about the community showcase, in which they share what they have learned at the end of the unit.

In many of the student paintings, the hope emerges from natural imagery. Birds take flight as students consider the possibility of healing, healthy relationships, and social transformation. Flowers blossom as students write about

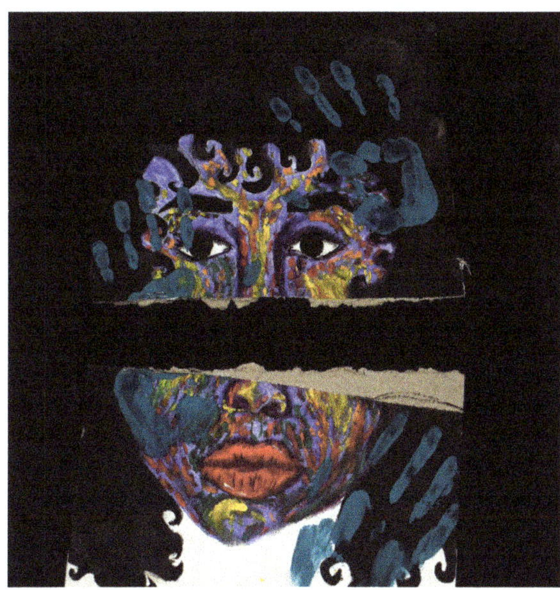

FIGURE 20.1 Violet captures in her painting the fear that students experience

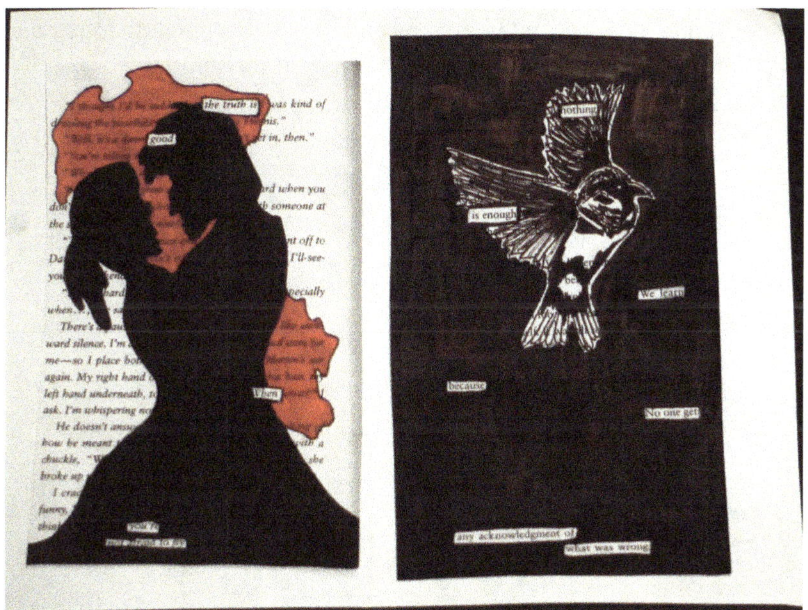


FIGURE 20.2 Ernest's blackout poetry conveys hopefulness through positive relationships and the image of a bird in flight

the ability to make the world a better place, connecting the program to the potential to change the world and recognising students' own power as part of this change.

*My students will change the world.* In the fall after the first year of the program, the Supreme Court confirmation hearing of Brett Kavanaugh (see Dickman-Burnett, 2019) took place. Nationally, a conversation arose about sexual violence. I returned to the school for the first time since the spring to meet with alumni of the program. A group of young women arrived to convey their commitment to the project. Throughout the school year, as the second group of students went through the prevention program, the alumni worked together with me to form a research project. One student, Wilhelm, found me in the hallway to tell me about his plans to use the program we developed when he becomes a teacher himself. Another student met with me weekly to serve as co-researcher on a project about training teachers. As we concluded the year, the art showcase grew to include a candlelight vigil during which the students conveyed their support for survivors of sexual violence and declared their commitment to change.

In his painting, Wilhelm conveyed the potential for learning about sexual violence through education. He followed this painting up with a group project about education in which he and his group members developed a survey to learn about other students' experiences with prevention education. Wilhelm is not alone. In final projects and interviews, many students reiterated the value of education and the belief that they can be a part of the solution.

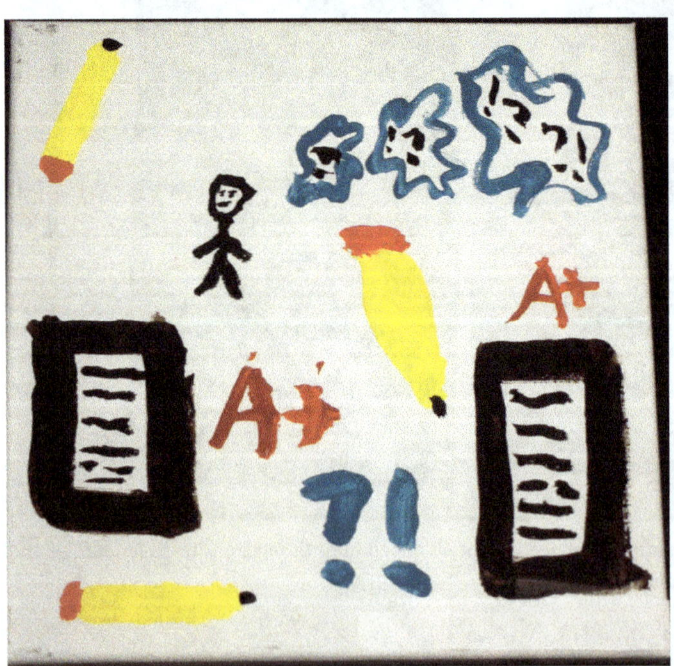


FIGURE 20.3 Wilhelm's painting highlights the role of social transformation through education

## 5 Creating Art in Response to the Program

*Hope and Nature.* After the community showcase at the end of the first year of the program, I went to the home of my mentor to make art. I decided I wanted to use natural themes to encapsulate the hopefulness I felt during the showcase as students, faculty, and members of the community came together to convey their commitment to preventing sexual violence. The goal of this art-making session was to create art to capture how I felt after the showcase as data centered around a particular moment. I created the art piece "Flowers of Hope" to represent this.

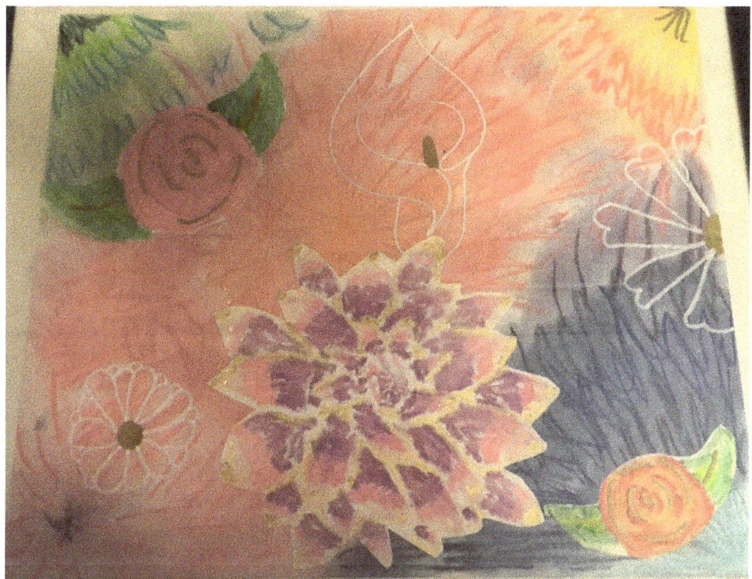

FIGURE 20.4 "Flowers of Hope." Mixed media on paper and plastic

Floral imagery recurred in my work surrounding the program. I believe this is because I had strong feelings about the potential for growth and transformation. As the program continued, this optimism grew. Students became involved in their own projects and remained committed to the prevention of sexual violence, showing the value of the program and the power of the arts.

*Mirror Silhouette.* As I analysed students' paintings for my dissertation project, I noticed how some students offered a human face to survivors, while others presented silhouettes, which point to survivors as an invisible population of which anyone could be a member. To represent these findings together, I made the mixed media artwork "Mirror Silhouette." The mirror asks viewers to empathise with survivors while the silhouette captures the nature of survivors

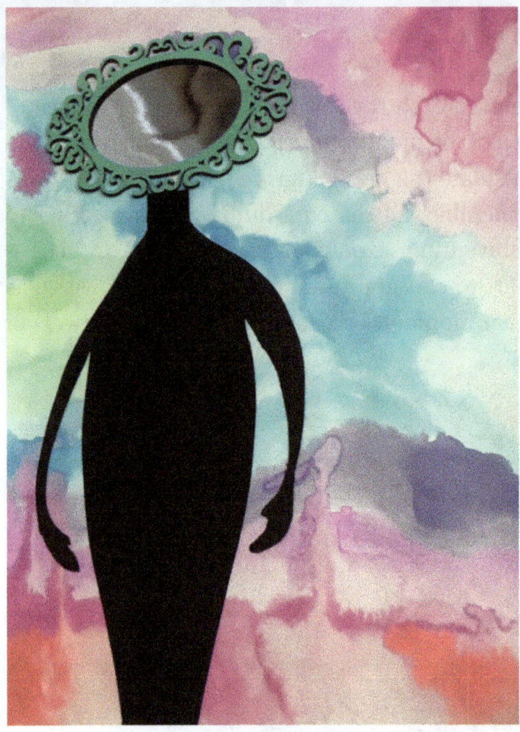

FIGURE 20.5
"Mirror Silhouette." Mixed media on paper

as a hidden population. In this way, the viewers can connect with the idea that sexual violence can affect anyone, though it may not be readily evident.

In humanising survivors, students showed their empathy, a potential source of social transformation. This capacity for empathy can change how students think about sexual violence. When sexual violence is presented with a human face, students can no longer ignore its realities.

## 6 Concluding Thoughts

As I draw this letter to a close, I am hopeful that there can be a better world than the one you knew, Artemisia. While my students are learning and growing, many of them began the program with attitudes toward sexual violence that already critically interrogated the roles of rape culture. As we went through the program together, I watched the students grow and gained hope for social transformation.

On my mantle is your painting, *Judith Slaying Holofernes.* I keep it there to remind myself that resistance can take on many different forms. I keep it there to remember that art has the power to transform and change the world. I keep it there to draw on your strength and remember my own. I may never change the world or eradicate rape culture, but I have seen the power of art to make an impact on youth.

Dear Artemisia, thank you for listening. Thank you for painting.

Love,
Victoria

## References


Buchwald, E., Fletcher, P. R., & Roth, M. (1993). Introduction. In E. Buchwald, P. R. Fletcher, & M. Roth (Eds.), *Transforming a rape culture* (p. vii). Milkweed Editions.

Carroll, K. (2015). Representing ethnographic data through the epistolary form: A correspondence between a breastmilk donor and recipient. *Qualitative Inquiry, 21*(8), 686–695. https://doi.org/10.1177/1077800414566691

DeGue, S., Valle, L. A., Holt, M. K., Massetti, G. M., Matjasko, J. L., & Tharp, A. T. (2014). A systematic review of primary prevention strategies for sexual violence perpetration. *Aggression and Violent Behavior, 19*(4), 346–362. https://doi.org/10.1016/j.avb.2014.05.004

Dickman-Burnett, V. L. (2019). Reflections on teaching sexual violence prevention after #MeToo. *Spark: A 4C4Equality Journal, 1*(1). https://sparkactivism.com/volume-1-intro/reflections-on-teaching-sexual-violence-prevention-after-metoo/

Fisher, B. S., Daigle, L. E., & Cullen, F. T. (2009). *Unsafe in the ivory tower: The sexual victimization of college women.* Sage Publications.

Gunnell, B. (1993, July 4). The rape of Artemisia. *The Independent.* https://www.webcitation.org/6V9q1a7fJ?url=http://www.independent.co.uk/arts-entertainment/the-rape-of-artemisia-four-hundred-years-ago-this-week-artemisia-genteleschi-was-born-in-rome-today-she-is-recognised-as-a-great-painter-but-for-more-than-three-centuries-her-works-have-regularly-been-attrib

Miller, C. (2019). *Know my name.* Viking Press.

Rape Abuse Incest National Network (RAINN). (2019). *Victims of sexual violence: Statistics.* https://www.rainn.org/statistics/victims-sexual-violence

Whitney, D. (2010). *The mockingbirds.* Little Brown.

CHAPTER 21

# Fiction for Social Change

*Addressing Gender in and through Popular Films*

*Esther Armaignac*

## 1 Introduction

What is the extent of the pedagogical power of fiction? Stories are part of our everyday lives and they address various subjects, often related to social change. Why do these stories matter? Studying fictional narratives in movies can allow us to question aspects of our social reality; this is particularly important when it comes to addressing critical issues such as gender-based inequalities and gender-based violence in work with adolescents in the context of effecting social change. Representations of women in popular films often simultaneously perpetuate and challenge norms related to gender, age, class, sexuality, and race (Armaignac, 2017), so these representations perpetuate these norms, maintain the established dynamics of power, and reinforce normalised representations of gender roles, all of which leads, often, to the validation of sexual violence in society. In this chapter, I focus specifically on two strategies for using fictional narratives to encourage adolescent students to challenge these gender-related norms and conventions: I have students engage in critical readings of popular films; and I have them engage in a process of creating narratives that express their own ideas and that challenge conventional norms. Both, I argue, could contribute to addressing the need for social change.

Teenagers, as a demographic, consume the most films in North America (Motion Picture Association of America, 2018), and studies show that they often learn and reproduce behaviors from popular films (Wasylkiw & Currie, 2012). At the same time, there is an emerging body of literature on the use of film narratives as a pedagogical tool in feminist practice in schools. Ncgobo (2016), for example used the South African film *Yesterday* (directed by Darrell Roodt, 2004) in a secondary classroom in South Africa to raise issues of gender in the context of the AIDS crisis. Analysing and producing fictional narratives in classrooms can enable students to think critically about gender-related issues and could lead them to engage in addressing social change (Leavy, 2013; MacDonald et al., 2011).

 | DOI: 10.1163/9789004442870_021

I am interested in how an understanding of gender through popular films could lead adolescents to challenge gender norms by taking on what Caron, Raby, Mitchell, Théwissen-LeBlanc, and Prioletta (2016) refer to as a "social change-oriented youth voice" (p. 2). The authors are "looking for what could be described as event-oriented content, or video commentary that responds to a prompt … and that has an obvious focus and commentary on a social issue along with an expressed desire for change" (p. 6). They observe the complexity and the diversity of youth perspectives by considering what they refer to as voice not only as an individual story but as a public event that delivers a message that often expresses personal concerns about gender. I explore how studying representations of women in movies could encourage students to think critically about the norms portrayed in them. In this chapter, I promote inclusive education, and I am advocating for a type of social change that benefits not only self-identified boys and girls, but also students who identify as transgender or non-binary.

## 2 Popular Films in the Classroom

Gender-based inequalities are portrayed in numerous ways in popular films. In the 200 most viewed movies in the world, only 12% feature women as main characters.[1] Some of these characters, for example Wonder Woman (*Wonder Woman*, 2017), Katniss Everdeen (*The Hunger Games*, 2012–2015), Ripley (*Alien*, 1979–1997), and Hermione Granger (*Harry Potter*, 2001–2011), are considered feminist in mass media (THR Staff, 2016). However, these female characters embody a striking paradox. These are so-called free women who engage in paid labor and are independent but, at the same time, they follow patriarchal norms, like, for example, entering into a heterosexual marriage to complete themselves, thus enacting normalised representations of gender roles (see, among others, Gill (2017), McRobbie (2004, 2015) and Butler (1990).

I am interested in how to use the complexity of these paradoxical representations of women in popular movies to engage adolescents and in how this critical engagement could support social change. Typically, popular films are considered to be entertainment, so students are not accustomed to looking at them with a critical eye and they do not always identify the problematic discourses perpetuated by representations of girls and women. Also, they may not want to criticise movies that engage them emotionally (Snowden, 2010; Marshall & Sensoy, 2009). I am interested in what might happen if they could continue to enjoy films *and* recognise the need to challenge gender norms.

## 3 Strategy One: Critical Readings through Critical Media Literacy

Critical media literacy consists in observing, studying, and discussing media content, so a promising approach to engaging students in critical readings is to give them this framework in which to conduct a gender analysis and then invite them to identify how female characters are portrayed and how norms are perpetuated or challenged in films. In practice, students might watch scenes, or entire movies in a classroom, and then engage in a critical discussion. For example, teachers can ask students to think about the physical presentation of women along with the dynamics of power between male and female characters. For example:

- How are women's bodies portrayed?
- Do male characters speak more than female characters?
- Do female characters talk to each other and, if they do, what do they talk about?
- If a character's sexual orientation is made explicit, are any hidden messages included in the portrayal?

When they learn to study film from a critical media literacy perspective, students become adept at seeing the norms portrayed in films, and they acquire the tools to adopt an intersectional perspective by looking at the dynamics of power related not only to gender but also to age, race, class, sexuality, and age. (Snowden, 2010; Marshal & Sensoy, 2009).

### 3.1 *Katniss Everdeen of the Hunger Games Movies in the Classroom*

*The Hunger Games*, one of the highest-grossing franchises of all time,[2] featuring the character Katniss Everdeen, is a science-fiction dystopian adventure series made up of four movies based on Suzanne Collins's books. Given the goal of this analysis, I will focus only on the portrayal of Katniss Everdeen in the four movies. Katniss is a young woman living in a dystopic world separated into districts, all controlled by the Capitol, the hegemonic power. The Hunger Games are a punishment devised by the Capitol: after an attempted rebellion led by the districts, the supreme authorities decided to sacrifice two so-called tributes, a boy and a girl, from each district every year, to remind everybody about who is in control. The 24 randomly selected candidates must all try to kill each other in an arena during the Hunger Games until only two, the Victors, remain. Katniss's sister is selected, but Katniss saves her by volunteering to be a tribute in the Games.

Katniss Everdeen's character is often considered feminist by the popular media (Tahir, 2018; Moore, 2013). In some ways, she does question and challenge conventional narratives in that she has traits conventionally attributed to men—she is the protagonist, the leader, the fighter. Accordingly, we could argue that this character challenges norms related to femininity. However, she embodies many conventions typically associated with women in relation to her romantic involvement with two young men, Peeta and Gale; she must overcome the problems of this heterosexual love triangle. She is also often in need of men's help and her body exemplifies the stereotypical Hollywood movie standard of beauty. Katniss Everdeen, therefore, simultaneously challenges and perpetuates norms related to gender; she is both empowered and hegemonised. After watching *The Hunger Games* (or some selected scenes) in class with their students, teachers could ask the following questions to engage them:

- Is it usual to see a female lead character in a Hollywood blockbuster?
- What is Katniss good at, and are these skills usually depicted in female characters?
- What is Katniss's goal?

These questions could allow students to understand how Katniss challenges norms related to gender: she has a leading role, which continues to be unusual for a woman; she is fighting against the Capitol; she survives; and she eventually becomes the face of the resistance. Katniss is also a very good fighter: she knows how to hunt; to make a fire; to use a bow. Several times in the films, she is shown leading military strikes.

Then teachers could also ask questions about the norms still perpetuated by Katniss:

- What does Katniss look like?
- Can you think of other female characters in Hollywood movies who look like her?
- What makes Katniss vulnerable?
- What is her relationship with other characters?
- What most occupies her thoughts?

Through these questions, students can identify norms portrayed in Katniss: she is a white, thin, young woman, she is part of a heterosexual love triangle, and ensuring the safety of two men is what makes her the most vulnerable. Her relationships with male characters are limited to lover or mentor: when in need, she reaches out to men for help. These elements illustrate how the representation of Katniss strongly perpetuates norms related to gender, but also to sexuality, age, and race. These questions enable students to navigate the complexity of the representation of Katniss Everdeen as they explore the characteristics that challenge norms related to gender, but also the conventions still being perpetuated. However, discussing the conventions perpetuated by the representation of Katniss Everdeen also enables students to notice conventions and dynamics of power that are present in other media discourses (for example, the news or social media), but also in their everyday lives. For example, students might notice that women of colour are generally under-represented in popular movies. Also, students can engage in a conversation about heteronormativity, and how heterosexuality is reinforced as a norm through movies and other media. Identifying and understanding these norms enable students to engage critically with popular culture and to participate in social change.

## 4 Strategy Two: Bringing Creativity into Classrooms

How do creative practices engage adolescent students in addressing social change? Earlier I refer to what Caron et al. (2016) term a social change-oriented voice. While Caron and her colleagues were referring specifically to youth-produced vlogs, the focus of much of their analysis on feminism aligns well with what interests me in terms of creative practices being used to address gender. Bringing creativity through cultural production into classrooms gives students an opportunity to develop discourses that correspond with their experiences and their newly acquired understanding. Through creating fiction, for example, teenagers can place themselves at the center of the discourse and can, thus, explore their own experiences (Macdonald et al., 2011) related to gender roles and gender norms. In this setting, the creative practice itself is simultaneously informed by a conceptual framework based on critical literacy and a critical discussion about popular culture's normative representations. In this way, they engage in the beginnings of effecting social change by participating in creating a narrative that challenges crippling conventions and norms. In this way creativity can be used as a tool of resistance against social injustices and can engage students in collective action that aims to generate social change (Mitchell, De Lange, & Moletsane, 2017).

With the development of online platforms and the strong involvement of teenagers with social media, we can see a shift in the way in which adolescent students consume popular culture and this shift needs to be considered when we are using critical media literacy in classrooms. Consuming popular culture has now become not only an active and creative practice, but also a participatory activity as students share, comment on, and produce content with and for their peers on online platforms. Consequently, combining critical media literacy with participatory and creative practices is a strong way to engage students in moving towards making social change possible.

Participatory and creative practices can take many forms including storyboarding, photovoice, performance, creative writing, video documentary, drawing, painting, dancing, and singing. Storyboarding methods, for example, associated with video are particularly relevant when combined with a movie analysis since storyboards are used in the film and TV industries. Storyboarding refers to a series of drawings, with some directions and dialogue, used to plan the order of action and events in a film or a television production. This method enables students to produce fictional narratives using different skills: writing; drawing; framing; planning; and so on (Labacher, Mitchell, De Lange, Moletsane, & Geldenhuys, 2017). As Patricia Leavy (2009) has highlighted, when we use stories as fictional practice, we create new forms of knowledge and we explore our own experiences through a fictional setting. Writing stories helps us to understand our environment and the norms with which we are confronted.

### 4.1 *Addressing Social Change through Creative Production*

As part of a previous research project, I wrote a fictional text built on the analysis of how four female characters (Katniss Everdeen from *The Hunger Games* (2012, 2013, 2014, 2015), Natasha Romanoff from the *Marvel Cinematic Universe* (2010, 2012, 2014, 2015, 2016), Rey from *Star Wars: The Force Awakens* (2015), and Imperator Furiosa from *Mad Max: Fury Road* (2015) simultaneously perpetuated and challenged norms related to gender since my goal was to write a fictional piece that challenged these norms (Armaignac, 2017). The story I wrote (in French) is titled *Zones Troubles* (Blurred zones). In a dystopic world, Alice, the main character, tries to understand why some issues related to gender, age, race, class, and sexuality still exist. She tries to understand why laws are so controlling and why governments are not doing anything to help people.

Alice, surrounded by other female characters, is bisexual and fluid (we know only that she has "curly brown hair" and "sharp brown eyes"). All these characteristics resist dominant discourses: Alice is not white; she is not the only female character in the story; and she is not heterosexual. Alice's world overflows with commonly accepted injustices. She is a fighter; she resists and tries to change her world. Alice's voice is often my own voice. Through the story, I express a need to resist conventional narratives and norms related to gender, age, race, sexuality, and class. This act of resistance contributes to social change by producing a narrative that challenges gendered norms. Moreover, Alice is going through several traumatic experiences: street harassment; sexual harassment at work; and sexual violence. Through having others read about Alice, I can condemn publicly some experiences I have been through. Writing this piece of fiction was an act of resistance, as well as an act of denunciation against what many women face throughout their lives. This piece of fiction was a way of exploring these norms, but also of participating in social change by denouncing the inequalities consequent upon these norms. Producing fictional stories could guide students through the process of finding their own voice. It might encourage them to explore personal issues but in a way that is less obvious because it is being done through fiction, thus creating both an intimate and anonymous space in which they can explore their past experiences.

In order to effect social change, fictional stories need to be shared. In my case, I have shared the fiction with other graduate students and professors at conferences or guest lectures. In classrooms, students could be invited to present their fictional pieces to the whole group. The presentations could be organised as informal discussions, or as part of a small exhibition that can be open to the rest of the students at the school. The goal is to generate a conversation about issues students are exploring and questioning through their fiction.

## 5 Discussion

Creative and participatory practices are particularly relevant when we are addressing gender-related issues, However, educators need to be careful when they invite students to produce fictional narratives related to their own experiences. Keeping students safe is a priority. Most students never talk about sexual assault with their parents nor in classrooms. Consequently, educators committed to helping students in such a situation might need to develop strategies promoting dialogue with adolescent students, and these strategies could include the use of fictional narratives such as books, films, and TV shows (Weissbourd, Ross, Cashin, & McIntyre, 2017).

Also, before implementing creative writing practices in classrooms educators must know the policies and resources that are available in schools and on campuses to help students who are victims of discrimination, sexual violence, or harassment. As Mitchell and Cheverie (1989) have pointed out, sharing personal stories in classrooms has ethical implications. What happens if students are telling real stories about their experiences of gender-based violence? Engaging in discussions about gender-related issues might trigger certain emotions in some students.

Both students and educators should be prepared to develop a dialogue that does not erase anyone's voice. They need to be aware of issues that often affect classrooms dynamics and that silence minorities and those who are shy or reticent. Using fiction in classrooms not only benefits self-identified girls and women, but also transgender and non-binary students. Creating fiction enables students to control their narratives. They can use creative practices to challenge norms, but also to explore their own experiences and to resist dominant discourses.

## 6 Conclusion

By working with representations of women in popular films and in engaging in their own creative practices, adolescent students can come to understand how norms and conventions related to gender operate. They can be given opportunities to participate in critical conversations that are key to addressing social change. By creating their own fiction, students challenge norms and conventions that affect them. They focus on specific social issues and, as observed by Caron et al. (2016), they express the "desire for change" (p. 6). In this way they are making use of their "social-change oriented youth voices" celebrated in the title of their article. By deconstructing norms related to gender and sexuality, students participate in creating an inclusive community. The two strategies explored in this chapter promote a type of social change that does not just benefit one group of students. Through creative and participatory practices, all students can be enabled to express their voice, regardless of their gender, race, age, class, and/or sexuality. To help counteract the ways in which schools are affected by strong normative dynamics of power and inequality, having students engage in arts-based endeavours like analysing representations of women in films and in creative story writing is a promising approach to promoting inclusive and equitable social change.

## Notes

1 https://www.boxofficemojo.com/
2 https://www.the-numbers.com/movies/franchises

## References

Armaignac, E. (2017). *La représentation des personnages féminins des « blockbusters » américains : Représentations et rapports de pouvoir* [The representation of female characters in American blockbusters: Representations and power dynamics] (Unpublished master's thesis). Université de Montréal, Montreal.

Butler, J. (1990). *Gender trouble: Feminism and the subversion of identity*. Routledge.

Caron, C., Raby, R., Mitchell, C., Théwissen-LeBlanc, S., & Prioletta, J. (2016). From concept to data: Sleuthing social change-oriented youth voices on YouTube. *Journal of Youth Studies, 20*(1), 47–62. https://doi.org/10.1080/13676261.2016.1184242

Gill, R. (2017). The affective, cultural and psychic fife of postfeminism: A postfeminist sensibility 10 years on. *European Journal of Cultural Studies, 20*(6), 606–626. https://doi.org/10.1177/1367549417733003

Jacobson, N. (Producer), Kilik, J. (Producer), & Ross, G. (Director). (2012). *The Hunger Games* [Motion picture]. Lionsgate, Alliance Films, Color Force, Criterion-on-Demand.

Jacobson, N. (Producer), Kilik, J. (Producer), & Lawrence, F. (Director). (2013). *The hunger games: Catching fire* [Motion picture]. Lionsgate, Color Force.

Jacobson, N. (Producer), Kilik, J. (Producer), & Lawrence, F. (Director). (2014). *The hunger games: Mockingjay part 1* [Motion picture]. Lionsgate, Color Force, Entertainment One.

Kilik, J. (Producer), Collins, S. (Producer), Lawrence, F. (Director). (2015). *The hunger games: Mockingjay part 2* [Motion picture]. Lionsgate, Color Force.

Labacher, L., Mitchell, C., De Lange, N., Moletsane, R., & Geldenhuys, M.-M. (2017). What can a visual researcher do with a storyboard? In E. J. Milne, C. Mitchell, & N. De Lange (Ed.), *The handbook of participatory video* (pp. 149–163). AltaMira Press.

Leavy, P. (2009). *Method meets art: Arts-based research practice.* Guilford Press.

Leavy, P. (2013). *Fiction as research practice: Short stories, novellas, and novels.* Routledge.

MacDonald J. A., Gagnon A. J., Mitchell C., Di Meglio G., Rennick J. E., & Cox J. (2011). Include them and they will tell you: Learnings from a participatory process with youth. *Qualitative Health Research, 21*(8), 1127–1135.https://doi.org/10.1177/1049732311405799

Marshall, E., & Sensoy, Ö. (2009). The same old hocus-pocus: Pedagogies of gender and sexuality in Shrek 2. *Discourse: Studies in the Cultural Politics of Education, 30*(2), 151–164. https://doi.org/10.1080/01596300902809104

McRobbie, A. (2004). Post-feminism and popular culture. *Feminist Media Studies, 4*(3), 255–264. https://doi.org/10.1080/1468077042000309937

McRobbie, A. (2015). Notes on the perfect: Competitive femininity in neoliberal times. *Australian Feminist Studies, 30*(83), 3–20. https://doi.org/10.1080/08164649.2015.1011485

Mitchell, C., & Cheverie, A. (1989). Now that we've them writing ... Addressing issues of ethics, aesthetics, taste and sensibility through student writing. *Reading Canada Lecture, 7*(3), 180–190.

Mitchell, C., De Lange, N., & Moletsane, R. (2017). *Participatory visual methodologies: Social change, community and policy.* Sage.

Moore, S. (2013, November 27). Why the hunger games' Katniss Everdeen is a role model for our times. *The Guardian.* https://www.theguardian.com/commentisfree/2013/nov/27/why-hunger-games-katniss-everdeen-role-model-jennifer-lawrence

Motion Picture of America. (2018). *2018 theme report.* https://www.mpaa.org/wp-content/uploads/2019/03/MPAA-THEME-Report-2018.pdf

Ngcobo, N. Y. (2016). *Adolescent readers' responses to gender representation in isiZulu texts dealing with HIV and AIDS: A case study in a secondary school in KwaZulu-Natal Province* (Unpublished doctoral dissertation). University of KwaZulu-Natal, Durban.

Tahir, S. (2018. October 18). Katniss everdeen is my hero. *The New York Times.* https://www.nytimes.com/2018/10/18/books/katniss-everdeen-hunger-games.html

THR Staff. (2016, December 9). Hollywood's 50 favorite female characters. *The Hollywood Reporter.* https://www.hollywoodreporter.com/lists/50-best-female-characters-entertainment-industry-survey-results-951483/

Raby, R., Caron, C., Théwissen-LeBlanc, S., Prioletta, J., & Mitchell, C. (2018). Vlogging on YouTube: The online, political engagement of young Canadians advocating for social change. *Journal of Youth Studies, 21*(4), 495–512. https://doi.org/10.1080/13676261.2017.1394995

Snowden, K. (2010). Fairy tale film in the classroom: Creating feminist cultural pedagogy. In P. Greenhill, E. Sidney, & Matrix (Ed.), *Fairy tale films: Visions of ambiguity* (p. 157–177). Utah State University Press.

Wasylkiw, L., & Currie, M. (2012). The animal house effect: How university-themed comedy films affect students' attitudes. *Social Psychology of Education, 15*(1), 25–40.

Weissbourd, R., Ross, T., Cashin, A., & McIntyre, J. (2017, May 1). *The talk: How adults can promote young people's healthy relationships and prevent misogyny and sexual harassment.* Talk presented at the Harvard Graduate School of Education. https://mcc.gse.harvard.edu/files/gse-mcc/files/mcc_the_talk_final.pdf

CHAPTER 22

# Unconscious Acts

## *An Auto-Ethnographic Investigation into Euro-Centric White Normative Consciousness in Theatre Training Programs in Canada*

*Makram R. Ayache*

## 1 Introduction

It is the first month of my actor training program and I'm performing a "Personal Mythology." I'm moving about on stage, emulating my twelve-year-old self playing in my best friend's yard. We climb trees and pretend we're action heroes. We bike through sparse streets, trade cards, and play our hand-held video games at the top of a hill until our parents come home from work. It was the perfect rural Albertan childhood. I emulate all of this with a simple sweeping gesture across the stage. I tucked into a playful roll and skirt across the stage with a blue cape. After the first showing, my professor offers earnest warmth with a desire to see me. She says, "I saw a child of war."

The story above is about an experience I had during my theatre training at the University of Alberta. On the surface, it is rather innocuous, perhaps playful. But what I attempt to investigate are the ways which a Euro-centric white normative consciousness manifests itself in Canadian theatre training programs. I make difficult and conflicting discoveries and what appears to be innocuous may indicate a more urgent issue that theatre training programs face. I look to answer the question, "In what ways does Euro-centric white normative consciousness manifest itself in Canadian theatre training programs?" through an auto-ethnographic analysis of one year at the University of Alberta's Bachelor of Fine Arts in Acting program. Through this inquiry, I reveal the ways in which unintentional and systematised structures continue to grate at the educational and artistic experiences of racialised students, even when so-called multiculturalism is invited into the room.

Multiculturalism invites a certain body into the room, but is it prepared for a new way of knowing? I am not sure. I am skeptical of this. At the risk of over-simplifying the complexity to a binary, we can either bandage the social issues of race and migration politics *or* work from both systematic and grassroots ends to radically transform it. Multiculturalism feels like the bandage. Perhaps the focus of Canadian Prime Minister, Pierre Elliot Trudeau on multiculturalism in the 1980s was an astute insight into the entanglement of our globalising world,

 | DOI: 10.1163/9789004442870_022

but we ought to consider it as a step in the right direction, *not* the solution we were looking for, because, indeed, we continue to be entrenched in the issues of a worsening economy, poverty, racism, and discrimination which have plagued Canada (and the Euro-colonised world) since European global colonisation began. Multiculturalism was the proper step, but are we outgrowing this ideology, and should we propose new imagined futures towards which we can work?

## 2 Theoretical Framework and Methodology

Daring epistemology ought to challenge conventional approaches to unconventional questions. Western colonial attitudes permeate beyond research content into research form, methods, and dissemination. My effort is to challenge my research investigation through an auto-ethnographic study situated in an anti-colonial framework. I argue that this will be where innovation is discovered.

My inquiry begins with typical research artifacts like journals, reflections, digital web sources, course outlines, and assignments, but also invites memories, conversation, and affective impressions to inform the discussion.

I situate the study of Canadian theatre training programs through my lived experience of one year in the University of Alberta's Bachelor of Fine Arts in Acting program. I do this through reflexive and reflective interrogation of the research artifacts. I began with an investigation of the linear progression of the raw material and tracked impressions and themes that emerge throughout. Then, I wrote down prompted memories and reflections. These became part of the material considered in this study. These materials are then supported, investigated, and considered alongside literature in education, theatre, and sociological theory.

## 3 Limits of Research(er)

This mythology comes with some risk. Certainly, challenging white supremacy and imperialist discourse through research content as well as methodology brings us into a new and volatile landscape. We do not know how to trust this work, but that is precisely the inquiry. How can we unveil other ways of knowing when we do not know how they work? I argue that this is more reason to keep going.

An important limitation I recognise is that my individual lived experience of the Canadian theatre landscape does not speak widely. This particular study faces the challenges that many issues of racialisation come up against; the way *I*, a queer Arab-Canadian who grew up in rural Alberta experiences white supremacy cannot be extended to all or even to most of the racialised participants of these training programs. This challenges the definition of ethnography with its etymological emphasis on culture and study.

And, of course, the limitation exists in the legitimacy of the content in journals investigated, experiences considered, course outlines and assignments explored, and the subsequent memories, affective impressions, and reflections that derive from them. However, this is where the research is most interesting; concepts of legitimacy are determined by "who defined whom, who interprets how, in what ways, and towards what end" (Crichlow et al., 1990, p. 101) and the entire enterprise of an auto-ethnographic study conducted by a queer Arab-Canadian on the relationship of white supremacy in Canadian theatre training programs is exactly a challenge to that dominant discourse and determination of legitimacy.

## 4 "I Saw a Child of War": An Incident of White Normativity and Its Implications of Racialised Students

In my first month of the program, I presented an assignment called the Personal Mythology. As described in the opening of this chapter, my professor said, "I saw a child of war." The residue of this memory exists in two ways. The implication closer to the surface is that my professor interpreted what my Arab body did through a very particular lens. Although I felt earnestness and camaraderie, and not malice in the misinterpretation, I also felt misrepresented. More importantly, I felt that this was another echo of white normative consciousness seeping into the most well intentioned of people. It is best here to iterate that one does not need to be white or intentional in reproducing imperialist, white supremacist heteropatriarchy. I do not mean to characterise my professor as maliciously or intentionally racist. In fact, this entire conversation is about combatting deeper socio-conscious manifestations of racism.

With that, then, was her comment racist? Was it an orientalist analysis of a brown body? I argue that it *was* racist. I suspect that if a white body performed my piece, it would have triggered a very different response (as would a black, Asian, or Indigenous body). Why "a child of war?" Because this was the encapsulation, domination, and strategic representation, which now operates organically, of the Near and Middle Eastern world that continues to manipulate the perceptions of the Western world (Said, 1978). And, since this discourse is predicated on domination politics of the white Euro-colonising world, I hold that the comment was racist. And it is important to remember that in the first showing, I merely flittered and rolled across the stage wearing a blue cape.

However, the more disturbing memory is that I did not correct her. Very little of my upbringing is directly related to war. Indeed, I had a perfectly average rural Albertan childhood. However, I felt a resistance to correcting her.

Why might I have felt that? There are several considerations at play. First, her being a cultural gate keeper (the professor and program chair), I am in a precarious position; I am taught through the overt and the hidden curriculum that we ought not to challenge our teachers. So, of course, this may be less race related and more teacher/student relationship related. The second consideration is the inherent domination psychology at play between white people and others. As Karen Pyke (2010) points out, "[superior and inferior social constructions] become habitual as they are constructed in and through social relations and organizations, causing *even the oppressed to have a stake in their subordinated identity*" (p. 557, emphasis added). As an Arab body in a predominantly white classroom, having grown up in a predominantly white culture, I had learned not to correct whiteness, not to call out racism, and to consider, beyond a shadow of a doubt, whether the tension I feel from essentialising comments like "I saw a child of war" is warranted or not. This is a consideration that I am still deliberating today.

So why hesitate to correct her? I cannot answer that question confidently. Perhaps it was student/teacher power politics. Perhaps it was a reproduction of internalised racism. Perhaps I felt that her heart was in the right place. Or perhaps I was simply tired that day. I am illustrating that it is difficult to conjecture and am reflecting a process of contemplation that an othered body might undertake in these situations.

An additional aspect of this moment is that in the second rendition of my performance, I added one more motion. I maintained the roll across the stage, but then I pretended to take aim with a toy rifle, then I ran across the stage in the blue cape. This additional *leaning into* the "child of war" comment is most peculiar. The same questions above belong here. Was this done to satisfy my teacher's needs? Or was this an internalised reinforcement of racist consciousness? *Give them what they want.* I suspect satisfying the teacher's needs and the reinforcement of internalised racial politics interact with each other quite closely. Educational research by Rachel Elizabeth Fish (2017) suggests this to be true, claiming, "teachers … appear to perceive students' abilities and motivations differently in ways that align with racist stereotypes" (p. 320). The implication is that racialised students consequently must work harder to become legitimised by their white teachers. It may certainly have been my experience.

What this experience most demonstrates is the kind of strain racialised students in these programs must consider when their professors are mostly white. My task was to create work that shares my experience for a Personal Mythology. However, when the cultural gatekeepers of these training programs are white, the perceptions of the racialised student are altered and the student's ability to represent themselves comes up against serious difficulty. This means I am not seen as I am but rather as I am perceived to be by the dominant moderators. But a brief exchange like this certainly cannot be representative of the totality of theatre training programs.

## 5 Legitimate Theatre: An Investigation into the Overt and Covert Curricular Objectives of Theatre Training

As part of the first year of the program, all students are required to do Movement, Voice, Acting, Singing, Dance, Fencing, and Production Lab. The structure of the program is based on a powerful European model of conservatory actor training and its roots are not so hidden. I am not interested in the destruction of successful, enjoyable, and creative European models of art, but I am interested in eliminating their domination over other models of art, especially if the Canadian theatre landscape (and its practitioner training programs) are invested in an authentic pluralistic paradigm shift.

Part of my research brought up reflections on fencing, ballet, classical singing, and Shakespeare in theatre training. I want to focus on these four units since they are glaring reflections of Euro-centric white normative consciousness that are idly accepted as necessary for the training. I recall holding the lunge position in fencing class on an early Saturday morning, my legs trembling, a film of sweat glazing my face, rage flushing my mind and body. Perhaps fencing was something I knew I would not take forward from my theatre training, but the necessary requirement of the course became more insidious than simply a personal aversion. The instructor proposed that the fencing salute was "to God in heaven, to the heart, and let's fight" alongside a sequence of lifting the foil to the sky, holding it against one's chest, then slashing it diagonally across the body until it is tip down along one's side. It is baffling that such an archaic and overtly Euro-Christian consciousness is unapologetically made a requirement of a program. It is not so different when Shakespeare continues to be a stringent requirement. And I recall being told that fencing and ballet would cultivate a solid foundation from which to perform. I was reassured that ballet, fencing, classical singing, and Shakespeare acting *optimised* the capacity of the body and that these techniques were the most effective, disciplined, and legitimate uses of the body from which an actor can spring.

This is precisely the dominant and normalised acceptance of white Euro-centric values that colonises the imagination of a racialised body. The implication is that these forms of art are the neutral base from which all theatre artists ought to begin. From there, we can deviate from the norm. And this deviation is an objectification of multicultural paradigms usually in the form of a tacked on "African dance" unit or some other. What I mean is that rather than allowing white Euro-centric structures to be a part of the richness of artistic expression, it continues to be the observer of all other supposedly diverse forms of *doing*. Although content is invited into the room (I was invited to do an Arabic poem for voice class), form, structure, and understanding certainly were not. And the legitimacy of Euro-centric models of theatre were reinforced and upheld through ballet, fencing, Shakespeare, and classic singing.

I suspect that a response may be, "But you signed up for a classical training program." This is a fair question, but I must ask, "Who's classical? Which version of who's history? Moreover, does classical equate with Euro-centric? Would a semantic shift to 'European Conservatory Theatre Training' be appropriate?" I ask because, currently, many (and certainly not all) non-European students hoping to enter the Canadian theatre landscape have an entire popular avenue of training closed off to their ways of being, knowing, representation, and learning because classical conservatory training programs hold the most potent *legitimising* gateway.

Mumbi Tindyebwa (2015) offers insight here:

> Companies such as Obsidian Theatre, Cahoots Theatre Company, Fu-Gen Asian Canadian Theatre, and Aluna Theatre are all producing consistently excellent work with a culturally diverse mandate. However, none of these companies own their own venues, and they often have to look for space to present their stories within the larger white institutions that have their own season programming and established audiences. (p. 25)

Even culturally specific training programs like that offered by the *Center for Indigenous Theatre* continue to be marginal, even if they are gaining legitimacy.

How can we invite authentic multicultural perspectives into university theatre training programs? Guillermo Verdecchia (2007) points to Kitchener, Ontario's multicultural theatre, *MT Spaces Theatre*, as a role model, saying "that's what—it seems to me—is going on here at the MT Space. Majdi Bou-Matar [Artistic Director] has insisted that the focus here is not on folkloric or static versions of culture. Instead, the emphasis appears to be on innovation, discovery, hybridity; this theatre seeks to generate something new" (p. 194).

However, I must stop this inquiry here. How to diversify theatre training programs is not the goal of this investigation, but I encourage others to take up this task. The purpose of this discussion is to highlight how the illegitimacy of 'other ways of knowing' begins in theatre training programs and cascades into the theatre landscape.

But as I present this information, I am aware of a deep discordance. Despite these minority stresses, I look at my theatre training at the University of Alberta with authentic fondness and gratitude. I go on to explore this dynamic.

## 6 An Available Spirit: An Acknowledgement of the Ways in Which White Normative Consciousness Is Being Challenged

I must recognise that the University of Alberta's theatre program is attempting to combat white normative consciousness in noticeable ways (as are many across the country). Although the scope of this research is limited to my experience in one year in the program, it is important to address, for a moment, my previous six years of study with the drama department as a Secondary Drama Education major. While the University of Alberta's conservatory acting program comes up against the issues discussed above, there are professors in the department at large who work with drama majors in non-acting streams, and who are doing innovative work with intergenerational theatre, Kenyan theatre groups, and more. Indeed, I developed much of my racially critical perspective with some of these professors. Further, even within the conservatory acting program, most professors were open to ongoing dialogue regarding many of these issues.

My relationship with the professors at the University of Alberta was beautiful, authentic, and it contributed to my growth in significant ways. Despite the systemic reduction of my experience as an Arab, I can say that I did not come across an educator at the university who intentionally or overtly limited my potential based on my ethnicity.

But the machine of white normative consciousness marches on. Often, oppression is not upheld by malicious intent but, rather, by convenience. Is it enough to have a spirit of change? Does a politics of convenience willfully obfuscate the affective response of the oppressed? I feel a sincere gratitude to my professors, but I am consumed by frustration at their change-is-slow attitude. Perhaps it is from our privileged perch in the academy that we could engage steadfastly in these discussions? Convenience shows its evil face when we confront it in the light of Indigenous homelessness and poverty, anti-Muslim violence, and the murder of trans women here in Canada. I hope it is clear that my argument is precisely against the white normative consciousness that permeates our educational, artistic, political, and cultural landscapes that scaffold the violence of overt oppression and white supremacy, so I can hold that my professors individually bolstered my academic, artistic, and personal development while recognising that the program engaged in a systematic and dangerous reproduction of Euro-centric ways of knowing.

## 7 Recommendations

I do not know if it is the role of the researcher to propose recommendations, but as I position myself as a praxis based academic, artist, and educator, I feel that it is my responsibility to add this section. Here, I offer a way into a different kind of reality. However, as mentioned earlier, we are embarking on a journey into new territory and the answers are not readily available since we are simultaneously inventing and discovering other ways of knowing.

The first recommendation is that without the radical transmission of authority of theatre training faculty from white, middle class men and woman to racialised people (among queer/disabled/and other marginalised ones), a systemic change will not happen. My first proposal is that stable, full time faculty members who are defining and designing these training programs become intrinsically diverse enough to offer meaningful organisational change. It may be a very different acting class if the professor at the helm is a black, Indigenous, brown, or Asian body. Indeed, it may be a different creative, performance, and knowledge space. Of course, this transition is in process, but I argue that it needs more urgency. In the liminal space right now, there is a variety of artistic practitioners who could come into programs like the one detailed in this chapter and guide several units. I agree that a systematic shift is not possible overnight, but more can and ought to be done if the commitment to change is serious.

The second recommendation is that existing professors take on the profound responsibility of complicating and deepening their understanding of systematic oppressions on the global, national, and local stage. Certainly not everyone can be thinking about every intersection of oppression always, but there is an onus on university professors, as cultural ambassadors in Canada, to undertake the labors of understanding the culture with which or against which they synthesise. A reflective and reflexive practice with systems of oppression is certainly understandable. And, perhaps even further, the leaders of these departments could present their faculty with professional development opportunities.

The third recommendation stems from a necessity to acknowledge my commitment to supporting Indigenous peoples in Canada. These issues are all the more complicated since I am an Arab-settler on colonised land and it is the responsibility of all of us to respond to, interact with, and honor the treaties that were signed with the First Nations, Métis, and Inuit (FNMI) peoples of Canada. Theatre departments ought to invite more analysis, different ways of knowing, and a much greater awareness of cultural difference into the theatre training area.

Finally, on the more affective front, what theatre training programs need most is what theatre does best in its willingness to embrace the unknown, to play, to welcome chaos into the room, to accept failure, to risk, to listen, to innovate, to invite the death of a certain way, and courageously make room for new ways. The same professor whose story opened this research taught me that between predictability and chaos, only one offers creation. Follow the line of predictability and you will get a linear, reductionist, positive conclusion. Dive into the unknown of chaos and the channel for discovery is unending.

## References

Crichlow, W., Goodwin, S., Shakes, G., & Swartz, E. (1990) Multicultural ways of knowing: Implications for practice. *Journal of Education, 172*(2), 101–117.

Fish, R. E. (2017). The racialized construction of exceptionality: Experimental evidence of race/ethnicity effects on teachers interventions. *Social Science Research, 62*, 317–334. doi:10.1016/j.ssresearch.2016.08.007

Pyke, K. D. (2010). What is internalized racial oppression and why don't we study it? Acknowledging racisms hidden injuries. *Sociological Perspectives, 53*(4), 551–572. doi:10.1525/sop.2010.53.4.551

Said, E. W. (1978). *Orientalism*. Vintage Books.

Tindyebwa, M. (2015). A multicultural stage. *Canadian Theatre Review, 163*, 25–29. doi:3138/ctr.163.005

Verdecchia, G. (2007). In the MT space. In M. McKinnie (Ed.), *Space and the geographies of theatre* (pp. 194–200). Playwrights Canada Press.

CHAPTER 23

# A Pedagogy of Presence

## *Attending to Context, Process, Being, and Belonging*

*Rébecca Bourgault*

Socially engaged art practices generate artwork centred around dialogue and interpersonal connections. The acts of social engagement, embodied dimensions of making, and critical discourse are understood to form an integral part of that artwork.

In the last decades we have witnessed an accrued variety of artistic approaches for which the significant values were found in the relational outcomes that brought the people and their projects together.

In such a context, artists place more importance on the methods of engagement than on making art products (Leake, 2014). Helguera (2011) suggested that the art object as the focus of making and participating leads to a depth of exchange that itself becomes the work of art.

If relational and social practices of art, including art for social justice, are understood to situate the heart of the artistic project in qualities of dialogical energy and sociality, what constitutes a successful work often does not register with definitions of artistic validity endorsed by an institutional expert culture. Rather, what is emphasised is the value of the communal exchange; this often dispenses with the conventional aesthetic function of art, altering its operation, and inserting other possibilities, say, its heuristic or epistemic purpose (Wright, 2014).

In *Aesthetic Perspectives: Attributes for Excellence in Arts for Change,* Laramee Kidd (2017) has suggested that the framework through which art with civic intent can be evaluated includes a broad understanding of the community's experience. What she refers to as aesthetic attributes include "emotional experience, sensory experience, openness, resourcefulness, coherence, commitment, and cultural integrity" (p. 4), to name a few. Indeed, the goals of art for social justice or art for change are often seen in contradiction to the values of artistic programs focused on developing artistic skills and art forms validated by a professional viewership.

In my experience, working at the intersection of artistic creation, andragogy, and community engagement demands a shift in perspective that is anchored in critical pedagogy and sustained by self-awareness and attention to context. Qualities of dialogical and relational development are possible when

 | DOI: 10.1163/9789004442870_023

participants invest a responsive, collaborative spirit and resourcefulness in the project, aware of ever-changing tones in the relationship between participants.

In many instances where work for social change is the goal, transformation happens in micro-steps so words or actions reflecting outcome may appear intangible and ephemeral, at times even stagnant. The question of relating aesthetic experience to everyday reality is answered differently by every participant. To Wildemeersch and von Kotze's (2014) question, "How does the art experience translate into a new way of relating to others, to objects, to the context in which the participants act and live, wanting to transform it so it may reflect [a] constructed transitional, potential space?" (p. 323), answers become observable in the unfolding of transference, such as when a reclaimed self-confidence is acknowledged and acted upon.

Advocates of social justice will argue that unless it is a project that becomes integrated in one's identity and activities, art for social change is difficult to evaluate and may have little long-term effect on the lives of the participants. This position maintains that as long as the process of change is framed within an individualistic understanding of self where the structural inequalities of the social, economic, historical, and institutional realms are not understood as defining one's relationship to the world—what Dej (2016) refers to as the "neoliberal obligations of personal freedom" (p. 22)—the transformational goals of art for social change risk remaining a naive and superficial fix applied to deeper societal problems.

In my view, recognising inequities and working for social justice begin with advocating for change through human encounters, artistic and otherwise, that establish communal and shared feelings of integrity, inclusion, and a sense of creative possibilities that reach both to the inner self and a societal dimension. Socially engaged artists are concerned with "emphasizing the practical, transformative, and activating power of art, and creating new space for social interaction" (Wang, 2017, p. 35). Artistic projects constructed through this goal offer a perspective or entry point that allows participants to reflect on their social and human conditions through art explorations.

What is at play and calls to be nurtured are qualities of authenticity and worthiness supported through a pedagogy of presence. Part social art practice, part meditation, and, borrowing from principles of critical pedagogy, a pedagogy of presence demands a mind that does not anticipate things to fix, but that is attentive to qualities that manifest.

## 1 An Open Art Studio at the Homeless Shelter

> If you have come here to help me, you are wasting your time. But if you have come because your liberation is bound up with mine, then let us work together.[1]

Recently, I initiated a creative work in the form of an open art studio at a shelter for homeless women. My inquiry and subsequent narration are informed by an understanding of life's unfolding as Ground, Path, and Fruition, a Shambhala articulation of the principle, substantiated with experiments with embodied presence and what Finlay (2006) has described as "reflexive empathy" (n.p.). I approach the inquiry from a philosophical perspective, eschewing the social science researcher's distancing approach that would make the participants of the open studio the object of my study. Situating a pedagogy of presence as a shared method of discovery renders possible a sense of solidarity that does not make assumptions about reciprocity with an Other. I remain ambivalent about naming the Other as such, preferring that the positionality of participants be defined relationally, from their own defined centeredness, through their own voice, knowledge, and experience. A pedagogy of presence intentionally engages into a co-constructed praxis that is not confused with the delivery of knowledge from teacher to learner. Participants pursue their own research and contribute knowledge through their personal experience. My role is that of a "context provider, avoiding representation, not speaking for others, but providing them with the means to speak for themselves" (Daniel, 2011, p. 65).

## 2 Ground, Path, and Fruition

Berkeley Shambhala Center in 2006/2007, points out that the "simplest form of logic is a three-fold analysis—any event or process has a beginning, middle, and end. We could also think of ground, path, and fruition ... as examples of three-fold logic." Mipham Rinpoche explains that it is "one of the key elements in understanding the principle of how we change."[2] If ground is where we find ourselves at the onset of experience and fruition represents the projection of a result, path suggests what we have to do to get there—the means of inquiry.

The model can be applied to the work of the social artist in the initiation of a project, and it also can be a way of interpreting the unfolding process engaged in with the participants. It suggests a paradigm that provides a perspective that ensures awareness of what arises in the relational exchanges as well as a tool to examine retrospectively the perceived changes. In more literal form, ground, path, and fruition offer a way to sense the development of an artistic work or a conversation. In this chapter, ground, path, and fruition provide a framework for writing, reflecting, and making sense of the open art studio experience. It starts with the ground of personal experience. Keeping in mind that "in Buddhism, the means of investigating experience starts with oneself ... It begins with mindfulness during which valid cognition is attained through paying attention to embodied experience ... Thus, knowledge is not confused with reasoning or intellectual constructions; knowing is through experience" (Rodriguez, 2005,

p. 40). Additionally, the Shambhala vision emphasises that inner work must be complemented with outer work—actions in the world at large.

## 3 Ground

### 3.1 *Presence*

Generally, presence is invoked in meditation practices, but its qualities are also examined by diverse practitioners such as therapists whose work is rooted in empathy and presence, which, in this situation, reflects an ability to listen and pay attention. Listening is also a fundamental exercise in the work for social justice and social change. As Butterwick and Roy (2018) observed, "We are familiar with the words usually identified with activism—*speaking out or standing up*; very few, if any, expressions refer to listening as a form of activism." Moreover, they note that "listening enhances inclusion" and that "listening is linked to a sense of collective identity and is about empowerment of those whose voices have been silent for too long" (p. 3, original emphasis).

Emphasising the importance of listening well, Rodriguez (2005) has also noted the need for a sustained witnessing that tolerates emotional states through a broad attentiveness and has said that "empathic connection is a state of being and understanding; it is knowing" (p. 139). In my practice and experiments with presence, the self-in-relationship situation of the open studio necessitates paying attention to the social and contextual factors brought in by the participants. Our group constitution, and resulting dynamic, is unpredictable and ever-changing.

## 4 Path

> In the studio, all of us connected today, in a simple and authentic way. We were, at that moment, all the same. We live differently but I did not feel a human distance. All women, more or less the same age, given a decade or two. We liked the calm and openness of the studio time. We just drew, cut, collaged, knitted, or painted stuff. F. was finishing a landscape drawing about memories of her Honduran home village. Then she drew a sky with birds and multiple colors. She called it her hope to fly, alto y largo, high and far away. Towards the end, we started to quietly converse. We found a space to exchange around languages and music. J. sang a love song in Portuguese. She has been studying the language. She says she wants to learn more and she wants to do humanitarian work. (Personal journal entry, March 8, 2019)

### 4.1 *Pedagogy of Presence*

A pedagogy of presence is grounded in an attuned, emergent, and responsive relationship with participants. The precariousness of a homeless person's life and disruptions of normalcy render this approach to the open studio both practical and reassuring. Often, sharing does not need to be verbalised; it is part of the mutual experience of the relationship. "Presence is knowing directly in the moment that we are what we experience" (McLeod, 2001, as cited in Rodriguez, 2005, p. 36).

The non-teaching approach stems in part from principles of critical pedagogy and adult education theories that establish that maintaining the relationship with the participant is the most important role for the facilitator whose embodied skills should include attitudes of genuineness, non-possessive caring, accurate listening, and empathic understanding (Rogers, as cited in Knowles, Holton, & Swanson, 2011, p. 84). More specifically in this project, as the climate of the studio became established, "the facilitator [was] increasingly able to become a participant, a member of the group, expressing his or her views as those of one individual only" (p. 85). Everyone can draw from the knowledge that everyone brings in from their life, family, cultural traditions, and experiences. Other key assumptions about adult participation in the open studio include the foundational understanding that adults are motivated to engage in new activities when prompted by life-centered needs and experiential interests (Knowles, Holton, & Swanson, 2011). Additionally, "adults have a deep need to be self-directing" (p. 39), hence the importance, in a pedagogy of presence, to be aware that participants bring in highly heterogeneous self-perceptions, beliefs, and intentions, and to engage in an intersubjective inquiry rather than a direct transmission of knowledge.

When explored from the perspective of occupational therapy, research with homeless persons shows that the contribution of arts occupations has a positive effect on health and wellbeing by supplying a sense of perceived control, a sense of self and purpose while building social support (Thomas, Gray, McGinty, & Ebringer, 2011). Silva, Silvestrini, Von Poellnitz, da Silva Almeida Prado, and Leite (2018) have found that shared art projects "promoted interaction, identification and socialization in the group" (p. 496), while artistic interventions favored the integration of other social functions and positions beside the person's own experience of disruption, "allowing both the expression of culture and its denunciation and criticism" (p. 497). Rose, Bingley, Rioseco, and Lamb (2018) have noted that for displaced persons, creating art in a group was "helpful in counteracting a sense of individual isolation, with the potential to enhance feelings of personal growth [and be] supportive of transition" (p. 105).

In trying to better understand what is meant by art and social change in an environment in which survival is a priority and in which the population is peripatetic, I experimented with approaches to setting up the open studio in response to the physical, emotional, and psychological situations of women who come for support at the shelter. The open studio aims to offer a normalising activity that provides safety, calm, and continuity in the life of participants. Often, staying at a shelter means experiencing noise, chaos, stress, and discomfort. One might be getting a bed on a lottery system, and, at night, fear of being robbed means that women sleep very poorly. In imagining a beneficial approach for the facilitation of the open studio, I imagined a pedagogy of presence to welcome participants into a community place in which I do not expect performance or skill nor dialogue or verbal exchange. I introduce basic art materials and tools at the onset with new additions available upon request. From its inception, the open studio has been free of educated hierarchies suggesting choices of artistic and technical approaches. Participants start where they are and change; growth (itself a value laden term) or conceptual curiosity come from witnessing each other's activities, conversations, and from private insights.

Finally, life at the shelter offers little privacy and an art studio time during which there is no need to talk is welcomed as a time for oneself. A pedagogy of presence is inspired by the suggestion that "rest, or pause, is intricately bound with our human sense of place and with the feeling that we are in touch with the meaningful center of ourselves" (Vandermark 2007, p. 243).

### 4.2 *Art, Displacement, and Belonging*

Homelessness affects a person's sense of self, place, and belonging (Vandemark, 2007), an impact that is felt more harshly by women for whom filiation and connectedness are paramount to a sense of self (Strauch-Brown & Ziefert, 1990). From its conception, the open studio was intended to provide a place in which their sense of self and belonging could momentarily counterpoise the uncertainty of living experienced by the women who attended. It would support participants' ability to engage in daily life by requiring them to make manageable decisions, thus gaining a sense of satisfaction that could bolster self-efficacy. In the words of Maxine Greene (1995),

> participatory involvement with the many forms of art does enable us at the very least, to see more in our experience, to hear more on normally unheard frequencies, to become conscious of what daily routines, habits, and conventions have obscured. (p. 378)

From previous experience facilitating activities at the shelter, I expected a sporadic attendance, but to my surprise a few women, in coming back weekly, became regulars, seemingly enjoying the routine and self-directed activities. The open studio became a refuge. It provided a distraction from symptoms and contributed to social belonging through group participation or presence (see Thomas et al., 2011). Other participants, seemingly in the throes of life upheavals and difficulties, came only once. Preoccupied, often tired and tense, they asked for something simple to do, looking to settle their mind for a little while, to sit still, to breathe.

> I also thought about the drawings left behind, most of them unfinished, and imagined making something with them for the Spring exhibition. In this place, I think it is possible to accept the reality of transience, how it impacts everything one does, leaving one in a situation of instability, of change, in constant search for balance in a life lacking a sure ground to stand on. For persons whose survival concerns are a constant struggle, art as an object ought to have limited value, but art as action and process offers moments of insights, pause, and silence that do not require completion, are in no need of aesthetic resolution. In this sense, the artistic activity that takes place does not have an end. In my view, these unfinished works are like interrupted conversations. They are moments that do not reach closure and they somehow reflect the life situation of their makers. (Journal entry, March 22, 2019)

## 5 Fruition

The open studio is in recess for the summer. At this time, the meaning of Fruition can be found encapsulated in small moments of realisation, many captured in my journal entries. As I got off the subway and walked down the street, as I did every Friday morning, I realised that the way I prepared mentally and emotionally for what one might think of as this class was so different from when I prepared mentally for a class at the university. For the open studio, my pedagogy is no longer a question of subject matter delivery, pacing, questions, assignments, and so on. When I walk towards the shelter in the morning, I can feel my mind softening, switching mode. I prepare by becoming totally present with my surroundings, the sights, sounds, and smells of the street. I beckon my patience and attentiveness, make them ready. This is my working pedagogy at the shelter. And it is a pedagogy that, as I mentioned earlier, can be expressed through many ontologies, a multiplicity to be explored in future research.

While I cannot speak for others, I believe that the open studio offers a meaningful resource for anyone who comes, and, more distinctly, for the women who return week after week. No matter who is coming, the studio allows everyone's presence in it. It always feels new, yet secure in the prospect of a time for oneself, engaging in an activity that provides a sensory experience, on a mode that impacts our state of being and of being together. Fruition is resonance.

> On the last day of the studio, before summer break, we were hugging and saying goodbye. I stopped myself short, realizing that I could not say: "See you next fall"! This community of reluctant residents could not possibly wish to be here in September. The only right time and place was "in the moment," on that day, drawing cards for well wishes to ourselves and the kids we missed, whose custody had been lost. (Journal entry, 17 May, 2019)

## Notes

1 lillianetwork.wordpress.com/about/
2 http://www.publishingbiz.com/bsc/3foldlogic.pdf

## References

Butterwick, S., & Roy, C. (2018). Introduction to finding voice and listening: The potential of community and arts-based adult education and research. *The Canadian Journal for the Study of Adult Education, 30*(2), 1–10. https://cjsae.library.dal.ca/index.php/cjsae/article/view/5443

Daniel, S. (2011). Collaborative systems: Redefining public art. In M. Lovejoy, C. Paul, & V. Vesna (Eds.), *Context providers: Conditions of meaning in media arts* (pp. 55–87). The University of Chicago Press.

Dej, E. (2016). Psychocentrism and homelessness: The pathologization/responsibility paradox. *Studies in Social Justice, 10*(1), 117–135. https://doi.org/10.26522/ssj.v10i1.1349

Finlay, L. (2006). Dancing between embodied empathy and phenomenological reflection. *Indo-Pacific Journal of Phenomenology, 6*, 1–11. https://doi.org/10.1080/20797222.2006.11433930

Greene, M. (1995). Art and imagination: Reclaiming the sense of possibility. *Phi Delta Kappan, 76*(5), 378–382.

Helguera, P. (2011). *Education for socially engaged art.* Jorge Pinto Books.

Knowles, M. S., Holton, E. F., & Swanson, R. A. (2011). *The adult learner.* Elsevier.

Laramee Kidd, S. (2017). *Evaluator/researcher companion—Aesthetic perspectives: Attributes of excellence in arts for change.* Americans for the Arts.

Leake, M. D. (2014). Social engagement with contemporary art: Connecting theory with practice. *Art Education, 67*(5), 23–30. https://doi.org/10.1080/00043125.2014.11519287

Rodriguez, J. (2005). *Presence, clarity and the space of receptivity in counselling: Shambhala Buddhist counsellors' narratives of experience.* (Doctoral Dissertation). Retrieved from ProQuest Dissertations & Theses Global (305354505).

Rose, E., Bingley, A., Rioseco, M., & Lamb, K. (2018). *Art of recovery: Displacement, mental health and wellbeing. Arts,* 7(4), 94–108). DOI: 10.3390/arts7040094

Silva, C. R., Silvestrini, M. S., Von Poellnitz, J. C., da Silva Almeida Prado, A. C., & Leite Jr., J. D. (2018). Creative strategies and homeless people: Occupational therapy, art, culture and sensitive displacement. *Cardenos Brasileiros de Terapia Ocupacional, 26*(2), 489–500. https://doi.org/10.4322/2526-8910.ctoRE1128

Strauch Brown, K., & Ziefert, M. (1990). A feminist approach to working with homeless women. *Affilia, 5*(1), 6–20. https://doi.org/10.1177%2F088610999000500101

Thomas, Y., Gray, M., McGinty, S., & Ebringer, S. (2011). Homeless adults engagement in art: First steps towards identity, recovery and social inclusion. *Australian Occupational Therapy Journal, 58,* 429–436. https://doi.org/10.1111/j.1440-1630.2011.00977.x

Vandemark, L. M. (2007). Promoting the sense of self, place and belonging in displaced persons: The example of homelessness. *Archives of Psychiatric Nursing, 21*(5), 241–248. https://doi.org/10.1016/j.apnu.2007.06.003

Wang, M. (2017). The socially engaged practices of artists in contemporary China. *Journal of Visual Art Practice, 16*(1), 12–38. https://doi.org/10.1080/14702029.2016.1179443

Wildemeersch, D., & von Kotze, A. (2014). Multiple interruptions: Creative encounters in public art and public pedagogy, a North-South dialogue. *Studies in Art Education, 55*(4), 313–327. https://doi.org/10.1080/00393541.2014.11518940

Wright, S. (2014). *Towards a lexicon of usership.* VanAbbemuseum.

CHAPTER 24

# Conceptualising a Black Feminist Arts Pedagogy

*Looking Back to Look Forward*

*Amber C. Coleman*

## 1 Introduction

My family members have always been supportive of my learning about the arts and Black culture, but the same level of engagement did not always present itself in my classrooms. During my master's degree, I contemplated my identity as a Black woman while thinking critically about my experiences with/in art and cultural institutions. I became intentional about my engagement with art and museums, working as an intern at The Columbus Museum (Columbus, Georgia) and the Georgia Museum of Art (Athens, Georgia). As a result, I was inspired to investigate the experiences of Black women in art.

Black feminism has resonated with my personal and academic interests. Feminism seemed promising in its rhetoric, but Black feminism helped me to think about how to support marginalised people in inclusive and equitable ways. The Combahee River Collective (1977/1995) states, "If black women were free, it would mean that everyone else would have to be free since our freedom would necessitate the destruction of all the systems of oppression" (p. 237); centering the experiences of Black women became new ground for my thinking and actions. Further consideration led me to become interested in how to expand conceptions of what art education pedagogy could look like. Here, I define art education as the theory, practice, and method by which visual arts, and other artistic forms, are: contemplated and discussed in ways that provide provocation about how people engage with art and visual culture; put into practice through instruction or learning opportunities in classrooms, art institutions, or informal art forums; and/or used as a medium for creating action or social change. Moreover, I define pedagogy as the methods an educator uses to teach; this can include choices for instructional content, approaches for learners' engagement with subject matter, and the creation of tasks during which learners can apply their understanding. My understanding of Black feminism guides how I see pedagogy affecting the understanding of marginalised experiences through art education.

Combining my understanding of Black feminism, art education, and pedagogy as a doctoral student, I ask, "How can pedagogical practice centre the experiences of Black women while critically engaging learners with these

 | DOI: 10.1163/9789004442870_024

experiences through art?" As I conceptualise what I call a Black feminist arts pedagogy, I recognise the importance of Black feminism to articulating and teaching about Black women's experiences, as well as those of other marginalised groups, with/in the arts. In this chapter, I look back at my master's research to show how I now understand the potential impact of Black feminism on the pedagogical practice of arts educators and how this practice can give voice to the experiences of marginalised groups.

## 2 Black Feminism as a Theoretical Framework

Black feminism articulates the connections of racism, sexism, and other forms of oppression experienced by women of the African diaspora. This theory emphasises the common challenges faced by Black women while allowing us the space to contemplate our own experiences (Collins, 1990/2009). In considering the inequalities that Black women face, Black feminism advocates for all people to engage in an ethic of caring (Collins, 1989). Proceeding from the knowledge that multiple oppressions exist, showing care means making a conscious effort to recognise the existence of oppressive environments and participate in thoughtful activism on behalf of those who navigate within them.

The ethic of caring for oneself, other women, and one's community (Allan, 1995) as a commitment to activism is important to understanding Black women's experiences and actions. With the commitment to self and others, Black women's activism is a direct response of resistance to our oppression (Collins, 1989). As the Combahee River Collective (1977/1995) has reminded us, Black women often lack opportunities to contemplate and define ourselves because of social politics that affect and inform our experiences. As Collins (1990/2009) has explained, "When Black women define ourselves, we clearly reject the assumption that those in positions granting them the authority to interpret our reality are entitled to do so" (p. 125). As Black women, we use our self-definitions to create conceptual, collaborative, and communal spaces, which prioritise our knowledge, wisdom, and experience.

## 3 Context: Reflecting on Black Women in Art/Education

The everyday experiences and artworks of Black women are often overlooked. Black female artists face challenges when they try to gain and maintain representation in cultural institutions like museums (Bobo, 2001). Comments and critiques of these artists by critics and viewers include assumptions based on their identity as Black women (hooks, 1995). Since Black women fall within the intersection of two cultural identity groups, being both Black and female means that we experience double marginalisation. Moreover, as Black women, we are often compelled to enact our own activism in response to our oppression. Just as I have had to do in my own art education, I assume that many Black women have to assert and prioritise their identities in theirs. In addressing the lack of representation in art, the artist Amy Sherald provides unique insight into her experiences as a Black female artist when she said,

> I was inspired to paint things that I didn't see within the art historical narrative ... It came naturally to paint people that looked like me ... I basically paint people who I want to see exist in the world, but then I also want to create a narrative that's extricated from a dominant historical narrative. (Khawaja, 2016, n.p.)

Narratives such as this are evidence of the impact of marginalising Black women's experiences in the art world and how this phenomenon is reflected in education. Scholars like Omolade (1987) have suggested the need to engage with Black feminist pedagogy to address historical experiences of oppression while expanding teaching methods to include many different perspectives and histories, especially of marginalised people.

As Acuff, Hirak, and Nangah (2012) have noted, the history of art education has been predicated on master narratives that perpetuate the subjugation of marginalised cultures in favor of dominant cultural norms. The lack of representation of Black women in the history of art education reflects the fact that the narratives of people of color are fixed to support these master narratives. Moreover, the challenges that Black women face are also found in the scholarly narratives of art educators like Wilson and Lawton (2019) who have stated that in their research, art-making, and pedagogical practices they are often compelled to refer to their racial and gender identifications and experiences as Black women in order to confront inequalities and issues that affect their communities.

Black female art educator/scholars, like Kraehe and Acuff (2013), have been advocating for the inclusion of diverse perspectives and critical theories and pedagogies as part of the narrative of sharing diverse experiences in art educational contexts. They have suggested the need for deeper theorisation of underserved populations through the use of critical theoretical perspectives such as critical race theory, intersectionality, critical multiculturalism, and social justice education. Furthermore, Acuff (2018) has insisted that Black feminist theory is a necessary theoretical and methodological approach for contemporary art education research because it values and validates Black women's knowledge and knowledge production. Thus, a focus on Black feminist theory can aid in decentring canons and traditional practices of art education that often omit Black women.

## 4 Looking Back to Look Forward

Before conceptualising a Black feminist arts pedagogy, I must look back on my own practice and theorise back (Tuck, 2009) by connecting experience, theory, and practice to look critically at dominant hegemonic perspectives and provide insight into the value of marginalised experiences. When art educators theorise back, they disrupt the rules and partake in practices that humanise marginalised groups. In my master's research, I investigated the representation of African American women's art in museums. My applied project, "Understanding Black Feminist Theory and the Representation of African American Women's Art in Museums: Engaging Black Women in Critical Dialogue"[1] (2017), explored how exposure to Black feminist theory, African American women's artwork, and contemporary museum practices could affect a group of Black women in understanding the artistic representation and output of other Black women.

The participants (Ashley Crooks-Allen, Karina Lewis, Monique May, and I) represented various identifications within the spectrum of Black/African American female identities. I acted as researcher, participant, and artist/curator as I explored three research questions relating to the participants' experiences of looking critically at the aforementioned topics, my application of theory in the facilitation of a critical pedagogical experience, and the visitors' experience with the exhibition that the group created.

We began by visiting two different museums, the Georgia Museum of Art (GMOA) (Athens, Georgia) and the Spelman College Museum of Fine Art (SCMFA) (Atlanta, Georgia). We saw the work of Kara Walker, Mickalene Thomas, Elizabeth Catlett, and other African American women artists. At these sites, we participated in activities such as talking with Black female museum professionals and rewriting artwork label text. In between visits, we engaged in a blog on which we posted our reflections. Next, I provided resources (slide presentations, scholarly and community-published articles, and YouTube videos) for us to use to explore Black feminist theory, African American women's art history, and contemporary museum practices. This information contextualised the experiences that we had at the museums. Altogether these experiences and new information aided us in creating our own artworks ("Wildflower" by Monique May,

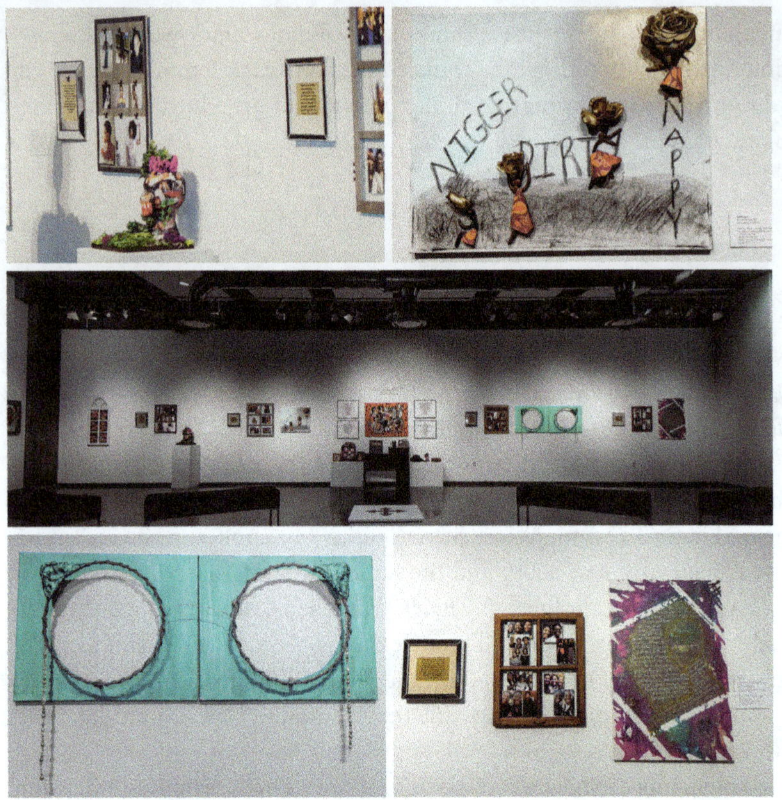


FIGURE 24.1 Images from the exhibition, *To Be Black and Female* (2017). Artworks by participants. (Photograph by Mikael Coleman)

"And Still We Rise" by Karina Lewis, "Soft Focus" by Ashley Crooks-Allen, and "MAGIC" by Amber Coleman) for our exhibition (Figure 24.1).

In October 2017, the exhibition, To Be Black & Female: Reflecting on Black Feminism and African American Women's Art in Museums, opened at the Lamar Dodd School of Art Galleries (Athens, Georgia), culminating our meaning-making about our experiences as Black women within a museum-like space. Our exhibition reflected our experiences and new knowledge from participating in the project (see Figure 24.2). We included a space to support the work of young Black female artists and made interactive spaces for our visitors. The exhibition hosted a station for visitors to write "Dear Black Woman" letters and take mementos (like bookmarks with Black feminist quotes and copies of articles and essays that we read) from our "Food for the Soul" table. During the opening reception, we served food that reflected Black women's culinary traditions and dietary lifestyles while playing music by Black female artists.

Overall, this study yielded some interesting results. With the participants, we re-envisioned museums spaces as places of belonging. Gaining comfort expanded our desire to engage with museums and see ourselves reflected in them. We also saw how various texts in museums could be re-interpreted. Through reinterpretation, we centered our own narratives and understandings through writing about art. In creating artwork for our exhibition, we used our experience and/as knowledge.

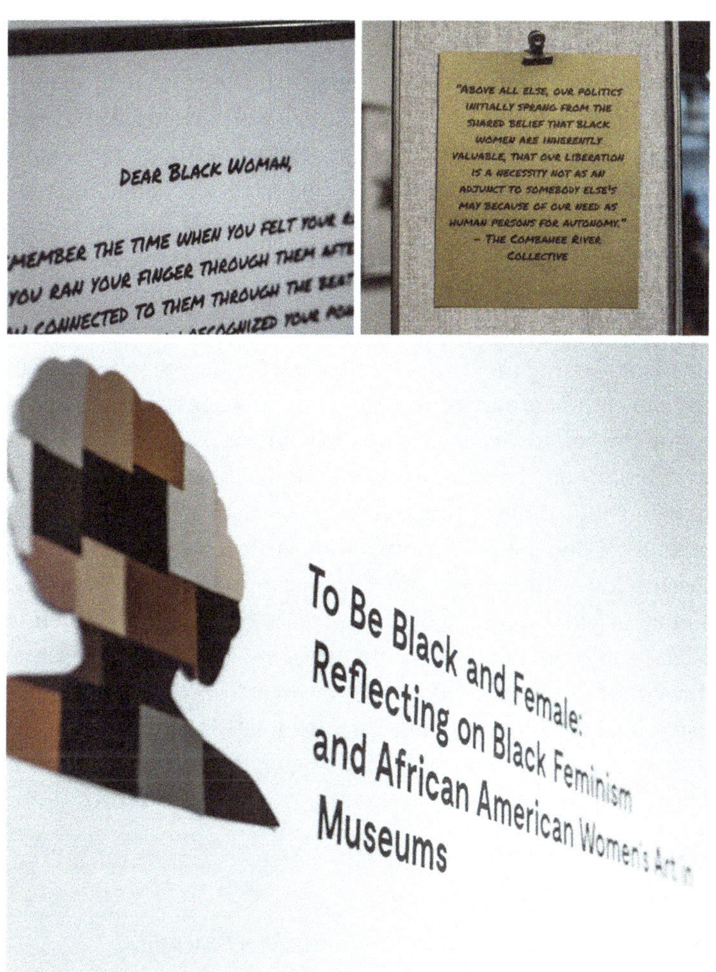


FIGURE 24.2 Images from the exhibition, *To Be Black and Female* (2017). (Photograph by Mikael Coleman)

I wanted to carve out space for us to engage with the topics by creating various activities and resources. Part of creating this learning space meant that I was an active participant, allowing other participants to express their thoughts on the direction of the project and exhibition. It was important for me to consider the possibilities of using theory while recognising the many kinds of texts and experiences that could be offered when curating. I did this by connecting our museum-visiting experience to our own exhibition. As a curator and artist, I sought to create forums of dialogue for and with our visitors. I wanted to emphasise Black women's empowerment and included visual and written texts that would showcase what we learned during this project.

Finally, the exhibition visitors responded to our call for engaging with Black women's art and experiences. They added to our work on empowerment by writing and leaving "Dear Black Woman" letters that expressed their experiences with and admiration of Black women. They also expressed gratitude for the work we shared during the exhibition. The visitors wrote about their enjoyment of the exhibition, left positive commentary in our visitors' book, and took mementos.

This project acted as a site of resistance to address the lack of representation of Black women artists and offered a group of Black women the opportunity to reflect, create, and empower themselves in museum spaces. Collectively, we found value in connecting theory and experience to practice in relation to Black feminism and contemporary museum practice. As a researcher, I found critical pedagogy to be helpful in creating meaningful and participatory learning experiences. Moreover, the museum, and similar spaces, can act as a medium to frame investigations of representation of Black women and other marginalised groups. When the perspectives from critical theories are implemented, representation in museums can become normalised in ways that allow Black women to feel valued and for audiences to be inspired by different experiences, ideas, and art-making. Museums also connect power, representation, and empowerment, so they should always be open to critique and change in order to reflect the lives and experiences of the public. By connecting to the public, museum exhibitions extend critical dialogue across multiple groups from the curators, educators, other museum professionals, and artists, to the general public.

## 5 A Conceptual Framework: Black Feminist Arts Pedagogy

I have begun to envision a framework for a Black feminist arts pedagogy. With this pedagogy, art educators can address and counter the predominance of Whiteness and other hegemonic categorisations that discriminate against Black women and other marginalised groups in art education. Collins (1989) has reminded us that the experiences of oppressed people may give them different perspectives from those of dominant groups, but hegemonic social structures get in the way of their articulation. While this control is difficult to negotiate, providing a framework that addresses marginalised experiences through theories of Black feminism and implements these perspectives in art pedagogical practice brings Black women from the margins to the center and sees such action as an ethical necessity.

A Black feminist arts pedagogy starts with the recognition of the ways in which Black women are marginalised in the field of art education. bell hooks (1995) has reminded us that identity categories shape art understandings and practices as well as call us to challenge existing hegemonic structures; as we know, Black artists are often aware of visual politics while actively working to change the hegemonic structures of the art world. The importance of these acts of resistance makes the representation of Black women's experiences and perspectives in art education pedagogy an imperative. Furthermore, a Black feminist arts pedagogy could be viewed as a strategy for art educators to show Black women and those from other marginalised groups how art can be "a psychological resource that [could] be used in a collective struggle against oppression and in a personal journey toward self-appreciation and good mental health" (Weber, 1998, p. 23). There are multiple uses for this pedagogy; I offer five starting points for this conceptualisation of a Black feminist arts pedagogy.

- *Representation matters*. Increasing recognition of marginalised groups and the representation of their experiences in art educational settings is important. Art educators should offer an array of examples of artists and models that reflect diverse experiences and connect to a variety of subject matters and big ideas.
- *Centering marginalised experiences and ways of knowing.* There is a need to begin with the inclusion of experiences of marginalised groups. When educators recognise diversity and different forms of knowledge that all learners have to offer, they validate the necessity of different modes of knowledge construction.
- *Creating space for collaborative construction of meaning.* Educators can create collaborative learning spaces to combat oppression and value everyone's perspectives. Providing opportunities for more equitable meaning-making about issues and topics relevant to the learners occurs when all members learn and work together.
- *Talking and walking social justice.* Social justice should be seen as a process, not just a project or a product. Educators are urged to practice what they preach and be open to the input and interpretations of others. Practicing social justice also means empowering and supporting learners to engage in activism on their own behalf.
- *Art-making as advocating for self/empowerment.* Learners can work toward their own empowerment through making art. Art-making can also inspire people to work toward the empowerment of those who identify differently from them and to create a bridge between art and their everyday lives.

## 6 Looking Forward by Looking Back

In the process of looking back and looking forward, I hope to have offered a conceptual framework for teaching practices that consider underrepresented and undervalued perspectives. Looking back at my own research helped me to think about what a Black feminist arts pedagogy could look like in practice. I realise that my applied project was not perfect, but it did provide an opportunity for me to consider the impact of critical and diverse perspectives and put this into action. This was a very meaningful and rewarding step that has led me to further exploration. With my emerging conceptualisation of a Black feminist arts pedagogy, I understand that there are many valuable perspectives to consider when one is teaching as an art educator and there is no simple way to capture them all. I offer this conceptualisation as a starting point for further discussion for arts educators as they seek to enact social change. This change can begin with educators and the ways we show how we perceive the world in our teaching. I plan to continue to refine this conceptualisation, personally and professionally. By outlining the concept of a Black feminist arts pedagogy, my hope is that arts educators will consider and implement pedagogical practices that center the need for more equitable engagement with diverse experiences.

### Note

1 The applied project used the term African American to refer to Black artists who were born and who lived or were living in the United States and who were described as such at the museums and in other resources that were used during the project.

### References

Acuff, J. B. (2018). Black feminist theory in 21st-century art education research. *Studies in Art Education, 59*(3), 201–214. https://doi.org/10.1080/00393541.2018.1476953

Acuff, J. B., Hirak, B., & Nangah, M. (2012). Dismantling a master narrative: Using culturally responsive pedagogy to teach the history of art education. *Art Education, 65*(5), 6–10. https://doi.org/10.1080/00043125.2012.11519186

Allan, T. J. (1995). Introduction: Decoding womanist grammar of difference. In T. J. Allan (Ed.), *Womanist and feminist aesthetics: A comparative review* (pp. 433–444). Ohio University Press.

Bobo, J. (2001). Overview: Art. In J. Bobo (Ed.), *Black feminist cultural criticism* (pp. 126–128). Blackwell Publishers.

Coleman, A. C. (2018). *Understanding Black feminist theory and the representation of African American women's art in museums: Engaging Black women in critical dialogue* (Master's applied project). http://hdl.handle.net/10724/37736

Collins, P. H. (1989). The social construction of Black feminist thought. *Signs, 14*(4), 745–773. www.jstor.org/stable/3174683

Collins, P. H. (2009). *Black feminist thought: Knowledge, consciousness, and the politics of empowerment*. Routledge Classics. (Original work published 1990)

hooks, b. (1995). *Art on my mind: Visual politics*. The New Press.

Khawaja, S. (2016, July 26). *Art talk with painter Amy Sherald*. https://www.arts.gov/art-works/2016/art-talk-painter-amy-sherald

Kraehe, A. M., & Acuff, J. B. (2013). Theoretical considerations for art education research with and about "underserved populations." *Studies in Art Education, 54*(4), 294–309. https://doi.org/10.1080/00393541.2013.11518904

Omolade, B. (1987). A Black feminist pedagogy. *Women's Studies Quarterly, 15*(3–4), 32–39. https://www.jstor.org/stable/40003434

The Combahee River Collective. (1995). A Black feminist statement. In B. Guy-Sheftall (Ed.), *Words of fire: An anthology of African-American feminist thought* (pp. 232–240). The New Press. (Original work published 1977)

Tuck, E. (2009). Theorizing back: An approach to participatory policy analysis. In J. Anyon (Ed.), *Theory and educational research: Toward critical social explanation* (pp. 111–130). Routledge.

Weber, L. (1998). A conceptual framework for understanding race, class, gender, and sexuality. *Psychology of Women Quarterly, 22*(1), 13–32. https://doi.org/10.1111/j.1471-6402.1998.tb00139.x

Wilson, G. J, & Lawton, P. (2019). Critical portraiture: Black/women/artists/educators. *Visual Arts Research, 45*(1), 83–89. https://www.muse.jhu.edu/article/731501

CHAPTER 25

# Working toward Sustainable Creative Social Justice Practices

## *Advancing Equity and Justice in the Academy*

*Amanda Claudia Wager and Kristen P. Goessling*

## 1 Introduction

We identify as white female scholars—activists—educators—artists who use the arts to engage students, staff, and faculty in social justice and equity initiatives in higher education settings. In this chapter, we ask:

- What are the challenges and triumphs we face related to fighting for equity and justice?
- How might we utilise the arts to infuse these actions with self-care and reflection?

We met in 2009 as doctoral students and developed a deep friendship grounded in humility, respect, and trust. Working together first as graduate teaching/research assistants and now professors/researchers, we celebrate our successes and commiserate over common struggles. Since we began our separate, yet intertwined scholarly journeys, we have explored and developed self-care strategies to sustain this work. We share stories, tools, and lessons learned through our use of the arts for social justice in the academy. Drawing on Greene's (1997) call for educators to grapple with notions of imagination, possibilities, and ethics toward a more socially just world, we often find ourselves "walking and talking our way to meaning-making" as a way of collaborative care (Goessling & Wager, 2020). Now, we collaborate from afar, nurturing and supporting each other through an ethical commitment to relationality and reflexivity in our work as critical scholars, activists, educators, and artists.

In this chapter, we describe, demonstrate, and reflect on an art practice to anchor the conceptual and analytical exploration. The discussion synthesises our artistic practice with experiences researching, teaching, and facilitating workshops using arts-based pedagogical practices in higher-education settings. We Illustrate the potential of incorporating arts into curriculum for generating social and personal change through a reciprocal process made possible through art-based pedagogical practices. We provide insights and inspiration for cultivating self-care via art to sustain the ongoing fight for equity and

 | DOI: 10.1163/9789004442870_025

justice within oppressive systems and structures, such as higher education. Following black feminist scholars, we argue that self-care is a key tool for individual and community transformation and healing (hooks, 1993; Lorde, 1988; Tillet & Tillet, 2019).

## 2 Theoretical Rootings

Our scholarship aligns in a shared view of art as a transformative tool, social justice aims, and a critical theoretical orientation. We view social justice as a commitment to human rights and equity based on the understanding that oppression and inequity are historically and contextually produced through systems of power (Talwar, 2019). Our four-part framework for arts-based pedagogical practices supports participants'

- identity construction
- self-awareness
- community-building
- critical consciousness

Identity construction is a dynamic, ongoing, socioculturally situated process of becoming (Lave & Wenger, 1991). Viewing identity as socially constructed reflects the understanding that social locations—such as race, class, gender, citizenship—are historically produced and maintained within systems of power and oppression. Broadly, self-awareness is understood as a process of getting to know oneself in and of the world (Freire, 1970). Critical self-awareness is a reflexive practice of how one's awareness is constituted through direct experiences, in particular social contexts that generate meaning-making (Ferreria & Ferreria, 2019). Community-building is key to the creation and progression of a collaborative learning environment where critical dialogue is built on the foundations of humility, reciprocity, and respect for each individual in the room (hooks, 1994). Freire's (1970) notion of critical consciousness reflects a dialectical epistemology applied through praxis geared toward identifying root and systemic causes of problems and taking action to effect positive social change.

## 3 Our Process

Using art practices for social justice in classrooms and educational settings requires intentional planning and preparation. Pedagogically, we begin by identifying the goal of the art practice. We ask and answer the questions related to *why* we are doing this specific practice with this group and *what* we want it to evoke in participants. Answers guide the selection of materials and artform, such as dry (markers) to wet (watercolor), two- or three-dimensional, performance, or photography, or video. Different art modalities and forms evoke unique sensorial embodied responses and will impact participants' experiences (Franklin, 2017). We use a three-part process to guide participants through transformative art-making. First, is preparing the art-making space, which is important when working in classrooms and non-traditional studio spaces. This begins building trust and a collective energy. Once participants arrive, we begin with a visualisation or meditation and intention setting activity. We explain what we are going to do and allow time for questions. Second, is art-making time. We continue creating the space with music or by using a meditation bell to signal participants to recall their intention. We pay careful attention to how individuals and the group are processing the activity. Sometimes we walk around the room, other times we maintain distance to ensure privacy and personal space for the practice. Third, is writing and reflecting. Translating the non-verbal activity to text format is crucial to the internalisation process (Hieb, 2005). In visual art, this involves non-judgmental gazing and observation of the creation. The written reflection or discussion can be scaffolded by a prompt or instructions. Provocations may guide deeper introspection throughout the reflective writing process, advancing from "What do you see?" to "How did and do you feel?" We illustrate this process in the mandala practice described below.

## 4 Mandalas for Self-Inquiry

Kristen designed the mandala activity to demonstrate the three-stage process. Mandala is a Sanskrit word for circle and in the Buddhist tradition symbolises wholeness or center. Carl Jung popularised the use of mandalas for personal growth and as a tool for consciousness-raising, self-exploration, and wellness. Mandalas have been used in teacher education to address issues of community-building through self-discovery that integrate both the head and heart (Young, 2001) and as a tool to facilitate college students' development and growth (Pisarik & Larson, 2011).

### 4.1 *Our Artistic Process*

*Stage I: Preparation*

- Schedule uninterrupted time for this activity.
- Create a space that inspires and allows you to connect to your inner self.

- Gather artifacts that reflect your values and commitment to social justice—things that are important to who you are, where you come from, and your imagined future.
- Gather your supplies—paper, pencil, paint, markers, pastels, tape, etc.
- Do a 10-minute guided meditation.
- End by setting your intention for the art practice that connects to your identities as scholars—activists—educators—artists; your "whys"; and possibilities and limitations of this work.

*Stage II: Creation*
- Trace a large circle for the mandala on a large piece of paper.
- Fill the page with lines, colors, shapes, patterns, symbols.
- Use any form or materials you like.
- Remember your intention and guiding questions.
- Let yourself go. Follow your intuition. Play.

*Stage III: Reflective Writing & Discussion*
- Gaze at your creation. Notice how you feel in your body.
- Look for meaning and significance in your design.
  - What do you see: lines? shapes or symbols? large/small? organic/geometric?
  - What colors did you use?
  - What relationships do you notice? Are some elements overlapping, far apart, dis/connected, messy? How do the positions of things enable you to make sense of them?
  - What emotions are coming up for you through this process?
- Dialogue: Take turns showing and sharing your mandala (in a class or group we would pair-share or ask for volunteers to share)

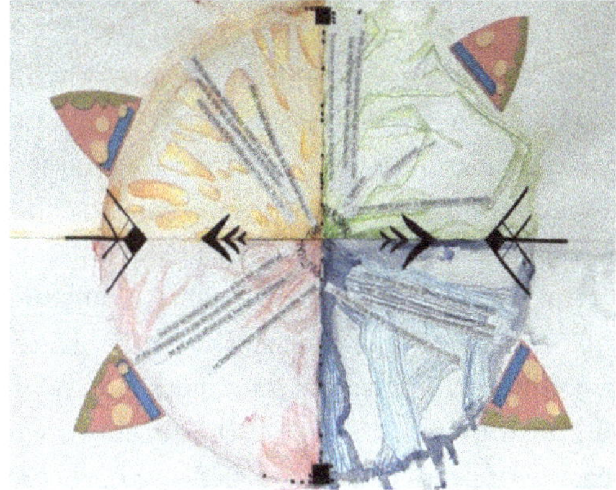

FIGURE 25.1
Kristen's mandala

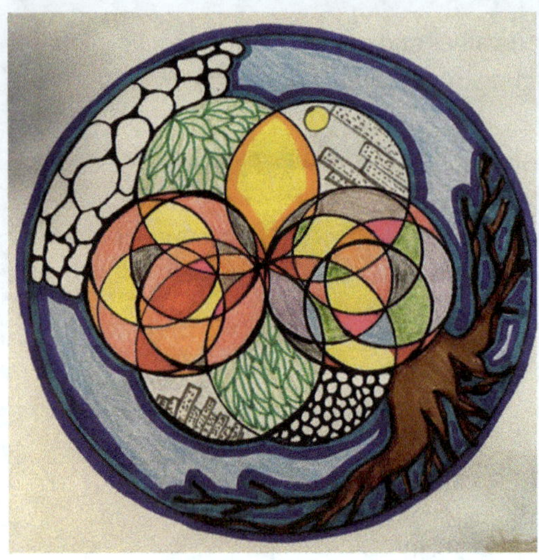

FIGURE 25.2
Amanda's mandala

## 5 Discussion

Amanda transcribed the recorded mandala discussion and then deductively coded the transcription into our four conceptual themes. The following discussion bridges our reflections of the mandala creation and our experiences doing this work in community and higher education contexts.

### 5.1 *Theme I: Identity Construction*

In the centre of Kristen's mandala are the words, "The Personal is Political." This phrase is a mantra in our lives, in the classrooms we teach, and in the workshops we facilitate. It signifies our awakening to feminism and our continued awareness of our privilege in society as white, middle-classed women. Our identities are co-constructed through dialogue (Stage III) about our art, reflecting important people, moments, places, and values of our lived experiences.

We grapple with the terms artist and activist since they are heavy with responsibility and cultural meanings. Having earned our scholar identities, we struggle with the elitism that accompanies the letters following our names. For us, activism is more about a worldview or a life-long commitment to community organising, rather than participation at a protest. It is a way of being, a way of thinking, a way of acting. Art is as well. It is a part of who we are and a way that we have learned to walk in the world and make sense of it. These identities inform our pedagogical choices. When we separate our scholarship from art or activism, there is something missing. As scholars, this form of creativity is outside the academy's measure of productivity and, in a sense, we are resisting through it, by practising what is central to us—we prioritise it and ourselves—in spite of the sociopolitical pressures of the institutions in which we are embedded.

Viewing identity construction as a situated, social, dynamic process that involves self-reflection and questioning over time, this discussion inspired a new curricular strategy of returning to participants' social justice art projects later in the term or having a follow-up professional development workshop for participants to review and question their artwork with a new perspective after taking in the readings and experiences from the course/workshop/term. This supports the idea that creativity and art—like identity—are living, dynamic, processes for world-building and meaning-making.

## 5.2 *Theme II: Self-Awareness*

Mandalas are understood as a symbolic representation of parts of the self that emerge from the unconscious. Creating mandalas can be a process of critical self-reflection and healing (Pisarik & Larson, 2011). Reflective creative work requires time and space, which can be a struggle. We have to prioritise creative work as a valuable practice; this means that sometimes we have to live in the messy, juggle our many responsibilities, and let some things go. Before producing the mandala, Amanda had not created a piece of art in a long time. Making the space to do this helped her negotiate family and work responsibilities and generated an enhanced understanding of her many different selves in the present moment. It is a reminder that although art and activism are part of our identities, they also take practice, nurturing, and habit to grow.

Critical self-awareness requires ongoing attention and practice toward understanding and unearthing unconscious aspects of ourselves. Art practices can help us feel or see in new ways. Kristen described participating in a poetry workshop with a student who has a twin sister.

> And this student read a line from her poem where she realised that she is pissed that people confuse her and her sister. It was this powerful statement that was like 'look at me, see me, I am not my sister.' I just got chills. Afterwards I was like, 'I think she just differentiated herself from her twin for the first time.'

Sometimes people choose not to share their inner experience because it does not feel safe to risk being vulnerable in front of peers or colleagues. Some people may need more time for trust-building. Diverse spaces in which there are many layers of power relations must be handled with the utmost care. We allow participants to choose what they want to share, and they may pass if they do not want to share with the full group. We support others to figure out what works for them and what feels appropriate to share or not. Art can help us understand this and ease the vulnerability of sharing ourselves in new or unfamiliar communities.

Facilitating these processes takes self-awareness and skill to carefully hold and support the many different people, perspectives, experiences, and relations of power and privilege within these spaces. There are many varied forms of participation and some may not participate, while others will take up too much space. Being a good leader is being able to move the discussion forward, gently interrupting, shifting directions, or checking in with participants afterwards.

We must know our triggers and blind spots as inevitably they will be shown to us. Facilitators must do the art practices first, in order to anticipate potential issues and emotional reactions. Setting community agreements and expectations that center those most directly affected by the issue of focus (like, for example, People of Color in a workshop on systemic racism) is one way to mediate some of these inevitable challenges. Although it is a collaborative space, a facilitator must make in-the-moment decisions to lead the group toward a critical awareness and orientation toward justice and equity while balancing divergent individual desires and experiences.

### 5.3 *Theme III: Community-Building*

Being in a community of artists, even in a studio with everybody doing their own thing, catalyses a collective energy. Creative activity provides a path for connection and community-building. In our communication and stories, we also move toward personal awareness.

Amanda uses a Life Map exercise during the first week of an online master's course, Teaching English to Students of Other Languages. Teachers in the course choose 7 to 10 pivotal life moments, represent them through drawn or digital symbols, connect them using arrows/lines, and explain why this would be important to do with students in their classrooms. The teachers post their maps on the discussion board and comment on each other's. Some people share vulnerable personal stories. Through this reciprocal sharing of self through a multimedia artistic practice, even online, a community is immediately being built.

Participation by everyone in the community, including ourselves, is important to the process. During the first class of Kristen's undergraduate Art and Social Justice course, she has her students do an opening art activity to build community and relationships. After the activity, she facilitates a sharing circle in which everyone has to share one thing; it can be about anything, but it cannot be about anyone else. Voicing and storying—being a presence in the space—is hard and important work. It fosters empathy and understanding because we hear parts of our stories in one another's art and sharing. This is especially powerful when the group is diverse, and participants find ways of relating through artwork.

Community-building is unpredictable. What worked last year might not work this year because every community is different (hooks, 1994). It is about every single person in that room and how they encounter, resist, appropriate, internalise, and process the work. We have to accept that not everyone will embrace this approach. Being able to communicate across differences, rather than trying to resolve them is essential to community building. As facilitators and community members, we are observers and participants, which can be challenging and exhausting.

### 5.4 *Theme IV: Critical Consciousness*

Critical consciousness can develop through creative praxis, during which individuals' creations and reflections are scaffolded to examine and re/present systemic oppression. In her mandala, Kristen highlighted James Baldwin's essay, The Creative Process (1962), about the moral duty of the artist: if we knew ourselves better, we would be much better off, and the artist's job is to provoke, challenge, and resist. Baldwin explains how the artists' duty to know themselves is also their duty to society.

We do artistic activist work in our classes and workshops because of its ability to spotlight and connect us to our humanness that is often overlooked in higher education settings. We ask:

- "How do you look inside yourself and understand what is important to you?"
- "How do you reflect on your childhood, family and culture?"
- "How does it inform who you are and how you make sense of the world?"

We recognise that these practices can be uncomfortable and sometimes jarring for participants. When we ask people to bring their full selves to the space, it is a request for the acceptance of vulnerability. We are asking people to trust us and each other. This is a significant risk that many do not want to take. We must honor individuals' resistance as a form of wisdom. We also have to trust the process.

In social justice workshops we have facilitated with faculty and staff, some people share too much. We can never walk in each other's shoes, especially when it comes to identities on either end of the power spectrum. There are different cultural ways of sharing. Some people take up too much space (often without even recognising their privilege). Some people are quiet while finding their place. Some people take time to accept other people's places (or not) and commit to sharing a personal part of themselves through an artistic medium that is new and intimidating. Again, this is messy work. We have to get dirty, sit with it, be uncomfortable, smile, and cry, and laugh and go through it or else we cannot make movement, make meaning, make change. There are times and contexts in which we should not lead this work, and topics we should avoid. We must leverage our power and privilege to lift up artists of varied backgrounds and experiences as experts. Our commitment to redistributing resources and opportunities to marginalised artists and activists is a practice of critical consciousness. We move through the messiness by practising self-awareness and helping each other know when it is time to step back or step up.

## 6 Conclusion

A final point is to note the importance of setting ground rules and post-activity discussions when doing arts-based social justice work. Collaboratively creating community agreements or ground rules from the start—reviewing, revising, and reminding each other of them—should be the opening ritual. Post-activity discussion is essential for internalising and meaning-making and too often gets overlooked because of time constraints. The solidarity created during the artistic activities can erode without discussion and intentional processing.

Our goal is that this work will be used to facilitate relationships, especially across differences. Without relationships and community, any progress toward an equitable and just world will be stymied. We hope that these brief examples of how we incorporate arts into different types of social justice curricula and how we use it to heal and connect, inspires our colleagues and friends. As bell hooks (1994) explains, we must begin with ourselves.

> Teachers must be actively committed to a process of self-actualization that promotes their own well-being if they are to teach in a manner that empowers students. (p. 15)

## References

Baldwin, J. (1962). The creative process. In J. F. Kennedy, Magnum Photos, & John F. Kennedy Center for the Performing Arts (Eds.), *Creative America* (pp. 17–21). Ridge Press.

Ferreria, S. B., & Ferreria, R. J. (2019). Fostering an awareness of self in the education of social work students by means of critical reflectivity. *Social Work/Maatskaplike Werk, 55*(1), 119–131.

Franklin, M. (2017). *Art as contemplative practice: Expressive pathways to the self.* State University of New York Press.

Freire, P. (1970). *Pedagogy of the oppressed.* Continuum.

Goessling, K., & Wager, A. C. (2020). Places of possibility: Youth research as creative liberatory praxis. *Journal of Youth Studies*, 1–19.

Greene, M. (1997). Teaching as possibility: A light in dark times. *The Journal of Pedagogy, Pluralism, & Practice, 1*(1), 1–11.

Hieb, M. (2005). *Inner journeying through art-journaling: Learning to see and record your life as a work of art.* Jessica Kingsley Publishers.

hooks, b. (1993). *Sisters of the yam: Black women and self-recovery.* Southend Press.

hooks, b. (1994). *Teaching to transgress: Education as the practice of freedom.* Routledge.

Lave, J., & Wenger, E. (1991). *Situated learning: Legitimate peripheral participation.* Cambridge University Press.

Lorde, A. (1988). *A burst of light: Living with cancer.* Firebrand Books.

Pisarik, C. T., & Larson, K. R. (2011). Facilitating college students' authenticity and psychological well-being through the use of mandalas: An empirical study. *Journal of Humanistic Counseling, 50*, 84–98.

Talwar, S. K. (2019). *Art therapy for social justice: Radical intersections.* Routledge.

Tillet, S., & Tillet, S. (2019). "Youth want to be well?" Self-care as a Black feminist intervention in art therapy. In S. K. Talwar (Ed.), *Art therapy for social justice: Radical intersections* (pp. 123–143). Routledge.

Young, A. J. (2001). Mandalas: Circling the square in education. *Encounter: Education for Meaning and Social Justice, 14*(3), 25–33.

www.ingramcontent.com/pod-product-compliance
Lightning Source LLC
LaVergne TN
LVHW010547110826
845149LV00003B/589

* 9 7 8 9 0 0 4 4 4 2 8 5 6 *